ONE SIGNAL
PUBLISHERS

ATRIA

BAD MEDICINE

CATCHING NEW YORK'S DEADLIEST PILL PUSHER

Charlotte Bismuth

ONE SIGNAL
PUBLISHERS

ATRIA

New York • London • Toronto • Sydney • New Delhi

ONE SIGNAL
PUBLISHERS

ATRIA

An Imprint of Simon & Schuster, Inc.
1230 Avenue of the Americas
New York, NY 10020

First One Signal Publishers/Atria Books hardcover edition January 2021

ONE SIGNAL PUBLISHERS / ATRIA BOOKS and colophon are trademarks
of Simon & Schuster, Inc.

For information about special discounts for bulk purchases, please contact
Simon & Schuster Special Sales at 1-866-506-1949 or business@simonandschuster.com.

The Simon & Schuster Speakers Bureau can bring authors to your live event. For more
information or to book an event contact the Simon & Schuster Speakers Bureau at
1-866-248-3049 or visit our website at www.simonspeakers.com.

Interior design by Dana Sloan

Manufactured in the United States of America

1   3   5   7   9   10   8   6   4   2

Library of Congress Cataloging-in-Publication Data
Names: Bismuth, Charlotte, author.
Title: Bad medicine : catching New York's deadliest pill pusher / Charlotte Bismuth.
Description: New York : One Signal Publishers/Atria Books, 2020. |
Includes bibliographical references.
Identifiers: LCCN 2019055582 (print) | LCCN 2019055583 (ebook) |
ISBN 9781982116422 (hardcover) | ISBN 9781982116446 (ebook)
Subjects: LCSH: Li, Stan Xuhui—Trials, litigation, etc. | Trials (Manslaughter)—
New York (State)—New York. | Anesthesiologists—Malpractice—
New York (State)—New York—Criminal provisions. | Opioids—
Law and legislation—New York (State)—Criminal provisions.
Classification: LCC KF225.L5 B57 2020 (print) | LCC KF225.L5 (ebook) |
DDC 344.74704/121—dc23
LC record available at https://lccn.loc.gov/2019055582
LC ebook record available at https://lccn.loc.gov/2019055583

ISBN 978-1-9821-1642-2
ISBN 978-1-9821-1644-6 (ebook)

For Joe, Buddy, Belinda, Bill, George, and the fifth-floor
team: wherever you are, there's hope.

With tender thanks to my parents, for their love,
support, and encouragement

There is no greater misfortune than greed.

—LAO TZU

Contents

The People

Names with asterisks have been changed to protect the privacy of individuals.

Raymond Belair, Esq., attorney for the defendant, Dr. Stan Li

Marlie Bensen,* friend of Nicholas Rappold, trial witness

Bridget Brennan, Special Narcotics Prosecutor for the City of New York

Michael Cornetta, brother, boyfriend, former patient of Dr. Li, deceased November 2010

Jon Courtney, investigative analyst and paralegal, Office of the Special Narcotics Prosecutor

Adrian Cruise,* former patient of Dr. Li, trial witness

Kristin Delumen, Joseph Haeg's sister, trial witness

Dr. Christopher Gharibo, Medical Director of Pain Medicine, NYU Hospital for Joint Diseases, medical expert for the prosecution

Seth Grant,* former patient of Dr. Li, trial witness

Xiao Yuan "Anna" Guo, wife of Dr. Li and office manager

Joseph Haeg, son, brother, uncle, former patient of Dr. Li, homicide victim, deceased December 2009

Senior Investigator Joseph Hall, Office of the Special Narcotics Prosecutor, lead detective on the case

Noah Hobbes,* friend of Nicholas Rappold, trial witness

Tracy Howard,* former patient of Dr. Li, trial witness

Andrea Howard,* mother of Tracy Howard, trial witness

Kevin Kingsley, husband, son, father, former patient of Dr. Li, deceased December 2010

Erin Kingsley Markevitch, daughter of Kevin Kingsley, trial witness

Anne Kingsley, mother of Kevin Kingsley, trial witness

Assistant District Attorney Peter Kougasian, Counsel to the Special Narcotics Prosecutor, trial partner

Dr. Stan Xuhui Li, doctor, defendant

Stefani Miotto, investigative analyst, Office of the Special Narcotics Prosecutor, trial team member, and witness

Lyle Park,* Joseph Haeg's friend, trial witness

Nicholas Rappold, son, brother, friend, homicide victim, deceased September 2010

Michael Rappold, Nicholas's brother, trial witness

Margaret Rappold, Nicholas and Michael's mother, trial witness

Nancy Ryan, former Chief of the Trial Division, Manhattan District Attorney's Office.

The Honorable Michael R. Sonberg, former Acting Justice for the New York County Supreme Court, Criminal Term

Sybil Stearns,* girlfriend of Michael Cornetta, trial witness

Jean Stone, former Director of the Northeastern Program Integrity Office for the Centers for Medicare & Medicaid Services (CMS), trial witness

Dawn Tamasi,* former patient of Dr. Li, trial witness

Armen Tamasi,* Dawn Tamasi's father, trial witness

Assistant District Attorney Joseph Tesoriero, Chief of the Investigative Division, Office of the Special Narcotics Prosecutor

Eddie Valora,* original complainant, former patient of Dr. Li, trial witness

Alli Walton,* former patient of Dr. Li, trial witness

Dr. Alexander Weingarten, anesthesiologist and pain medicine physician, medical expert for the defense

Kaci Yates,* friend of Nicholas Rappold, trial witness

Lydia Yates,* mother of Kaci Yates

About This Book

This is a true story.

I have changed or omitted certain names. While witnesses agreed to testify at trial, it was my decision to write this book. I used real names for individuals appearing in a professional capacity, the deceased patients listed in the indictment and for others, only when I obtained specific permission to do so.

All exchanges that occurred in the context of the trial are directly quoted from trial transcripts. Outside of the context of the trial, scenes and conversations featuring witnesses from the case were reconstructed using dialogue lines from trial transcripts. Other dialogue, including lines attributed to me or my team members at the Manhattan DA's Office, has been reconstructed, to the best of my ability, from memory.

Other than the occasional "[*sic*]" where a quotation may appear to be grammatically incorrect, and therefore may cause confusion, I have remained true to the transcript. In the instances where I needed to shorten a quotation, I used brackets and ellipses to indicate any omitted text and took care not to compromise the intended meaning.

The narrative scenes involving trial witnesses were reconstructed solely based upon the facts set forth at trial and recorded in the transcript.

A portion of my proceeds from this book will be donated to charity, in support of families and individuals affected by the opioid epidemic.

Any and all errors are mine.

CHAPTER 1

The One to Start With

Aren't opioid pain medications like OxyContin© "addicting"?
Even my family is concerned about this.

Drug addiction means using a drug to get "high" rather than to
relieve pain. You are taking opioid pain medication for medical
purposes. The medical purposes are clear and the effects are benefi-
cial, not harmful. If you or your family have concerns about addic-
tion, please talk to your doctor or another member of your health-
care team. This fear should not stand in the way of relief from pain.

—LATE 1990S PURDUE PHARMA PATIENT BROCHURE:
OXYCONTIN: A GUIDE TO YOUR NEW PAIN MEDICINE

NOVEMBER 27, 2010: 1,209 DAYS UNTIL TRIAL

Alli Walton couldn't take the pain anymore. Her limbs ached. Her bones
hurt. Her head throbbed. She was sweating, shaking, and anxious, a
mess of cravings and illness. She called her doctor—he was on vaca-
tion. She went to the hospital—they refused to give her what she knew
she needed. There was only one place left to go.

There were men and women waiting, chatting, smoking, and wheeling-dealing outside of 132-59 41st Road in Flushing, Queens. Alli recognized some of them and kept her head down. There were rules in this place and she was about to break every one of them. She stepped down the dirty concrete stairs, past the graffiti and urine stains, to the basement level. There she opened the door and hurried down the hall, then to the right, toward the green metal door, darting past all the other patients. The closer she got, the harder they glared. Would anyone call her out for cutting when they had all been waiting since the early morning? She couldn't care—she felt like her body was giving up, and there was no other way. It wasn't about feeling good anymore. That had ended ages ago. It wasn't even about feeling normal anymore. She couldn't even remember "normal." The first time she'd come, just over a year earlier, she'd been a healthy nineteen-year-old, with a loving family, a boyfriend, college ambitions, and a future in the family business. Now all she wanted was to survive. To stop the tailspin, to hold still, to breathe, to quit the consuming, hungry pain of withdrawal. It used to be about the feeling she had when she took the pills—they numbed everything in her body and she just drifted out of reality. Now the only thing she felt was *not* having them, never having enough.

The receptionists stared at her. "I need to see the doctor," she told them. "I'm sick. I need to see him now." The receptionists glanced around the waiting room, filled with others who looked just like her: tense, pale, anxious, impatient. They looked up her name. You've been discharged, they said, you can't see him. She knew it was useless to argue with the receptionists—she'd been there often enough to know it wouldn't get her anywhere, and she didn't want to risk drawing the attention of other patients. Without another word, she turned and ran down the hallway toward the office where she'd seen the doctor go on his lunch breaks. She opened the closed door. He was there, in his white lab coat, sitting at the table and eating.

"I'm sick," Alli said. "Please help me." She couldn't hold herself together anymore and began sobbing. "I'm so sick. I need more; please help me. You started me on this, and now I can't stop anymore. I tried everything. I can't get another doctor; I can't get more pills."

"I told you not to come back," he said. "It wouldn't look good. I told you not to come. You're not my patient anymore."

"I know," she cried. "I know, but you don't understand, I'm so sick."

The doctor pulled out his prescription pad and pen. He began writing, then stopped. "You have the money?"

"I'm short," she said. "Please."

He stopped writing. He returned his prescription pad to his pocket. "No, no, no," he said. "No. I can't give it to you. This is not a free service. You have to pay."

"Please," she begged. "I'll get more. I'll go get more."

The doctor waved his arms, gesturing at her to get out, go away.

She ran out, past the receptionists, down the hall, up the stairs, down the street. She ran until she found a cash machine, hoping she'd have enough. Once she finally held the cash in her hand, she ran back to the office, down the steps, down the hall.

Lunch break was over. "He's with a patient," one of the receptionists said. "You have to wait."

"I have the money," she said, holding the cash. "I need to see him."

She hovered by the door to the office where the doctor saw patients, trusting that she wouldn't have to wait long. The door opened, a patient emerged, and she swooped in, unfolding the bills on the desk in front of the doctor: $150 in cash. "I need my prescription," Alli said. "Please, if you just give this to me you will never have to see my face again."

The doctor took the money and put it into the pocket of his white coat. Without another word, he wrote out a prescription for oxycodone.

• • •

On that Saturday, November 27, 2010, I did not know Alli Walton. I did not know the doctor or his practice. In that moment, everything and everyone remained unconnected, unexamined. There was no team and no investigation. All the facts and records were out there, accumulating: cash transactions, patient files, prescription forms, prescription data, witnesses, bank records, autopsy reports, and insurance claims. Dozens of human lives intersected in the Flushing clinic: some unraveled as others thrived; some already had been lost while others still might have been saved.

In November 2010, I was a rookie ADA in the Office of the Special Narcotics Prosecutor (OSNP) for the City of New York, on assignment from the Manhattan DA's Office. I'd just taken on my first pill case, involving a Russian supermodel, forged prescriptions, and a lot of Vicodin. Even as an ADA and a thinly stretched, separated mother of two small children, I lived in a state of privileged innocence: I believed neighborhoods were safer without drug dealers and that those suffering from addiction could find help; I had faith in lawyers fighting for justice and I trusted doctors to do no harm. On Saturday, November 27, 2010, specifically, I was four days away from launching an investigation that would consume the next four years of my life—and that doctor in Flushing, Queens, with a roll of cash in the pocket of his white coat, was three years, three months, and twenty-two days away from being the criminal defendant in a groundbreaking legal case.

DECEMBER 1, 2010: 1,205 DAYS UNTIL TRIAL

It was dark outside. I'd been working late. Piles of paperwork required attention and, regardless, I didn't want to go home. I could bear my empty office more easily than my empty apartment.

The long, wide hallways that during the day echoed with the hurried footsteps of ADAs, the sputter of police radios, and our civilian-alert system for undercover detectives ("UCs, clear the halls!") had gone silent. Any ADAs still around worked quietly at their desks, writing motions, preparing trials, or filling out indictment paperwork that still involved carbon-copy forms.

On my way to the ladies' room, I passed my bureau chief's office and was surprised to see her sitting at her desk after hours, illuminated by a reading lamp. She was rigorous in her use of office time, relentlessly organized, and committed to her family dinners. Also, rumor had it that "ice-cold water" ran through her veins and that she sometimes did a few minutes of yoga behind closed doors. In other words, she was an excellent and efficient boss who happened to be a working mother.

My chief spotted me and waved. From the far reaches of her oblong office, a Red Sox outpost in Yankee land, she stretched out her arm to hand me a tiny yellow Post-it.

"I got a call from an NYPD detective," she said as I took the note. "They've received a complaint." This was it:

Dr. Stanley

41st Rd

She'd scrawled the detective's name and phone numbers in the margins.

"It's about this Dr. Stanley," she said. "According to the complainant, he is prescribing medication to young kids who don't need it. Can you look into it?"

To this day, I don't know whether my assignment to this case happened by mere coincidence. Had I done a good job on my other pill case? Or did she pass me the tip simply because I happened to walk by?

What kind of medication? I asked. Did we know anything about the tipster? Is the doctor selling pills or just writing prescriptions? The chief's smile and expression revealed that she had no further information. It was up to me to find the answers. I returned to my office, armed with the tiny square of paper that would change my life.

In that moment, the doctor's world and mine intersected for the first time. Although he long may have feared the authorities, he did not know there was a prosecutor in an office just a few miles from his clinic who was about to start asking a lot of questions.

When I first spoke to the NYPD detective, he gave me the street address and told me that the doctor's name was, in fact, Stan Lee, "like the Marvel guy." We agreed to name the case Operation Marvel, even though it wasn't a formal investigation yet, just a new, empty folder on my desk.

Days passed. I called the detective again. When could I meet the complainant? The detective assured me he would set up the meeting soon, but there were just a few bureaucratic hurdles to overcome first, just "routine." Then—nothing.

Turning away from my chipped wooden desk, toward the computer table to my right, I decided to do some research. My children had scotch-taped drawings to the wall on either side of my screen during a visit to the office, and now their love always framed my work. I found a pain management practice at 132-59 41st Road, but the doctor's name wasn't Stanley or Stan Lee: it was Stan Xuhui Li.

The fifty-seven-year-old physician had excellent credentials: medical school in China, a fellowship at the University of Pittsburgh Medical Center, a residency at the Rutgers New Jersey Medical School, board certification in Anesthesiology and Pain Management, a license to practice medicine in New York and a job as an anesthesiologist at a teaching hospital in New Jersey. How did he run a pain management practice in Flushing if he was employed full-time by a hospital in New Jersey? Could this really be the guy?

I took a virtual stroll down 41st Road: Dr. Li's clinic occupied a quiet section between College Point Boulevard and Flushing's Main Street. Around his block, an adult daycare center, an office for the National Committee of the Democratic Party of China, a dental practice, and a pharmacy adjoined small residential homes and low-rise apartment buildings. Li's office was on the basement level of a beige brick residential building, which also held an internal medicine practice. A gray cement staircase descended from the street straight into the basement, with a small sign in Chinese and English indicating the pain clinic.

What defined the specialty of pain management? I wondered. What kind of conditions do pain management physicians treat? What are the range of available treatment options and common medications used? Apparently, these included opioid painkillers, such as oxycodone and morphine, as well as other medications I knew to have addictive potential and high street values, such as Vicodin and OxyContin.

I read about Purdue Pharma, the manufacturer of OxyContin. A page on their website proclaimed partnerships with law enforcement to prevent diversion and abuse of the medication. This seemed curious. I tracked the initiative back to the 2007 settlement of "misbranding" lawsuits brought against the company and certain executives for having misrepresented the drug's addictive potential. I read about the company's relentless, misleading, and highly effective marketing of the drug, which included the slogan "OxyContin: *The One to Start With and the One to Stay With.*" Partners from my own previous law firm had represented one of the Purdue executives. Gulp. How had I not known about this? Had I been so deep in document review, marital strife, and maternal guilt? My former law firm's involvement did not sit well.

Reading about the appeal of cheaper, more accessible heroin for those who had first become addicted to opioid painkillers, and the increase in supplies of heroin on the streets, I realized this meshed with what we'd been hearing and seeing as Special Narcotics ADAs—but there was still so much that didn't make sense. If these cases were settled in 2007 with a clear understanding that the medications were, in fact, addictive and easily abused, how, in 2010, could overprescribing and addiction still pose such a problem, where an increasing number of Americans were dying of accidental overdoses?[1] Hadn't this case pointed to clear areas requiring oversight and caution? Of the more than thirty-seven thousand drug overdose deaths in 2009, almost twenty thousand had involved at least one opioid—nearly two thousand more human beings than in 2007.[2]

Was there any treatment for opioid addiction? I discovered that Dr. Li, of all people, was an authorized prescriber of buprenorphine and Suboxone, medications used to treat opioid addiction—he even appeared in an online directory of opioid addiction treatment providers. I made a note to follow up: at the very least, this additional licensing might indicate that he had been trained in the diagnosis and treatment of opioid addiction. What did this training entail? More cynically, I wondered about Dr. Li's application of this knowledge: If, in fact, he sold prescriptions without a medical basis, did he also treat patients for addiction in order to profit on both ends? This would be a new low.

It was an unlikely scenario. After all, I was dealing with a well-educated, well-trained, licensed *physician*. He was accused of writing prescriptions for patients, but that's what doctors *do*. The complaint alleged that the doctor sold those prescriptions in exchange for cash, without medical reason, but from this distance I couldn't verify his rationale for the prescriptions or even the form of payment used at the clinic. All I had was this tip—a Post-it note and a few words—and I didn't even have the tipster.

MARCH 20, 2014: DAY 1 OF TRIAL

The Criminal Branch of the New York State Supreme Court shared the dark, glassy building at 111 Centre Street with the New York State Civil and Housing Courts. The Honorable Michael R. Sonberg, a graduate of Harvard Law School and former president of the New York Association of Gay and Lesbian Judges, presided over "Part 21," the vast courtroom at the end of the hall on the ninth floor. Compact and keen, with his natty bow ties, long black robe, and neat goatee, Judge Sonberg held an iron grip on all proceedings and unleashed sharp commentary on unprepared attorneys. Under his supervision, and as soon as we had picked a jury, my team and I would try to reconstruct the events that had taken place years before in Dr. Li's basement clinic. For the unforeseeable future, the courtroom, with its long, empty wooden benches and high ceilings, was about to become our second home. As I waited for the trial to begin, I read, over and over again, the brass letters on the wall: "In God We Trust."

I sat at the prosecution table, in the part of the courtroom near the judge's dais we called "the well," inside the barrier that separated us from the public seating area. Our table was closest to the jury. Dr. Li sat next to his attorney, at the defense table to my left, near the court clerk. Between us, a chasm: he resented our prosecution and we rejected his brand of criminal indifference.

From the original tip I received in December 2010 to the execution of a search warrant in Dr. Li's office in November 2011, through two indictments and hundreds of hours of work, the case had grown from a team of one to a team of many, from a few questions to an indictment, from a tense and suspenseful investigation conducted in secrecy to a high-stakes public trial. It was the first time in New York State that a doctor faced homicide charges related to the overdose deaths of his patients—and those were but two of the 211 counts we would seek to prove at trial.

My earliest partner on the case, Senior Investigator Joe Hall, a veteran NYPD homicide detective, had gumshoed his way through the boroughs of New York City with his fellow investigators for years, tracking Dr. Li's patients, his employees, the relatives of his victims, and all the people who had tried to warn or stop Dr. Li along the way.

We'd rounded up seventy-two witnesses and enough physical evidence to weigh down a rickety two-tiered, four-wheeled, four-foot-long cart. This cart, sagging under the weight of several bulging boxes, would soon take its place between us and Dr. Li. We believed the documents would prove Dr. Li's guilt. He and his lawyer believed they would exonerate him; more accurately, they believed that some of the documents would exonerate him and fought to keep the others out of the jury's sight.

For the next eighteen weeks, the evidence cart would roll into court every morning under the custody and watch of an investigator. Over the course of each day, we discharged some of its contents onto our table, into the hands of the defense attorney, up to the witness stand, and onto the projector. At the end of each day, we gathered up all the exhibits and folders and replaced them onto the cart, and off it went with its official escort, laden with boxes full of patient files, boxes full of manila folders, boxes, boxes, and more boxes, everything labeled and stickered and carefully preserved and piled up high. When our first cart crumbled, we received approval to replace it with a tougher model, a sturdier cart that had mountain-bike wheels we hoped would survive the trial.

Each box, each folder, each slip of paper, each witness, resulted from years of work. Not just my work—the work of a small, committed army of professionals and civilians determined to seek justice and outraged by the damage that Dr. Li had caused.

After each day in court, we'd emerge to find Joe waiting in the hallway. From our years spent working together on this case, he could always tell just by looking at me how the day had gone. He raised an eyebrow. I shrugged. We checked the hallway for jurors before speaking.

"That good, huh?" He gave a chuckle and tried to relieve me of the giant binders I carried. I resisted: "It's the only exercise I get!" Joe and I walked as a pair, while our analyst, Jon Courtney, steered the evidence cart and maintained a sarcastic banter with my trial partner, Assistant District Attorney Peter Kougasian. Much as I enjoyed Joe's company, I knew he wasn't there to mingle. Instead, he ensured chain of custody for the evidence and never let it out of his sight, except when it was in court or locked up for the night.

At the end of our trial days, the four of us always rode the elevators down in cautious silence, then swept out of the building for the short, liberating two-block walk from the courthouse to our offices at 80 Centre Street. Under Joe's eye and with his occasional assistance, Jon wrangled the cart over and around bumps, curbs, and potholes. We all enjoyed a few rare minutes of "fresh" New York City air as we crossed between the two buildings where we spent the majority of our time. Once in front of our office, Jon and Joe veered off to make the dicey descent down the steep driveway with the cart, while Peter and I rode—again in silence—up to the sixth floor, to the OSNP where we all worked, to prepare for the next day of trial. We were just another two tired schlumps in the elevator, sharing a lot of responsibility and a mercurial working relationship. For all the years I'd been working in the office, working with Peter, working on this case, I still wondered when it would all get easier—or if any of it would ever get easier.

SEPTEMBER 2, 2008: 2,025 DAYS UNTIL TRIAL

The first time I had entered this building, I'd ridden up to the eighth floor, crammed in with a bunch of fresh-faced law school graduates in brand-new suits. Despite emerging from more than four years in a law firm as a married thirty-four-year-old "lateral" with two children, I was just another rookie Manhattan ADA. My fellow rookies, most of them a decade younger, were excited, energetic, and looking forward to the social lifestyle that came with the job as much as the job itself. I, on the other hand, was distracted by tricky timing—the overlap of my first week in a new job with the first week of my kids' school—and shell-shocked by the recent realization that my marriage was in tatters.

While the other rookies compared assignments, traded rumors about the various trial bureaus to which they had been assigned, speculated about the cases they might expect to have on their dockets within a few months, and planned the evening's drink outings, I checked email to make sure I had given the babysitter the right information for my elder child's school dismissal and wondered how I could fix my life. Public service had been my goal and dream for years: I had always wanted to work on behalf of crime victims. I was finally in the right place, especially with my first assignment to the Appeals Bureau, but my head and heart were torn.

My husband and I had been together for nine years. We used to laugh together until we cried. We'd adored, understood, and found solace in each other. Shortly after our marriage in 2001, my French-Tunisian grandmother yelled, "Bébé! Bébé!" at my new husband over a long-distance call, making clear her impatience for great-grandchildren. My husband and I laughed, confident that it would all work out, that we would be great parents *together*.

Unfortunately, my grandmother died when I was eight months pregnant with our first child. I'd missed so many opportunities to go see her in France because it was never "the right time." I was so angry at myself for having let that happen. Was it an accident, one of those things in life you can't control? Was it the result of my bad choices? Was it an early symptom of the expanding deadlock that would eventually condemn our marriage?

In the meantime, my husband and I were lucky: we had two healthy babies. In September 2008, our son, Charlie, was two years old. He had curly brown hair, the softest cheeks in the world, and a tiny little huggable body. He didn't speak much yet, but he loved to sing—especially "Hit the Road, Jack," in his phonetic toddler mumble. His big sister, Nina, was about to turn five. She spoke French with me, English with her dad, and both languages at the same time when she really, really needed something—like chocolate. She loved everything about school—the fresh pencils, the glue sticks, the songs, the lunch boxes— and hated bedtime.

More than anything, I wanted to be a good mother and have a happy, steady family. I had a pretty good idea of what that should look like, from movies and books and childhood, so why wasn't it happening? Well, I worked long hours at the law firm despite my "part-time" status; I couldn't seem to help Nina feel safe and comfortable at bedtime; I couldn't fix my husband's work conflicts, prevent his unhappiness, understand our complicated relationship, get enough sleep, make one week go by without having it all rip at the seams, shake the feeling of guilt and anguish that gutted me every morning the minute I woke up and caught me in the throat during the day or in the middle of the night when I wondered who I was, what I was doing with my life, and why everything felt so frantic and so wrong and so unstable. Was there someone to blame? Was it me?

By the time I joined the DA's Office in September 2008, my husband and I couldn't seem to have a simple conversation or plan a simple outing. We'd lived in several apartments and never managed to settle in any of them: we'd start with big ideas and end up with temporary arrangements, tangled cables, unpacked boxes, and unfinished projects. We couldn't align our schedules and lifestyles enough to share a meal or agree on even the smallest parenting decisions, like whether the kids were hungry or tired. We both had such clear ideas of what a relationship and family should look like, but we'd just never realized they were so different. Like tectonic plates, we were out of alignment, each resistant and defensive and aggressive in protecting our turf, occasionally building up so much tension that it all exploded. Our incessant, cumulative conflicts suffocated me, but I clung to our children and our fantasies of a happy family life.

The month of August had been raw, unpredictable, scary, and demoralizing: incompatibility had turned into outright hostility. With my insides jumbled and my home life uncertain, the predictability and community of rookie training offered relief—and over time the job got better at providing the purpose I needed to survive.

During my first two years at the DA's Office, in the Appeals Bureau, I studied New York State criminal law and wrote briefs, emerging only for short bursts of adrenaline-fueled arguments in the Appellate Division's ornate courthouse near Madison Square Park. With the help of an antidepressant, my blind anguish gave way and I became functional again. With functionality, however, came the stark realization that my marriage might be over. My work was taking shape—but was my life about to fall apart?

JUNE 14, 2010: 1,375 DAYS UNTIL TRIAL

The OSNP unfolded around a lengthy ring of hallway, with certain sections extending so far that, seen through the haze of late-night eyes, they seemed to bend at the end like a mirage. Even at its busiest, the place never quite bustled, but I suspected there was a lot happening behind all those closed doors.

The City had founded the OSNP in 1971 in response to a sweeping heroin epidemic. As we learned in OSNP rookie training, Governor Rockefeller's vision of curing addiction through institutional residential treatment had failed, his eponymous drug laws were about to take effect, and the office was expected to either handle or coordinate all of the City's felony narcotics prosecutions. While the other boroughs agreed to participate to varying degrees, the Manhattan DA's Office channeled their entire felony narcotics caseload to OSNP and continued to do so until the crack epidemic in the late 1980s overwhelmed OSNP's capacity. Through the stories, photos, and archives of old-timers, we learned about those times: undercover officers wearing bulky recorders taped to their chests; the office's first surveillance van, upholstered in plaid fabric; the ravages of heroin abuse and crack addiction on human bodies, on families; the outdoor drug markets; the days of nonstop court appearances; the stark rise in incarceration rates. Nobody viewed them as glory days: those were hard, dark times and their legacy was under constant scrutiny. The agency was committed to learning, evolving, and doing everything within its power to protect the public from another epidemic.

The 1970s left their mark on our office décor, if nothing else. The wooden doors had pebbled glass cutouts with old-fashioned lettering; large offices had high ceilings, drab upholstered chairs, and banged-up metal filing cabinets. With warm amber lights, a quick polish of the wood, some steaming white take-out containers, and a group of photogenic ADAs debating the law around a table, you'd have gotten close, if you *really, really* squinted, to a classic crime procedural movie scene. But in real life, we worked in dusty offices, snagged our budget suits on peeling laminate strips and rusty fixtures, wondered why the electrical sockets on our walls stood at eye level, and found 1980s-era Chinese food menus stuck behind our desk drawers, along with hairballs and old pennies. Bedbug-sniffing beagles were called in at least once a year, and when we worked late we budgeted ten to fifteen minutes round trip to pick up our food deliveries from the security desk downstairs because the hallways were so darned long and most of the elevators went to sleep in the evening.

My boss, Special Narcotics Prosecutor Bridget Brennan, occupied a corner office overlooking Foley Square. Bridget was the first woman to serve in her position. She had been appointed by the elected district attorneys of the five boroughs in 1998 and continued to lead the agency with a discreet and innovative efficiency. A former journalist from Wisconsin who'd served as a homicide assistant in Manhattan during the crack epidemic, Bridget had two compulsions: fact-checking and public safety.

She created the Narcotics Gang Unit, the Money Laundering and Financial Investigations Unit, and expanded the agency's commitment to drug treatment programs as well as community outreach, reinvesting forfeited funds back into the affected neighborhoods. With OSNP indictments down from seven thousand a year in the days of the crack epidemic to under two thousand and a renewed focus on treating addiction as a disease rather than a crime, the office developed a specialty in prosecuting violent drug organizations and identifying emerging threats.

When I joined in June 2010, Bridget was as much of a mystery to me as she was to many assistants: while she addressed us with warmth and often walked the halls, stopping to inquire about cases of interest, her attention and concern seemed trained on a longer horizon. In fact, Bridget was on high alert: she had been tracking the emergence of a grave threat.

"Typically," she later testified before a New York State Senate Committee Roundtable, "our work has involved illegal substances [. . .] which come in from outside the country. And there are relatively predictable organizations behind the distribution of these drugs—cocaine and heroin primarily. With prescription drugs, it's a whole different ballgame. [. . .] [W]hen I reviewed our cases [in 2010], I saw a good 15 to 20 percent of our cases involved opiate drugs, opiate drugs mixed with heroin and cocaine, opiate drugs mixed with guns, opiate drugs found in search warrants, all over the city. And it was clear to me we had a problem. I then tried to figure out the source of the problem because there is a very robust black market in these drugs. But I was [. . .] stunned to learn that the number of opiate prescriptions in New York City had increased by about 100 percent, between 2007 and 2010. So I knew that, while we may have a black-market problem on our hands, we also had a problem with respect to the drugs being prescribed."[3]

Bridget had access to the latest, freshest data about illegal drug supplies, suppliers, and drug-related deaths. Nevertheless, she labored to make sense of the numbers. While we all sensed danger, we had no idea of the horrors that lay ahead. All of us would have been sickened to know that, by 2016, the death toll in the United States would have doubled that year alone. By 2016, more than sixty-three thousand human lives would be lost from drug overdoses alone, and that more than forty thousand of those deaths would involve at least one opioid.

If anyone out there had enough information to understand what was happening, to stem the tide and save those lives . . . why weren't they doing so? That's the painful reality of prosecution: as we try to piece together the past, criminals are still hard at work profiting from future disaster.

CHAPTER 2

Sick Little Body

A right to jury trial is granted to criminal defendants in order to prevent oppression by the Government. [. . .] The framers of the constitutions strove to create an independent judiciary, but insisted upon further protection against arbitrary action. Providing an accused with the right to be tried by a jury of his peers gave him an inestimable safeguard against the corrupt or overzealous prosecutor and against the compliant, biased, or eccentric judge. [. . .] Fear of unchecked power, so typical of our State and Federal Governments in other respects, found expression in the criminal law in this insistence upon community participation in the determination of guilt or innocence.

—*DUNCAN V. LOUISIANA*, 391 U.S. 145 (1968)

FEBRUARY 12, 2014: 36 DAYS UNTIL TRIAL

All I could think about was my opening statement. I'd just finished the first full draft and I would write a dozen more versions in the next few weeks.

I caught myself drafting sentences in the shower, on the train, in my head at night, or when reading bedtime stories to my children. I shared drafts with friends and co-workers. My mind flooded with names and numbers, dates and faces, dosages and documents. I wrote and deleted page after page after page.

An opening statement introduces the case to the jury and previews the evidence. It tells the jury what they can expect—or should not expect—to see and hear. Some say that the opening statement is more important than the closing argument, but junior attorneys are more likely to be assigned to do the opening, so I'll let you puzzle over that one. In this case, I was possessive and passionate enough about the case to want to do both the opening and summation (though I knew that wasn't going to happen), but given a choice between the two I'd prefer the opening: I'd lived with this case for a long time, since its earliest days, and wanted to introduce it to the jury. Also, the long, de- tailed work of weaving together the strands for the jury offered relief: it helped me get my thoughts and evidence in order for the trial.

You can't just read an opening statement—you have to "deliver" it, with eye contact and honesty and humanity and integrity. Legally, it's a minefield, since you can preview some of the evidence but mustn't draw conclusions or make arguments or go outside the evidentiary bounds set by the judge, at the risk of incurring an objection or—worse yet—a mistrial. It's a challenge and a nightmare, all rolled up into one, especially when you remember that you're only standing there because someone else got hurt.

I indulged in the fantasy of clear, flowing, well-structured oration but also wondered if I was kidding myself about my capacities or my competence and feared that I would end up as a ridiculous figure—small, squeaky, monotone, a caricature of my idealized lawyer self and a disap- pointment to the folks counting on me. Fortunately, the text itself would be subjected to intense supervisory scrutiny, so I was less concerned about substantive errors, but I thought about all the times I'd heard—in horror and dismay—my recorded voice or seen myself on video and hoped that maybe this time I could do better, sound better, because there was so much at stake. I felt like a liability to my own work.

In our justice system, the burden of proof lies with the prosecution. The accused person is presumed innocent until proven guilty, which means that unless, and until, the jury finds that the prosecution has proved every element of each charge brought against the accused, the accused is, and remains, innocent of that charge. Defendants have no obligation to mount a defense or testify at trial. Even still, the prosecution's proof may fall short, their burden may be left unmet, the accused may be found "not guilty." On the flip side, the prosecution could, in theory, come into a courtroom, read the indictment to the jury, present barebones proof of the necessary elements, and ask a jury to convict. But I've never met a trial attorney who recommended such an approach—especially not in a complex, tragic, long, and novel case such as this one.

Beyond the anxieties about my performance, the task itself was arduous: I needed to set the jury's expectations, lay out our burden of proof and describe how it would be satisfied, introduce our victims and witnesses, explain the charges in our 211-count indictment. In so doing, I could earn—or lose—the jury's trust, and I would get just one shot.

A doctor on trial for prescribing medication? It wasn't the first such case in the United States—federal prosecutors and a handful of state prosecutors had introduced Americans to this new brand of criminal years before, in cases where doctors dispensed controlled-substance pills directly to patients in exchange for cash out of "pill mills." Some of those cases even involved overdose deaths, but federal criminal laws provided for a sentencing bump when death resulted from the crime. In New York State, however, a doctor had never been charged with homicide for the overdose death of a patient—*until now.* And we were asking the jury to find, based on the evidence we planned to submit, that Dr. Li had caused the deaths of not just one but *two* patients with his reckless prescribing.

Homicide charges were a grave undertaking in any context.

According to the New York State Penal Code, "[h]omicide means conduct which causes the death of a person." In accordance with the tradition of the Manhattan District Attorney's Office, homicide cases were handled only by the most experienced ADAs, listed on a mystical, mythical "homicide chart."

And yet here I was. I'd investigated the case since day one, we hadn't known it would turn out to be a double homicide case, the office had assigned a senior trial ADA—but I, a relative rookie by the office's standards, was still slated to deliver the opening . . . *and it was the first such case in the state*. So—just a bit of pressure.

I could barely sleep.

I wanted the jury to understand the case as we had come to understand it: a human tragedy brought about by one man's greed. So much was at stake and I struggled to find the right way to explain it. As prosecutors, we carried the entire burden of proof on all the charges: there were many, and it was a weighty burden. Sequence and context were crucial. It mattered what Dr. Li knew, when he knew it, why he nonetheless acted the way he did. Certain specific details were crucial for meeting our burden. How could I possibly draft an opening statement that could retain the jury's attention, capture the tragedy of the case, and preview the proof with accuracy?

I enlisted the help of one of my colleagues in the DA's Office who had an uncanny emotional intelligence about jury trials. We hunkered down in his office one afternoon in early 2014, recalling salient facts as a way to prompt our minds to find the best starting point—the hook, the image or line or word or person that would speak to the jury, that would tell them what this case was about and why it mattered. Every time we conjured up one of the victims and marveled or mourned over their survival, grit, or pain we would think of another one and follow that trail. How could we choose among all these tragic stories? What tied them all together?

"She was Dr. Li's first victim," my friend said. Say their names, he said, tell their stories and enumerate them for the jury. That was it.

Once I had the hook, the writing flowed. When I had the first draft of the final version of the opening statement, I submitted it to my exacting editors: Nancy Ryan, the legendary former Chief of the Trial Division whom Bridget had hired as a consultant on this case, and ADA Peter Kougasian, my trial partner. I rewrote, incorporating their edits. I read the revised version aloud and rewrote it again. I circulated a new draft and received more edits, then rewrote some more.

We were more than three years into the case, but there was neither relief nor satisfaction nor excitement in the prospect of a trial: Just fear and suspense. And a lot of preparation.

MARCH 15, 2014: 5 DAYS UNTIL TRIAL

On a quiet Saturday afternoon, I stood in the IT department's empty open workspace. Peter wedged himself between cubicles in the back while I stood in the hallway area and hollered yet another revised draft opening aloud in his general direction. I was apprehensive—and not just about the possibility of errors in my opening statement. The whole point of this practice session was to vet my draft for potential mistakes, of the sort that might trigger an instant mistrial and flush several years' worth of work down the drain. Still, the Court's judgment was less imminent—and less intimidating—than Peter's.

"Ladies and gentlemen," I started, to which Peter responded, "LOUDER!"

"—this is a case about a doctor who put money before lives. And not just any lives—"

"LOUDER!"

I dissolved into awkward, miserable laughter. I can't do this, I thought. But there was no avoiding this. Ugh. I started yelling.

"—the lives with which he was entrusted. The defendant, Dr. Stan Li, is a board-certified anesthesiologist and pain management physician who had a full-time job in a well-respected New Jersey hospital near his home in New Jersey."

As I continued, Peter interrupted with suggestions, questions, comments, and I stopped myself to try out different fixes for the snags we encountered. We went through it twice, three times . . . again and again until we could no longer process the words and needed to put out other fires. Somehow, he and I had managed to sustain a productive truce for a few hours, avoiding the danger zones of our working relationship.

The setup for our vaudevillian partnership was clear: I served as his foil, his square and fussy opposite. It was a familiar role. As a child, I had changed schools six times and endured, over and over again, the indignities of being the "new girl"—and a small, weird one at that, by the standards of the 1980s. I wore glasses; I raised my hand a lot in class and felt the sting of constant, *constant* teasing. Peter made me feel like that kid again, every day. He seemed to see past my thirty-nine years, my two kids, my divorce, my suits, my heels, my degrees, my work, and revealed to everyone around us the same "little," "overly sensitive," "bossy," and "stubborn" "French girl" who'd landed in an American elementary school at age eleven with collared blouses and socks pulled up to her knees, to the amusement of much cooler classmates. I was embarrassed to be embarrassed.

I kept a constant tally of Peter's and my differences and run-ins, which was not unlike the evidence I'd assembled for trial on our rickety cart, hoping to make some sense of them at some point or reach some definitive understanding. I convinced myself that this was a professional analysis: I questioned my own assumptions and tried to remain unemotional, since I knew, as a prosecutor, that I shouldn't ignore exculpatory evidence or prevent myself from recognizing it. For instance, I suspected Peter suffered from an anxiety as virulent and painful as my own (even though clearly it didn't manifest as compulsive neatness). Perhaps that's how he knew that forcing me to yell out a draft and face direct feedback might be the best and only preparation for what lay ahead.

The following Monday, with just a few days left before trial and mere weeks before I'd deliver the opening, I sent out a mass email to my fellow Special Narcotics ADAs, asking if anyone would be willing to hear my latest version and critique it. A few days later, I recited it before a dozen attorneys in our conference room.

"You will hear that he made several hundred thousand dollars a year working in that hospital as an anesthesiologist, full-time. But that is not why we are here. We are here because of what Dr. Stan Li did on the weekends. You will learn that on one day every weekend between 2004 and 2011 Dr. Stan Li ran a pain management clinic out of a small basement office in Flushing, Queens. That is why we are here. That is the scene of the crime, that weekend basement clinic."

I sent out a call to the entire office staff, begging for non-lawyer volunteers to provide feedback. When we were able to gather a critical mass, I stood at the lectern in an unused grand jury chamber and presented the latest version before twenty or more of my fellow employees at Special Narcotics: our devoted human resources staff, administrative assistants, paralegals, and operations team. I knew they wouldn't go any easier on me just because we worked together. I watched their expressions as I moved through the different sections of the opening, making notes in the margins.

"In that weekend basement clinic, you will hear that the defendant saw up to fifty, sixty, seventy, eighty, ninety, or more patients a day, one after the other. And we will prove that he committed numerous crimes out of that basement clinic.

"We will prove that the defendant sold one hundred and eighty controlled-substance prescriptions for drugs, including oxycodone and Xanax, to twenty of the patients from that basement clinic in Flushing.

"We will prove that the defendant recklessly endangered the lives of four patients, recklessly caused the death of two patients, and put three additional patients at risk of death."

At the end, my colleagues gave me profound and constructive commentary. I rewrote and reworked.

All that preparation was just for the opening statement—just one hour of court time. There was also, of course, the entire rest of the trial to work out: witnesses, exhibits, questions, motions. We thought the trial might last three months, and there were very few things we could leave undone before it all started.

MARCH 19, 2014: DAY 1 OF TRIAL . . . ?

We were slated to begin jury selection. In negotiation and collaboration with the defense attorney, Raymond Belair, we had developed a questionnaire devised to surface the biases and preconceptions of potential jurors, whether about law enforcement, physicians, addiction, opioids, or chronic pain. Regardless of their life experiences and beliefs, would they be able to follow the judge's instructions and apply the law?

I had been living with the facts and the witnesses for so long that by the time 2014 rolled around the case felt like an extension of my mind. This was my third trial ever. Every single day I reminded myself that Bridget trusted me and trusted the team. I had to trust her about trusting us, I decided.

During the preceding months, weeks, days, and nights, the trial appeared in my mind as a systematic unfolding of facts. A million pieces came together as one story woven from the strands of multiple stories. I imagined that everyone involved in the trial would operate in good faith toward a common goal of setting forth the truth, making sure we all came away with an understanding of what had happened in that clinic. It is an understatement to say that I did not have a lot of trial experience.

We were supposed to start on March 19, 2014.

But we didn't. Word came down from the judge's chambers that we'd start the next day. Those twenty-four hours felt like a year.

MARCH 20, 2014: DAY 1 OF TRIAL

I met Peter at the elevator bank on the sixth floor of our building. "At the end of the day," he said, "we will know more." And off we went.

Jury selection was a puzzle, a challenge, a potential trap—and a pleasure. We began with a pool of more than one hundred New Yorkers called in for jury duty, filling the courtroom's benches. The judge and his staff went through the grueling task of confirming eligibility for jury duty and hearing from jurors who could not commit to a trial of such anticipated length. We spent hours in the small jury room with the judge and Belair hearing further, private appeals from jurors who sought to be excused for personal reasons ranging from illness to weddings to medical practices and acting schedules. I watched Judge Sonberg's face, in turn understanding or frustrated, as he processed the pleas. Over and over, he worked to articulate a fair reasoning and make consistent decisions. I was exhausted on his behalf and gratified when he explained to a few entitled attorneys in the group, with mounting impatience, that they had a particular obligation to serve. In this way, we sorted and sifted through the large group of humans, filtering down to a few dozen who were qualified and available.

The "lucky" survivors got to work on our exhaustive questionnaire. When they were done, the judge's staff made copies and we all pored over them after hours. Peter and I drew up lists of questions and I dug frantically around my office for my rookie training notes. Aha! At last, I found them: "Make eye contact! Start a conversation! Teachers make great jurors! Don't commit reversible error! Don't forget to return seized vehicles to their rightful owners!"—*Oh no, wait, that was from another lecture*—

There were so many rules and recommendations and warnings and pitfalls. How do you translate training into practice? How could I remember all the advice? How inevitable was it that I would make mistakes? Why can't humans learn and make progress in a perfect, linear, coordinated way, from person to person within consecutive generations, without having to wait for centuries of zig-zaggy evolution?

In the next phase of our jury selection, the court officers called fifteen to twenty prospective jurors at a time into the box. We took turns addressing the group. The judge introduced me as "Ms. Fishman," my married name, which I had kept for professional continuity. More than ever, it felt like a stage name: if and when the trial ever ended, I decided, I would shed it.

As do all humans, the prospective jurors each harbored unspoken identities, feelings, thoughts, memories, and sentiments. It was our job to create discussion, to learn their thoughts on the issues relevant to our trial. Voir dire, the process of jury selection, was a singular opportunity to *hear* from prospective jurors, because if selected they would be restricted to listening for the duration of the trial. Moreover, our voir dire discussions were designed to uncover unspoken truths: Are there groups of people you just don't believe? Are there groups of people you always believe? Are there topics that make you so angry or upset that you can't think straight? It was impolite conversation conducted in the most polite and formal manner, all in direct service of the Constitution.

When I asked the jurors if they could see beyond their experiences and biases, I asked the same questions of myself. When I asked them to pledge to follow the judge's instructions and apply the law as he explained it to them, I reminded myself that this was my duty as well. Would I make mistakes? Yes. Was it possible to sustain an unbiased, impartial perspective in such a long and complicated trial? We would strive to do so. We would help each other to do so. The promise was meaningful. The effort was meaningful.

After each round of questioning, the jurors filed out of the courtroom and we debated whom we would seek to exclude with "peremptory challenges," whom we would exclude in agreement with Belair, and then made our arguments before the judge.

Day by day, we assembled a group of civilians who potentially would hear the story and decide a man's fate.

The judge hoped to have a jury impaneled and opening statements on March 28. On the night of March 27, I could not sleep. On the morning of March 28, I tried to turn my nerves into a teachable moment for my children. "See," I told them, as I stood pale and shaky before them, "Mommy's about to do something scary and I'm just a little nervous, but it's all going to be fine." I ran into the bathroom and bent over the toilet, my stomach seizing with cramps.

I arrived at the office just before 9:00 a.m. At the top of the hour, Jon, our paralegal, shimmered into my office. He was the man who did it all: the analyst, the document guru, the unofficial prosecution team therapist. He managed the evidence cart, witness wrangling, the discovery process by which we shared records with the defense, and any last-minute trial emergencies. The discovery process in itself was laborious and painstaking: when Jon handed me the discs containing scanned images of every single document that had been produced on the case in the last week or so, each page bearing its own unique identifying number (the legendary Bates numbers that populated my nightmares), he was handing me dozens of hours of work, but never with a single complaint.

Whenever I saw Jon appear, I breathed a sigh of relief.

"Ma'am," he said.

"Sir," I responded.

We debriefed on the day's plan: if we proceeded with openings then he would need to bring over the evidence cart and coordinate with Joe Hall to make sure our first witnesses were ready. We had never done this before and I was terrible at delegating, but I left it all in Jon's reliable hands.

I met Peter at the elevator bank. "At five o'clock," he said, "we will know more." We crossed the street and passed through security, pulling our black rolling briefcases behind us. As we entered the courtroom one of the court officers glanced back at us, looking up from his newspaper. "Oh," he said, with cruel nonchalance, "one of the alternate jurors called in sick."

It was Friday. Now opening statements wouldn't take place until Monday, March 31, leaving me with an entire weekend of anxious anticipation. I reminded myself of the others who were also awaiting and dreading this trial: the defendant, our witnesses, the victims' families, our team.

On Sunday night, I couldn't sleep. I was shaking again on Monday morning but didn't get sick.

"Ma'am?" said Jon, at 9:00 a.m. on the dot.

"Sir," I responded, and we debriefed.

When Peter and I entered the courtroom, we learned that the same alternate juror was still sick and another juror had taken his wife to the hospital. We decided to cut the absentee alternate loose and give the other juror until Wednesday, April 2, to see if the situation resolved. One more try, the judge decided. He called in the jurors and apologized for the delays. "It is like I tell lawyers never to say, 'This is my last question,' because it invariably isn't, but I can't—unless, you know, four of you call in sick on Wednesday, I can't see any circumstance under which we are not going to start on Wednesday."

With that delay and those remarks, he guaranteed my insomnia for the next two nights.

APRIL 2, 2014: DAY 14 OF TRIAL

I picked what I hoped would be a lucky outfit: a black-and-white sheath dress with a white blazer. This would be my trial uniform, I had decided: a dress and a blazer. I had a few of each. I would mix and match. I would put my hair up in a bun every day. I was in control of at least these aspects of the trial. My kids hugged me tight. Nina wanted to skip school to come watch the opening: Nice try, kid, I said.

Once again, I met Peter at the elevator bank on the sixth floor of 80 Centre Street. "At five o'clock," he repeated, "we will know more."

We settled at our table in the courtroom, the one closest to the jury. Peter sat in the senior trial counsel spot on the left, Jon sat on the right, with the projector, and I planted myself in the middle, trying not to shake. It was happening.

The judge called in the jury and offered a few preliminary instructions on opening statements, reminding them that the burden of proof rested entirely on the prosecution. And then it was my turn.

I walked over to the lectern positioned in front of the jury box, taking in the jurors' faces, wondering for the first time—but not the last—what they were thinking and whether they would understand. I opened my thin black binder where I'd concealed, in the left-side pocket, a Xeroxed photograph of Nicholas Rappold at twenty-one years old, the last year of his life, staring straight into Dr. Li's office camera, intent and scruffy and alive and beloved. Seeing his face kept me grounded and reminded me of our purpose.

As I spoke, I was aware of the silence. I was facing the jury but could sense the presence of many others in the courtroom. The jury watched and listened, with impassive faces. I reminded myself to project and breathe, but my nerves were still raw, and every word felt effortful.

I repeated the first lines from memory, having practiced them so often, in front of so many others, but my voice cracked. A few paragraphs in, fueled by the years of work and heart we had poured into this case, I hit my stride and began telling the jury about a young woman named Dawn Tamasi.

"You will hear that in 2007 [Dawn Tamasi's] family found her unconscious and learned that she was abusing both prescription drugs and heroin," I said. "Stan Li, the defendant, was [her] doctor, but she was the defendant's first victim."

JANUARY 2012: APPROXIMATELY 800 DAYS UNTIL TRIAL

Dawn Tamasi's file had been the thickest of the bunch. Our team and law enforcement partners had seized more than twenty boxes' worth of patient records from Dr. Li's office, along with other items, such as posted signs. All the materials were stored in a gated, locked storage cell on the fifth floor, near Joe's office. We met there almost daily for several weeks, in between court appearances. He'd unlock the gate and then we'd fight over how many boxes he'd let me carry. We'd each haul a few into the large investigators' conference room, covering the long wooden table with boxes and notepads. Joe and I were always there, with Jon Courtney, our paralegal, and a rotating cast of investigators temporarily reassigned from other cases to help us sort through it all.

We began by taking an exhaustive inventory, listing each item in an Excel spreadsheet while the radiators cranked out dry, heavy heat, making the room unbreathable. We'd creak open the windows, the glass clouded with the residual crust of city grime stirred up by countless rainstorms, welcoming in the frigid winter air and a sliver of sunlight. Outside, just across Worth Street, sat the ornate court buildings of Foley Square.

Jon's job was to enter and organize the information while we read names, descriptions, and box numbers out loud. There were more than one thousand patient files, but we didn't have much time: the "speedy trial" clock was ticking—and we were commandeering one of the office's only laptop computers.

Our group sat together around the long table, folders in hand, for hours at a time. Reading the files was like playing a memory game with more than twelve hundred pieces. We would see a note or a name or a date and remember that we'd seen something meaningful with the same notation in another file. When a member of the team called for everyone's attention, we stopped and listened.

"Take a look at this one."

That was the lead-up to our discovery of a damning piece of evidence demonstrating "notice"—that Dr. Li had been warned about his patients' abuse of his prescribed medications, their addictions, and even their overdoses. The name on the tab of the thick file was Dawn Tamasi. The page was covered in large, uneven handwriting. I read the letter out loud. "*Attention Dr. Stan X.*," it began.

"*This letter is in regards to our daughter and your patient [. . .], as she is in very bad shape both mentally and physically as well. [She] is a drug addict who has had a pill and hard substance problem for over five years already. [. . .] [I]f you haven't noticed [she] is not healthy at all and she does not eat normally, sleep normally or breathe and think normally.*

So it's obvious that if you are a doctor of pain therapy, then you must be able to see the pain our daughter is dealing with."

My eyes skipped ahead. These were the words of a desperate parent, but as I read them out loud, in our conference room, they took on another significance: this was proof that Dr. Li knew his patient, Dawn Tamasi, was extremely vulnerable. As I came to the next line, I looked up at Joe and read louder, with more emphasis—

"Please you must stop prescribing these deadly doses of drugs ranging from Methadone to you name it."

What kind of doctor receives a letter like this? I thought as I kept reading. Was he devastated? Did he stop prescribing? Despite my impatience to look through the rest of the file, I continued reading:

"[She] has come close to OD'ing. She has been found in our closet with her mouth open and lying in bad condition. She has also been found on numerous occasions lying in the bathroom, toilet, or anywhere else her sick little body gives out on."

"Her sick little body." I could see it—I could feel the fear. As a parent, I could not fathom having to write a letter like this.

"[. . .][She] is one foot away from a serious OD," the father pleaded. *"We will follow up with you on this and make sure that this is given immediate attention!!!"*

The letter was undated, but maybe something in the file would reveal when Dr. Li had received it? Had there, in fact, been any follow-up? We flipped through the sheaf of papers chronicling Dawn's visits to Dr. Li dating back to August 5, 2006. We found another letter, and a staggering record of the prescriptions she'd received from Dr. Li. Under his "care," she had floated from one potent medication to the next, while making no secret of her opioid addiction (for which he prescribed methadone at one point) or her kidney disease.

"This is insane," we kept saying. We weren't physicians. We needed an expert to give us some markers, to tell us if what we were seeing was, in fact, as wrong as it seemed.

According to the doctor's notes, Dawn Tamasi, then thirty-four, told Dr. Li that she was experiencing pain in her elbow, knees, and fingers. It was arthritis, she told him; she'd been tested, she said, but the chart didn't include any diagnostic test orders or results.

When she first came to see Dr. Li, Dawn Tamasi was taking forty milligrams of methadone, a synthetic opioid, three times a day. Methadone is prescribed to treat moderate to severe pain. It also treats addiction to other opioids, such as heroin, despite itself being a Schedule II controlled substance, which means it is also associated with a high risk of dependence or abuse.

During Dawn's first visit in 2006, Dr. Li had completed a three-page intake and examination form. A cursory note indicated she'd denied any substance abuse history, but there was no indication of follow-up questions about the methadone. Dr. Li's diagnosis was "arthritis, on methadone." Was that a diagnosis? Joe and I wondered. We would come to learn that, at some later point in Dawn's treatment, Dr. Li revised the intake form, writing "cervical radiculopathy." He made no referrals for diagnostic tests or specialty treatments. Instead, on her first visit, he prescribed the same medication she claimed she'd been receiving: forty milligrams of methadone, three times a day.

The first year alone, Dr. Li prescribed a variety of additional medications, at different times and in varying doses, ranging from Neurontin to Vicodin ES to Suboxone.

The chart also listed Dawn's complaints over the same period: she had difficulty sleeping; she complained of a burning pain in both hands; she came to see him every two weeks; she lost medication; her pain was never under control; she had anxiety; her anxiety was never under control; her shoulder hurt; both legs hurt; she refused injections; she had back pain; she had hand pain; she lost medication; she had hepatitis; her medication was taken away; she didn't want to take Suboxone; she had leg pain; she tripped and fell; she was robbed of her medication; her teeth hurt; she had pain all over her body; she was afraid of needles; she was a heroin addict.

Wait—what? We had so many questions, but the file contained no answers.

APRIL 28, 2014: DAY 40 OF TRIAL

Peter pulled Dawn's file from the evidence cart. He brought it to the lectern, preparing to question Dawn's aging father, Armen Tamasi. Small, strong, with white hair, Mr. Tamasi seemed reluctant to bring himself—and his private struggles—into this public courtroom.

In his accented English, Mr. Tamasi gave punchy responses to all questions, whether they came from Belair, the defense attorney, or Peter, a fellow Armenian.

"What languages do you speak, sir?" Peter asked.

"I speak Armenian and Russian and English, of course," answered Mr. Tamasi, arms crossed.

"What dialect of Armenian do you speak?" Peter pressed. "What dialogue? Do you speak Eastern or Western Armenian?"

"Both."

The judge smiled. He'd known Peter for a long time, and anyone who knew Peter knew that he was Armenia's most fervent unofficial ambassador. "This is of interest to Mr. Kougasian," the judge joked.

Peter asked about Dawn's living arrangements. "Does she live on the same floor that you live on?"

"No, she living in basement." As Mr. Tamasi spoke in the courtroom I recalled our last visit to their home, a neat gray house with potted plants visible through the windows. We had not been invited to enter.

"For how long has she lived with you?"

"All life she lives with me," Mr. Tamasi groaned, turning to the jury, confident that they would understand his feelings about it. "She didn't get married and she still live with me." He was complaining and yet he wouldn't have it any other way, if it meant putting his daughter at risk.

"Now," asked Peter, "did there come a time that you learned that your daughter was seeing a doctor named Dr. Stan Li?"

"[S]ometime when I see her bad condition, I was going to the basement," said Mr. Tamasi, with a pained shrug. "I see her prescription and container and I find out she's seeing Dr. Li."

"Could you describe her condition during those years?"

"She's very bad condition," Mr. Tamasi repeated. "[. . .] She does everything, heavy drugs, everything, and violence, fighting. [. . .] Many times I call the cops. They come. They will discuss—they say, 'Enough, don't call anymore,' because they know what's going on."

I couldn't imagine having to call the cops on my own daughter. Having the cops tell me not to call them anymore.

"How about her health during those years?" Peter asked.

"Health is no good. She's very bad. Health is very bad. She has too many diseases in herself right now. She can't cure herself. She don't want to cure herself. That's why I was worried all the time until now I'm worried to get well and I can't—I can't do anything."

My duty was to sit there with a poker face. Still, it was overwhelming to hear this father describe a purgatory of worry.

"Now, during the time that your daughter was seeing Dr. Li," Peter continued, "can you describe for us her physical appearance during that period?"

"Horrible, unclean, very thin, she wasn't eating. The only thing she would eat was ice cream or candies. She wasn't eating at all."

"Did she sleep?"

"She sleep daytime. She's awake in the night. All night she's awake. She'd sleeping daytime. Opposite. She's living opposite. Regular people sleep nighttime. She sleep daytime."

"Did there come a time," Peter asked, "when your daughter [. . .] was seeing Dr. Li that you found her unconscious?"

"Before Li or after Li, of course, I saw her many times. She was not only unconscious. Sometimes she fell on the floor. Sometimes she fell in the house. Sometimes she was in the bathroom sleep there two hours, you know. I'm a parent. I'm following her."

He often had called for the police and ambulances. "Maybe three, four times, many times," said Mr. Tamasi, with resignation. "I find her many times unconscious, yes. I—I mean unconscious. Um, she was very bad condition almost she's not breathing and I call ambulance. They took her to hospital two, three days and leave her home again."

All I had to do was turn my head to the left in that courtroom to look upon the face of the man responsible for this father's agony. He was a middle-aged Chinese man of average height and build, with gold-rimmed glasses and a thinning head of hair. Dr. Li had sworn an oath to do no harm. He lived in New Jersey with his wife and two children. As an anesthesiologist in a nearby hospital he had guided countless patients into and out of unconsciousness.

Peter asked Mr. Tamasi about the letters. Why had he written to Dr. Li?

"Because I can't find a solution," answered Mr. Tamasi. "I thought maybe I write a letter to the Dr. Li. [. . .]. And I start writing letter. I can't write it. I speak Armenian and I ask my son, please, could you help me to do that. And he write it, whatever I say. [. . .] After then, even one time I went to see Dr. Li."

A hush took over the courtroom as Peter read the first letter out loud, the one I'd read in the conference room years earlier. "[D]oes that sound like the letter that you dictated to your son in Armenian?" he asked.

"Yes." Mr. Tamasi nodded. "Yes. I dictate and whatever I said, my son write."

There was more. Peter pulled a second letter from the evidence cart and read it out loud. Some of the sentences still gave me chills, for the horrors they described as well as for their significance. As early as 2007 Dr. Li had known the risks: How could he have continued?

"[. . .] I'm the parent of [this young woman], who is currently a

patient at your office. [. . .] She is abusing what you prescribe her and taking them without the proper doses cocktailing/mixing them and since you give her more dose than she should receive. We have seen her get worse in front of our eyes, month by month. [. . .] Instead of helping her, you have been fueling her needs with the overprescribed amounts of pills you dispense to her in the side for cash thus bypassing the Medicaid card she normally should get prescribed with. [. . .] She is not healthy at all, very skinny, does not eat often, and only takes pills or does the drugs she buys from her dealer. She has a heavy crack usage along with occasional heroin as well, we believe. [. . .] Please consider this a way to make good on a patient. You cannot [not] only impact her life in a positive way but also help our family who is coping with this life-draining situation. The stress is unbearable [. . .]. She can't help herself. So we need to help her by all means necessary at this moment. Because the next step we are very afraid for her is fully to collapse from weakness and maybe even death. [. . .]"

"Now again," Peter asked, "does that sound like the letter that you dictated in Armenian to your son?"

"Yes, I dictated whatever you said, everything I dictated to my son, and he wrote it in English."

"Thank you. Now, after you sent those letters did Dr. Li call you?"

"No."

I knew this, and I knew that HIPAA rules limited Dr. Li's ability to communicate with a patient's family, yet I was livid all over again. There were ways for a doctor to respond to such a stark warning and desperate request. I took a deep breath that I hoped would go unnoticed and glanced at the jury. Their faces were set and stern. What were they thinking? Feeling? Many months would pass before we might find out.

"Did there come a time that you saw Dr. Li?" Peter continued.

"Yeah," said Mr. Tamasi, "when I didn't have an answer from Dr. Li, I decide to see him."

"What did you do?"

"And with my daughter I went to doctor office," he explained. It happened in December 2007. Dawn let him speak to the doctor alone. "I said, please, Dr. Li, I need your help. Just give it whatever she need, not more. And he said, yes, I'll do [. . .] whatever you want."

When the judge finally released Mr. Tamasi from the witness stand, Peter called Dawn to testify. She took her turn in the courtroom as she had in Dr. Li's office, so many years earlier: weary, unapologetic, and blunt.

Dawn recounted to the jury her conversation with Dr. Li. "I said, I said don't listen to my father, that, you know, I am an adult and I will make my own decisions on what I want to do with my life. And I want the medication."

"And did Dr. Li continue to prescribe to you?"

"That day he wouldn't," said Dawn, "but I went back again. I was very persistent to getting the medicine because at that point I was addicted."

Her father was no longer in the courtroom when she said this—none of the witnesses were allowed to listen to another person's testimony. He'd spoken his truth, and then she'd come in and said hers. We were hearing from two people who loved each other but had been set on a track for constant conflict. It was heartbreaking.

"I just felt just really like a zombie," Dawn said about using fentanyl, which she tried for the first time after Dr. Li wrote her a prescription. "I went out to celebrate," she continued, describing her thirty-ninth birthday, "and my idea of celebrating was taking pills. And I, myself, decided to put on two fentanyl patches, I took fifteen Xanaxes, and also I did cocaine with that." Somehow Dawn didn't die that night, but she did wind up hospitalized. "For three days," she told the jury, "I couldn't even wake up."

Dawn was not pathetic—far from it. She was a miracle of the human body's ability to keep living. She was superhuman for having survived. And yet, when Peter asked her to describe her current life, we all could measure the extent of the damage. "I go to the clinic," she said, in a flat voice. "I come home and I just watch TV and mostly I fall asleep because I can't sleep at nights. I have severe anxiety so I stay up all night just watching TV and then when I get home I am really tired and I just sleep and then I just get up and watch TV. I don't go out anywhere; I don't do anything with friends."

Dr. Li continued seeing Dawn for three years after her father's letters and visit, prescribing fentanyl, morphine, Vicodin, Xanax, Kadian, Opana, Percocet, oxycodone. When he discharged her from his practice on December 26, 2010, he made a note in his chart: "Patient will move to Utah." Where did Dr. Li get this? Was this something Dawn just made up in the moment? Did he even pretend to believe her?

When Peter had asked Mr. Tamasi where Dawn had been living during this time he replied that she was still living in the basement. "I don't want to throw her out," said the aging man. "Many time I ask help. They come to me. They said only solution you have to throw her out. Homeless. I don't want to do that. And I still keeping and I suffering until now from her. That's it."

For us, the trial was a reenactment—a look back to a messier, more dangerous time when Dr. Li's clinic was still open, when we were just beginning to understand what he was doing, when there was no certainty that we would ever be able to gather any proof or ever make it this far in this new kind of case.

For this beleaguered father, though, the past kept continuing into the present. His daughter was still in danger—and always would be. The jury may have been looking back at a human tragedy, but he was still living it every day—and he wasn't alone.

CHAPTER 3

One of the Good Ones

A Queens man was slapped with a parking ticket as he lay dead in the driver's seat of his car, cops and family said Wednesday. Nicholas Rappold, 21, of Flushing, was slumped across the front seat of his Jeep Cherokee on 165th St. near 35th Ave. Tuesday morning when a traffic agent wrote him up for being illegally parked during street sweeping, cops and family said. [. . .] The cause of death is still to be determined by the medical examiner, but investigators believe Rappold died hours before the ticketing from an overdose. Police voided the parking summons after they released the vehicle to the family.

—*NEW YORK DAILY NEWS*, SEPTEMBER 16, 2010

APRIL 2, 2014: DAY 14 OF TRIAL

Belair pushed his burly pinstriped frame up out of his chair and ambled to the lectern carrying a yellow legal pad, its crinkled pages covered with handwritten notes. "Good morning," he murmured. "Let me tell you something very important. You have heard a little bit about pain management, you have heard a little bit about opioids, but you haven't heard the whole story.

"There is something I want to tell you very clearly," Belair asserted. "The proof in this case will show . . . that no one who took the medications that Dr. Li prescribed the way that he prescribed them got into any sort of trouble in this case. Nobody died because of anything that they took as he prescribed them. It is because of a number of other things that these people got into trouble, principally by disobeying his instructions, principally by not following his instructions when there were problems and by going and doing things that Dr. Li had no way of knowing about."

Dr. Li, Belair said, was "one of the good ones."

And there it was. For so many months—*years!*—Joe, Peter, and I had wondered whether Dr. Li would present a defense and, if so, what it would be. We knew Belair only by his acidic letters and his impenetrable demeanor. He sat on the bench outside the courtroom before we started in the morning, and then sat on the benches inside the courtroom before we were allowed to move into the well, and then sat on his chair at the defense table during the proceedings, always a physically imposing figure, like a nineteenth-century drawing of a lawyer, in custom pinstriped suits, the fingers of his large hands braided together and resting on top of his stomach. When we learned tidbits—He loves Oscar Wilde! He writes with a wide-nibbed fountain pen!—we shared and examined them with glee, like children savoring a rare sweet. This opening statement was an unexpected reveal—we hung on every syllable. But words like these—"Dr. Li was one of the good ones"—were hard to swallow.

Belair staked out the grounds for his argument: this would be a battle of the experts, a discussion about the legitimacy of opioid treatment for pain and what Belair perceived to be a prosecutorial vendetta against a legitimate, caring physician. It was a binary landscape: there was truth and there were lies; there were "good ones" and bad ones; there should be guilt . . . but not for Dr. Li.

In a neutral tone, Belair reset the medical goalposts for the jury. What was tolerance? "You prescribe to a certain level to reduce the pain. After a period of time that same level of medication is not going to produce the relief from pain that it did the first day because the body gets used to it. That is called tolerance. That is expected. [. . .] That is not addictive behavior; that is a physiological response that is expected in every patient who receives chronic opioid therapy for chronic pain. [. . .] It means that you'd have to increase the dosage somewhat in order to be able to deal appropriately with the pain. That is not addiction."

Of course, the devil was in the details. As our medical expert, Dr. Christopher Gharibo, had explained to us and would explain to the jury, opioid receptors are present throughout the human body, especially in those areas and organs susceptible to pain or pleasure. Our bodies produce their own opioids, but not enough to block all pain or to depress breathing. When natural or synthetic opioids are introduced into the body, with chemical structures designed to imitate our natural neurotransmitters, they plug into the receptors, triggering a release of dopamine into the body and a feeling of euphoria. Tolerance happens when the body desensitizes to the effects of the opioid, such that patients need a greater and greater dose to achieve the same pain-relieving effect—but without ever experiencing that first, blissful dopamine release again. Tolerance is a dynamic process that happens to all opioid users to varying degrees: in fact, in the absence of opioids, the body could revert to its baseline of low or no tolerance.

"There is something else called dependence, physical dependence," Belair continued. "Physical dependence is the patient has grown used to the medication in order to get relief from pain. That is not addiction."

I thought about some of Dr. Li's patients, who had described the need to keep taking opioids just in order to "feel normal." In medical terms, as Dr. Gharibo had clarified for our team, dependence was "imprinted tolerance": it happened when opioids became part of the body's biochemistry. Without the medication, dependent patients experienced withdrawal—a flu-like, ill feeling of the body, with pain and unpleasant sensations inside and out and a feeling of deep physiological instability.

"There is something else called pseudoaddiction," Belair added with the slow drone of a lawyer weaving a fiction into fact. He'd pulled this one straight from the Big Pharma playbook. "Pseudoaddiction is when the patient [. . .] is under-treated for pain, not given enough medication for the pain that he or she is experiencing, and therefore the patient is always asking give me more, the pain's not going away. That is not addiction. And what I am telling you is agreed in the medical community. Pseudoaddiction is not addiction."

Pseudoaddiction is a fraud, I thought to myself. But, in that moment, my job was to sit at the prosecution table, listen, take notes, and maintain an expressionless face. Belair had reached the climax of his argument.

"What is addiction?" he asked the jury, with a suspenseful pitch. "Addiction is when you want medication not for the relief of pain, not for the function that it gives you, not for the better life quality that it can give you, but because you like to be high."

Because you like to be high. I glanced at Peter. He was staring at the desk with an air of studied neutrality.

Belair pointed to his client. "Dr. Li, obviously he was born in China," he began—why "obviously"? I wondered—but Belair was pressing on, reviewing Dr. Li's background, rolling the crinkled pages of his legal pad over and under as he finished each one, sometimes tricking us into thinking he was done with a page . . . lifting it up and up and up . . . and then dropping it down again.

Dr. Li attended nursing school in China, worked in a psychiatric hospital for several years, then spent five years in medical school to obtain his first advanced degree. After training in pulmonary medicine, he moved to the United States and passed qualifying exams for graduates of foreign medical schools. He competed a three-year residency in anesthesiology, then a fellowship in pain management at the University of Pittsburgh Hospital before obtaining Board Certification in Anesthesiology and Pain Management. Fully accredited, Dr. Li began working in the Anesthesiology Department of St. John's Episcopal Hospital in Far Rockaway, New York, and later Robert Wood Johnson University Hospital, in New Jersey.

So, Dr. Li was qualified, I thought. We can all agree on that—but didn't this mean he should have known better?

Apparently not. "His personal life suffered," Belair segued: Dr. Li's wife, who'd been a doctor in China, struggled to adjust to life in the States. Unable to find a job, she divorced him and moved back to China, where she gave birth to their child. According to Mr. Belair, Dr. Li opened the pain clinic in Queens in an effort to reunite the family. Belair was careful to avoid providing a precise timeline. Dr. Li remarried his wife and gave her the task of managing his Flushing clinic.

Peter and I absorbed this twist. Was Dr. Li blaming his wife? Belair pressed on, leaving us to bookmark this curious motive for later discussion.

"Listening to what your patient has to say is something that the doctors are taught, taught from the very beginning," Belair lectured. "Your patient holds the key to how you can help him." But the patients in this case, he warned, were different. "There are a lot of liars and there are a lot of addicts in that group. Some of these people took advantage of Dr. Li." In fact, Belair reassured the jury, referring to Dr. Li's frequent pairing of oxycodone with Xanax, these combination prescriptions were "all very mainstream in pain management."

"At the end of this case," Belair said as he reached the last page in his legal pad, "what you are going to see is a progression of things that have been proved. A doctor who gives reasonable dosages, a doctor who cares about his patients . . . And everything that he said, everything that he's done, everything that he's recorded, is going to point to one thing when you analyze it. He was acting in good faith."

Dr. Li, insisted Mr. Belair, was "trying to do his best, documenting what he was doing, doing things that somebody who was not acting in good faith would not be doing."

Here the defense had touched on a perplexing reality of this case. Why had Dr. Li kept the records as he had, including the handwritten notations of dollar amounts in the margins, the letters from parents, the misleading claim forms, or even the prescription price lists?

And those were just the records that we had seized from his office three years before this moment in the trial. A year into our investigation, we'd finally amassed sufficient probable cause to apply for a search warrant. From that point forward, Dr. Li's unusual record keeping would create many more opportunities for surprise.

NOVEMBER 19, 2011: 852 DAYS UNTIL TRIAL

"Police!" Joe Hall announced in a loud voice, just after 9:00 a.m., startling the patients in the waiting area. "Police! We have a search warrant! Everybody stay where you are! Nobody move!"

As Joe pressed forward, other members of the team took charge of the patients. Joe was heading up a team of investigators from Special Narcotics, as well as agents from the DEA and the IRS and our Medicare team partners from the Office of the Inspector General at the U.S. Department of Health and Human Services. Earlier that Saturday morning, they had watched as patients began gathering outside the building at 132-59 41st Road. When one of the two young receptionists arrived to open the office, she entered the building with a line of patients falling in behind her. They had watched Dr. Li pull into the parking garage across the street, then enter the clinic with his wife. The team allowed a few extra minutes before moving in.

Two officers remained outside to secure the location and handle any incoming patients. We did not want to leave patients in the lurch, suffering from either chronic pain or withdrawal. So, at Bridget's instruction, officers handed out forms listing legitimate medical offices in the neighborhood as well as substance abuse treatment facilities. They also provided a contact number within our agency in case any patients needed copies of their medical records.

Joe strode up to the reception area where two young women stood frozen behind the desk. He displayed his badge and asked for Dr. Li. "He's with a patient," one of the young women said, pointing to a closed door. Dr. Li's wife, Anna Guo, and Anna Guo's sister also were in the office: Joe instructed the four women to step away from whatever they were doing, leaving everything as it was. Then he opened the door and found Dr. Li sitting across from a patient.

Even as he was advised of his rights and being placed under arrest, the doctor asked no questions and made no complaints. Had he expected this? Joe wondered. Ever since the horrific events of June 2011, Dr. Li must have known that law enforcement would, one day, come busting through that door. Joe searched Dr. Li: he found two hundred twenty-five dollars in cash in the right-hand pocket of Dr. Li's white medical coat.

Before the team began searching and seizing the office, a videographer recorded everything: workplace information placards on the bulletin board, customized signs taped to the reception window, the contents of the supply closet, and every drawer and cupboard in the office. Among the items seized were prefilled prescription sheets containing the patients' names, addresses, and medications but lacking Dr. Li's signature. The patients had signed in but had not yet seen Dr. Li. The team also found handwritten instructions, in Chinese and English, containing insurance billing codes, filing cabinets full of custom-made medical forms, and more than one thousand patient files. The Medicare team scanned the patient files and took custody of all records pertaining to the seventeen Medicare beneficiaries whom they had identified as Dr. Li's patients. Investigators seized the rest of the records, packing them into cardboard boxes.

Joe called me while the search was under way. I could tell from his voice that something big had happened. "Charlotte," he said, "there's a sign. Remember how we heard about the prices, per prescription, per pill? There's a sign."

"Take the sign!"

Joe laughed. "Who do you think you're dealing with here?"

The team packed away the sign that had been posted in the reception area, along with Dr. Li's prescription pads and that morning's patient sign-in sheet. Dr. Li watched in grim silence as the team dismantled his office. A plexiglass plaque displayed on the counter in front of him celebrated his status as "Best Doctor in America 2003." But that day, Dr. Li left his office in handcuffs, arrested pursuant to a New York County Grand Jury indictment and a lawful warrant.

Finally, as a result of months of legwork and the swift and successful execution of the warrant, our team had safely stored in our evidence locker Dr. Li's "fee schedule": a document that might just convince a jury that Dr. Li was nothing more than a glorified pill dealer.

JANUARY 2011: MORE THAN 1,100 DAYS UNTIL TRIAL

All this had started with that Post-it note—the tiny yellow square containing Dr. Li's misspelled name, the street where his practice was located, and contact information for a New York City Police Department detective. My research had uncovered red flags about Dr. Li's practice, but the NYPD wouldn't grant me access to the tipster.

That's when Joe had come on the case. He'd walked into my office at the start of 2011, a slim and athletic man with close-cropped gray hair and rounded wire-rimmed glasses. "Charlotte?" he'd asked, with a slight New York accent. "I'm Joe Hall, one of the investigators." We shook hands. Given his outstanding reputation, I'd been expecting a brash or gruff larger-than-life character, but instead I was faced with a careful thinker and quiet listener.

Within a few days, Joe had cleared the hurdles and tracked down our tipster: Eddie Valora, a young man in his thirties. Valora's life hadn't been perfect or easy—but if there was one thing he couldn't stand, it was to let someone get away with wrongdoing.

When Valora first stepped through the door of my office, the smell of cigarettes followed, along with a palpable physical tension. He was in his thirties but looked older, with a tight, tense frame, deep creases in his face, and bags under his eyes. His thin, sinewy arm muscles twitched under his skin, and his fingers beat a rhythm against each other as he fidgeted to find a comfortable position. He spoke in a staccato voice, interrupting himself when his train of thought outpaced his speech. He had a million questions for us. Who were we? What did we want to know? Where should he start? Did we know about his pending criminal case? He didn't care if helping us helped him with that; he just didn't want Dr. Li to get away with fraud or dangerous prescribing.

"Hold on," we said, Joe and I both reaching toward him, arms outstretched. We had spoken to his attorney to understand the nature of Valora's arrest and make sure it was okay to meet with him, but, we told him, we couldn't talk to him about that case without his attorney present.

I pulled out a chair for Valora, picking the most stable one from my collection of discolored brown-upholstered seats in various states of disrepair. I explained that we had received his tip but needed more information to determine whether we could pursue a case. Valora told us his story. We listened, interrupting only to keep him on track; then we went back over every detail from the beginning and opened up countless lines of inquiry. What he told us launched a long and secret investigation, of which only the parts ultimately disclosed at trial ever may be known other than to the judges, attorneys, and prosecutors and, of course, the witnesses and Dr. Li.

At the end of our meeting, Valora repeated that he didn't care if helping us made a difference in his own case. After his last visit to Dr. Li, he had overdosed on Xanax. He just didn't want anyone else to get hurt.

"Have you heard about any other overdoses?" Joe asked. It was a key question—one that he would end up asking many times, of many different people. Valora gave Joe just enough to keep him on the road pursuing leads for the next few weeks: a first name, a neighborhood, and a rumor. He also remembered a sign he'd seen in Dr. Li's office—something about prices per prescription. Sounded too crazy to be true—no doctor would ever do that!

We asked Valora about his health. We had saved these questions until the end. Of course, this was necessary information if we were to understand Valora's interaction with Dr. Li, but there were other questions in the back of our minds: Was Valora strong enough to go forward? Would it be ethical to expose him to the type of scrutiny and pressure that might be involved in testifying about the case in an eventual trial? As Valora spoke about his illness, Joe and I took in its physical manifestations: foreshortened arm muscles; swollen and stiff hands; body mass reduced to the absolute minimum. Valora had been a body builder, so he was now left with a defined but atrophied body. He'd also struggled with addiction in the past and still denigrated himself for some of the choices he'd made. In body and spirit, he was a man under relentless attack by an unavoidable foe: himself.

Nevertheless, Valora assured us that he was determined to go forward. I explained what this meant: At some point, his identity and testimony would be a matter of public record. Should we ever go to trial, Valora would be cross-examined on the stand by Dr. Li's defense attorney, including about his criminal record and credibility. We're far from that now, I explained, and we'll work with you to prepare if it happens, but it's not easy. You'll have to be up-front about all of it. Are you up for it? Yes, he answered. When I shook it, his hand was clammy and cold, but his grip solid.

Afterward, alone in my office, I wondered whether *I* was up for it—whatever "it" was. Where was this case going? At the time I couldn't know. Valora's story raised the possibility of criminal behavior, ranging from prescription sales to health-care fraud, but there also was the possibility that Dr. Li was just a bad physician, running an unprofessional and lax—but not criminal—practice. It would have felt irresponsible to just stop, without a proper resolution or answer, but the uncertainty made me anxious, especially now that Joe, too, was clocking so many hours on the case.

Valora also presented a particular challenge. He was an important fact witness but had vulnerabilities ranging from his criminal record to his health. If I wanted to preserve him as a witness, I'd have to strike a balance between warning him of the difficulties ahead and guiding him through with a steady and neutral hand. It was not my job to protect him—in fact, I had to be level-headed, transparent, and direct about the challenges he would face down the line. And I would have to subject him to the toughest questioning myself.

You would think that this comes naturally to prosecutors. To some, maybe it does. To others, like me, this kind of questioning is an acquired skill and a significant challenge. When you have grown up seeking to avoid conflict at all costs, it takes deliberate effort to speak awkward truths and accept discomfort. That is precisely why I wanted this job: I hoped and expected it would force me to counter my deep-rooted instincts to put everyone at ease and keep every situation conflict-free. Call it voluntary aversion therapy for a lifelong people pleaser. My old way of functioning would be unethical and unprofessional in the context of my work. I had to let it go. It certainly hadn't served me well in my personal life, either. At tense moments throughout my workdays, as I realized that I was, yet again, trying to appease or avoid tense situations and emotions, scenes flashed through my mind, warning me away from the old trap.

I'd catch myself studying body language for signs of annoyance, frustration, tension, wondering if someone hated me or was angry at me—those fears and feelings then sent me into a spiral of anxiety and paranoia. For too long, I had learned to watch for danger signs, detect the signals, and ward off trouble by any means necessary.

AUGUST 16, 2008: 2,042 DAYS UNTIL TRIAL

On my thirty-fourth birthday I was sitting on a beach on Long Island next to my then husband, suffocating under a tense weight of silent discord, apprehension, and resentment. I watched our kids—Nina, then four, and Charlie, just two—dig in the sand. The last golden rays of the setting sun outlined their little noses, lips, and curly hair against the sunset. I hoped (in vain) that they might always remain so oblivious to their parents' exhausting drama. They were the only element of love and peace left in my life.

On the drive back to my parents' house, a car followed us: it was a family friend, who'd recognized us on the road. My parents were away, so I was glad to see him. I prayed silently that he would invite himself over or invite us out, anything to escape the imminent storm. But our friend soon drove away with a smile. While I managed to hustle the kids to bed almost without incident, the rest of the night was a blur of tears and slammed doors. We were in the final throes of our marriage.

The situation had been growing steadily worse over the past few years. There were the mundane moments of parental rivalry: on so many weekends, when I'd been up with the kids since dawn, my husband would emerge from our room in the early afternoon to thank me for his extended sleep: "I really needed that," he'd say. I was beyond exhausted myself, even with my "part-time" law firm job. "I'm doing my best," he'd say, seeing the look on my face—but I'd stopped believing him, and speaking up was a bad idea, even if it was to ask if he was feeling unwell.

We also had moments of unintended tragicomedy, when I wondered what, if anything, the universe was trying to say to me, if, indeed, the universe was in the business of communicating with a frazzled Franco-American working mom. There was, for instance, a road trip home after a "romantic" weekend away—another futile attempt to get our marriage back on track. I drove while my husband yelled. His face was turned toward mine, mine was turned toward the road ahead, and I felt like a character in a cartoon, speeding forward while pushed sideways by a gale of wind. I needed out. Surreptitiously, I set our GPS to the closest train station. He didn't notice the change in route until I pulled up short in front of a quaint railroad structure, grabbed my bag, and ran out of the car, to the door.

"What are you doing?" he asked.

"I'm going home," I said, so impressed with myself. "I'm done. We'll talk later." I strode toward the train station.

I could see the clerk through the window. He looked strangely rigid.

I pushed open the door: the clerk was made of wax. It was a railroad museum. I turned back toward the car. Luckily, my husband hadn't understood the reason for the stop or my dramatic declaration. I buckled back in for the rest of our ride.

There was also despair, plain and simple. One fight, in our Vinegar Hill, Brooklyn, apartment took us past midnight and well past my limits. Our cozy bedroom, with thick wooden beams, went from a sanctuary to a cell. At one o'clock in the morning, I gave up on everything and ran out to the car, thinking about driving to the nearby dock at the end of Old Fulton Street to do something, I wasn't sure what. I didn't wake up my one-year-old daughter. I drove away wondering how I possibly could drive away from her. I got to the dock and sat there in the dark, unsure whether I should do something stupid with the car or get out of the car and *then* do something stupid, or whether, most likely, I wouldn't do anything at all, in which case I wasn't sure if I even deserved help. I called my best friend.

"Hi," she said, in a sleepy voice.

"Hi."

"What's up?"

"I don't know." There was a long silence. "But—thanks for picking up. Love you. Sorry." The water looked cold, I knew how to swim and I had an inkling that I'd fight like hell to stay alive: so this was not the answer. I hung up and drove home. I couldn't leave my little girl. *But I already had.* But I couldn't. *But I did.* The evening counted as another notch of failure.

Going back to her meant I had to go back to all of it. Okay: it was worth it. And maybe I could still fix everything! I micromanaged daily schedules and weekend plans, minimized outings and family expectations, and adjusted my own hopes as I tried to eliminate the opportunities for conflict. It always backfired. "Get over it," he'd say, when we talked about his anger. I was too sensitive; that was the problem. I seethed and moved on, pushing myself into exhaustion—and out of love. Sitting in the passenger seat one day a few years later, this time with two kids in the back seat, I realized that I had lost all agency and felt cut off from my origins, my traditions, my values, and my friends. The future years of our marriage spooled ahead of me like a prison sentence. Was this how it was supposed to feel?

In February 2009, I went to California by myself to visit a friend. It was my first weekend away from the children and my husband. I cried myself to sleep on her couch every night. On my last day, I received the unexpected gift of a smile from an old acquaintance. I was embarrassed to have had to wait for some sort of sign, but there it was: I was not entirely numb, yet. I wanted to love and feel loved again. "I think I need to leave my husband," I told my friend as we sat in Los Angeles traffic. Even then, I was relying on signs and signals from others to make important decisions about my life.

I came home and asked for a divorce. It was the middle of the night in February 2009. We both cried. I heard a little voice and turned around to find our five-year-old daughter standing in the doorway. "What's going on?" she asked. "Go back to bed," I said. "Everything's okay," I lied, and ushered her back to the room she shared with her little brother. By the time I'd tucked her back in, my husband was on his way out the door.

My request and release carried a high cost. My children would go from having one home to two. They'd always be missing one parent. Would it be easier or harder for the kids? We'd never fought in front of them, but our marital tension smothered any joy. I rationalized the decision: My husband adored the children and they were his family's kin. They wouldn't feel like outsiders. They were better off with happier parents. *Right?*

We "mediated" our separation over a series of raging and tearful sessions. The mediator watched us in disbelief. Even after the papers

een found dead in his car. Something about a traffic

was just the first step, and it was not easy. Joe finally
to a big, proud house up on a hill in one of the outer
tone lions guarding the gates. Seth was a pale young
us energy. He hesitated to confide in Joe at first but
med that he had, in fact, overdosed after abusing the
scribed by Dr. Li and that his father had written to
esitated to go further. After all, we were asking him to
s. Weeks crawled by.
e from the road.
ou'll never guess—"
letter?"
arked another big break. I held it in my hands—another
nt. It was generic fax cover sheet template, with a mes-
the box. It was dated September 4, 2009, addressed to
signed by Seth's father.
is in reference to my son [. . .]," the father wrote. "You
scribing him some serious pain medications for an ex-
zed period of time now with unwarranted use. It
[he] obtains pill presc

simple.
had staked
Sometimes
faces; sometimes
whom to visit next
Two names kept c
Nicholas hadn't. There wa
ened Dr. Li. Or written him a
knew his last name and he d

were signed, there was
time?" my kids would a
learned that my daughter
ule" for her two besties th
my face burning: the chil
decisions.

We renegotiated a cus
but still my ex-husband ch
and even after, for years, c
respected and hated him f
too, suffered being away fr
whelmed any empathy. We
we each wanted more than
sadness, couldn't have both
competition. We both fough

MAY 2011: APPROXI

Joe and I spoke several times
linger on it until he had all th
if he'd made significant progre
get back to the office to tell me
"Charlotte," he would say, t
If I guessed right, he woul
I knew he never cut corr
out the clinic and ca
olks let them in; s
they wouldn't s
r who might
ming up:
s a rum
lette

rumor was he'd
ticket.

Finding folks
had tracked Seth
boroughs, with
man with nerv
eventually confi
medications pre
Dr. Li. Still, he l
revisit hard tim
Joe called m
"Charlotte,
"You got th
The letter n
indelible mom
sage typed int
Dr. Stan Li, an
"This letter
have been pre
tended prolon
knowledge tha
other offices a
half snorts up
[my son's] pri
and medicati
mixed with o
that there is s
ute medicatio
will be made
ment, attorn
As prom
vate attorne
ance compa

were signed, there was no moving on. "Why doesn't Daddy get equal time?" my kids would ask me whenever we were reunited. When I learned that my daughter had established a rotating "best friend schedule" for her two besties that closely matched our custody schedule, I felt my face burning: the children were suffering the consequences of *our* decisions.

We renegotiated a custody agreement with the help of our lawyers, but still my ex-husband challenged its fairness, before the ink was dry and even after, for years, day by day, email after endless email. I both respected and hated him for fighting so hard. While I knew that he, too, suffered being away from them, my anger and lack of trust overwhelmed any empathy. We couldn't both have the kids all the time, but we each wanted more than what we had. And the kids, to their great sadness, couldn't have both of us together ever again. Love had become competition. We both fought for more of them and less of the other.

MAY 2011: APPROXIMATELY 1,054 DAYS UNTIL TRIAL

Joe and I spoke several times a day. If there was tough news, he didn't linger on it until he had all the facts and we could discuss it in person; if he'd made significant progress, I trusted that he would never wait to get back to the office to tell me.

"Charlotte," he would say, then pause, "you'll never guess—"

If I guessed right, he would laugh: "How did you know?" It was simple: I knew he never cut corners and never gave up. Joe and his team had staked out the clinic and canvassed the five boroughs for witnesses. Sometimes folks let them in; sometimes they shut the door in their faces; sometimes they wouldn't say much about themselves but told Joe whom to visit next or who might have overdosed.

Two names kept coming up: Seth and Nicholas. Seth had survived; Nicholas hadn't. There was a rumor that Seth's dad might have threatened Dr. Li. Or written him a letter. Seth was from Queens. But nobody knew his last name and he didn't see Dr. Li anymore. As for Nicholas, rumor was he'd been found dead in his car. Something about a traffic ticket.

Finding folks was just the first step, and it was not easy. Joe finally had tracked Seth to a big, proud house up on a hill in one of the outer boroughs, with stone lions guarding the gates. Seth was a pale young man with nervous energy. He hesitated to confide in Joe at first but eventually confirmed that he had, in fact, overdosed after abusing the medications prescribed by Dr. Li and that his father had written to Dr. Li. Still, he hesitated to go further. After all, we were asking him to revisit hard times. Weeks crawled by.

Joe called me from the road.

"Charlotte, you'll never guess—"

"You got the letter?"

The letter marked another big break. I held it in my hands—another indelible moment. It was generic fax cover sheet template, with a message typed into the box. It was dated September 4, 2009, addressed to Dr. Stan Li, and signed by Seth's father.

"*This letter is in reference to my son [. . .],*" the father wrote. "*You have been prescribing him some serious pain medications for an extended prolonged period of time now with unwarranted use. It is my knowledge that [he] obtains pill prescriptions from your office as well as other offices and sells half of the prescriptions on the street and the other half snorts up his nose. [. . .] I am puzzled why you have never contacted [my son's] primary care physician when prescribing such serious pill[s] and medications that could ultimately lead to death when misused or mixed with other medications that [my son] may be taking. [. . .] It seems that there is some type of conspiracy to illegal [sic] prescribe and distribute medication from your facility [. . .]. This type of negligence and abuse will be made known to the proper authorities, including police enforcement, attorneys and insurance company.*"

As promised, Seth's father copied several people on this fax: his private attorney, the family's primary care physician, their health insurance company, and a detective from their local precinct. We never were able to confirm whether any of those parties had taken further action against Dr. Li, but this family was nevertheless one of the lucky ones: their child lived. By putting his concern and anger into words, Seth's father also had tried to help—and had, in fact, helped other families. The letter had been a cry for help and a warning, but now, sadly, it simply was more proof that Dr. Li had been aware of the risks. Dr. Li could have read the letter and thought twice about his practice, or looked differently at the young men and women who came in asking for opioid painkillers. I wish he had.

NOVEMBER 16, 2009: 1,585 DAYS UNTIL TRIAL

A few years into his "treatment" of Dawn Tamasi, Dr. Li received a visit from the Drug Enforcement Administration (DEA). When a Special Agent and her colleague, a Diversion Investigator, arrived on November 16, they revealed to Dr. Li that the DEA had received a complaint: specifically, that he was writing controlled-substance prescriptions in exchange for cash and without doing a medical exam.

It wasn't true, insisted Dr. Li: He performed medical exams on his patients and always got the proper documentation for every new patient, like X-rays. He made his patients sign a narcotics agreement form. He charged only one hundred dollars per visit. "Screen your patients," the agents warned him, at the end of the twenty-minute meeting.

MAY 2011: APPROXIMATELY 1,050 DAYS UNTIL TRIAL

Joe walked into my office. I looked up, ready with a smile and a warm greeting, but stopped short when I saw his face.

Joe repeated the first name that we'd heard through the grapevine: "Nicholas." Now he had a last name to go with it: Rappold.

It was not yet a familiar name to either of us.

It was not yet a name that echoed in my head every day.

I swiveled my chair toward my computer and typed the name into the Excel spreadsheet containing every controlled-substance prescription written by Dr. Li since 2008. Would I find it?

I found it.

Did Nicholas Rappold receive prescriptions from Dr. Li?

He did. I read them out loud to Joe.

"July 11, 2009: Roxicodone thirty mg, ninety pills.

"August 8, 2010: Roxicodone thirty mg, one hundred twenty pills, and Xanax two mg, sixty pills.

"August 14, 2010: Percocet ten/three twenty-five, one hundred twenty pills, and Xanax one mg, ninety pills.

"September 11, 2010: Roxicodone thirty mg, one hundred twenty pills, and Xanax two mg, ninety pills."

I searched for the name on the Internet and pulled up a *Daily News* story about a traffic agent who had issued a parking ticket on the morning of September 14, 2010. I read the article aloud to Joe. The agent hadn't realized that the car's driver was still inside—or that he was dead. We peered at the fuzzy photo together: the driver was a young man with a smile, a backwards baseball hat, and a black hoodie. Cause of death? Suspected overdose. Three days after he'd filled his last prescription from Dr. Li.

I don't remember what Joe and I did or said. I do remember the cold, somber feeling of that moment. Our evolving investigation, our busy lives, the natural constant movement of life itself, had touched and connected with death. With this news, our responsibilities had changed. Our attention shifted toward a grieving family and so many questions to be answered. Who was Nicholas Rappold? What was his story? Nicholas Rappold was Dr. Li's patient: Could he have been Dr. Li's victim?

CHAPTER 4

Three Years, Eight Months, Two Days

The primary operational mission of the sales organization is generating the sales that are the lifeblood of the company.

—"SALES CAREERS AT PURDUE," PURDUE PHARMA WEBSITE, 2010[1]

MAY 16, 2014: DAY 58 OF TRIAL

Every morning of the trial, from March 20, 2014, until July 18, 2014, I woke up with a pit in my stomach. This morning was no exception—but it was worse.

Trial life had its own routines and rhythms. On the mornings when my kids were with me, I woke at six and scrambled to get the three of us out the door. I walked them to school, then hustled in the other direction to the subway to press into a train car, or if I was crunched for time, I hailed a cab and shot downtown, emailing frantically the whole way. On the mornings when I woke in an empty apartment, I showered and left, running to my second home—my office at 80 Centre Street—

to catch up on calls, emails, conduct witness prep, or organize the day's exhibits.

After work, there was also much to do and think about. (That is, if you can call it thinking when it is not a deliberate action but rather the pursuit of half-formed thoughts.) My mind whirled through reminders and tasks until I fell into anxious sleep plagued by nightmares. Before my eyes even opened, worries about the coming day flooded my mind again. When we had a roster of document witnesses, such as bank representatives or IRS agents, I worried about efficiency, the jury's attention span, laying the proper foundation, assembling the correct and complete sets of evidence. On days when we were bringing in doctors and Medicare experts, I worried about making the testimony clear, simple, and relatable; I worried about my own understanding of the issues; I worried about hitting all my marks because I knew I couldn't bring these witnesses back in. Micro-achievements were the only measure of our work given that we had no guarantee of the jury's decision. Every day, I also still worried about childcare, custody negotiations, calls from the nurse's office, and emails from my ex-husband.

The hardest mornings preceded the testimony from patients or family members. We brought in folks who had purchased prescriptions from Dr. Li or whose loved ones had overdosed on those medications. We asked them to tell a courtroom full of strangers, including four lawyers, a judge, several court officers, and a jury, about their addictions or their grief or sometimes even their crimes. It was a lot of pressure on them, which meant we felt the pressure as well: we had to elicit certain facts and keep the witness on point; we had to tell the jury a story and abide by the limits of admissible testimony; we had to be firm, get to the truth, and show respect; we had to ask simple, straightforward questions and refuse to settle for ambiguity; we had to remember everything we knew about them; we had to keep the record clear. We also had to be mindful of the appropriate boundaries between a prosecutor and a witness—we weren't there to fix their problems or to be their friend.

Still, their stories haunted me—and the entire team. My job, however, required me to put them through the wringer, both as my witnesses and as targets for the defense's cross-examination. It wasn't my duty to win at any cost: it was my duty to do justice.

On the morning of May 16, I was bracing for one of my toughest direct examinations. Margaret Rappold's eyes already were rimmed with red when she took the stand. She sat and stared straight ahead. At the lectern, I arranged my notes and prepared to lead her back through every terrible detail of the worst moments of her life.

In the weeks leading up to this moment, I'd imagined there was an optimal flow of questions. Yet it eluded me. I agonized over the wording. Perhaps the facts were sufficiently dramatic that the order wouldn't matter? Maybe there was no way for me to protect my witness? Knowing her, she would want me to focus on what was most effective—and we both knew it would be difficult, no matter which questions I asked first or how I worded them.

"Good afternoon, Ms. Rappold," I started.

"Good afternoon."

"Who do you live with?"

"My son Michael and my mother, Mary," she answered. Michael was waiting outside the courtroom. He was our next witness.

"Do you work?" I asked. I wanted the jury to understand Margaret's family responsibilities, her work ethic, and her character.

"Yes, I do," she answered.

"Would you please tell the jury where you work?"

"I work at [. . .] a special education school, all special ed, and I'm a cook there."

"How long have you worked at the school?"

"Twenty-five years."

"Have you had any other jobs at the school?"

"Yes."

"What other jobs have you had?"

"After my day ended in the kitchen I worked as a custodian part-time."

I thought about our tendency to describe other people as "strong" when they are responsible and persisting through difficulties. I thought about how Margaret Rappold could be perceived as "strong" or "tough" for her blunt manner, her tenacity, and her charge as a single working mother with an aging parent. I thought about how calling that strength would deny her the credit she was due. Margaret's perseverance, hard work, and survival was a moral choice. It was a refusal to quit, a refusal to abdicate her responsibilities, even when she didn't think she could keep going. It made me want to fight for her, as hard as I could.

It was time to talk about Nick.

"What is your relationship to Nicholas Rappold?"

"I was his mother." *I was his mother.* Her use of the past tense threw me. Wasn't she still? Wouldn't she always be his mother? "Was his mother" made sense if she had been the one to die, not him. . . . But maybe that was the truth of it.

We talked about Michael and how he was eighteen months older than his brother. I asked Margaret Rappold to describe Nick's personality to the jury. The defense attorney objected. Belair delivered this objection as he did most—without moving. He remained hunched over his papers, fountain pen in hand, his voice booming out in the courtroom. The Court allowed the question.

Margaret Rappold described a young man "full of life," a "jokester" who helped out the elderly in the neighborhood but also was keen on "looking good for the babes." Nick, she explained, was "impeccable" and fussy about his appearance. He played ice and roller hockey for three different teams, as well as softball, handball, and basketball.

I was trying to do three things for the jury at that point: introduce them to Nick as a person, set a baseline point of physical well-being for him, and establish a timeline for the changes that occurred in his interests and his health. Nick's athleticism would lead into his addiction, its effect on his appearance and life, and his mother's awareness of the problem. I tried to ask how often Nick played sports, but on an objection from the defense attorney, the Court interrupted that line of questioning.

So I asked about Nick's education—he was attending a local community college after high school, she said. Now it was time for a transition.

"When did your son pass away?" I asked, expecting the date: September 14, 2010.

"Three years, eight months, and two days ago," she replied, straining to hold her voice steady. The courtroom fell silent and heavy. I considered how long each one of those days must have felt: it was the continuing sentence of her life without him.

JUNE 2011: APPROXIMATELY 1,023 DAYS UNTIL TRIAL

Less than a year after Nick's death, I stood on a green hill in Queens, looking at his youthful face in an array of photos. In some, he had spiky hair; in others, his hair was combed back. In some photos, he looked intent; in others, he grinned, his face full of mischief, about to burst into laughter. The photos were propped up against a gravestone, along with baseball knickknacks and handwritten notes: "I love you," "I miss you." It was like a teenage boy's bulletin board, but for the wilting flowers, the cold stone, the short-cut grass, and the domino lines of graves spooling out in every direction. Nicholas Rappold, who had lived, breathed, loved, slept, eaten, hugged, studied, driven, partied, dreamt, and suffered during his twenty-one years on earth, lay somewhere below, in the permanent silence of Flushing's Mount St. Mary Cemetery. Glancing at the gravestones around Nicholas's, I saw he was by far the youngest at the time of his death. It was like seeing a kid in a nursing home. He was an outlier. It was an error. More than that—an injustice. A crime.

Joe Hall stood beside me, his mouth set in a straight line. This wasn't his first homicide investigation, far from it, but we were both at a loss for words. We'd spent the drive talking, as we always did, about his old cases. He answered my questions with patience and reflection. Were there scenes he wished he could "unsee"? Were there crimes he'd never cracked? Killers who got away? How do you stay sane when you see the worst of life? This case, Joe always insisted, was one of the hardest—if not the hardest. So many lives and so much potential lost for nothing—actually, worse yet, for *money*.

I crouched by Nicholas's grave. I was about to meet his mother for the first time. In fact, it was time. We left.

The public school where Margaret worked was just down the street from the cemetery. When we first entered, we noticed the cinder-block walls and the distinctive, sharp smell of government-issue disinfectant. As we walked toward the principal's office, a group of chattering, smiling kids filled the hallway and we recognized the spirit of a school.

The principal waved us into her office, then disappeared. Buddy LaSala, one of the senior investigators from our office and Joe's steadfast partner, was already there, sitting at a small, round conference table. He nodded at us. Joe made a joke about Buddy having worn a suit for the occasion—and waited a beat before turning to me to explain: "That means he's wearing a T-shirt without holes in it." With that joke, he took our collective level of stress down a notch, but just a small notch—we were all bracing for this meeting. Joe and I were conscious of the responsibility we would bear for reopening the wound in Margaret's heart if we didn't handle this conversation—or the case—the right way. I was also terrified of saying the wrong things, of giving her any false hope.

Buddy sized me up with a wary eye. I knew that his presence at this meeting was, to some extent, to protect Margaret Rappold from the possibility that I might mess up. Buddy didn't know me at all, Joe hadn't known me very long, and none of us knew where this case would lead. Buddy was there as an additional bulwark against any potential bullshit. He'd met her before, he knew the map to her pain, and he wasn't going to let me stray.

MAY 16, 2014: DAY 58 OF TRIAL

The jury remained silent and attentive. I asked Margaret Rappold if Nick had continued to play sports until he died, but Margaret Rappold said he was "just getting back into it." He had lost interest for a while, she said, "when he was doing painkillers." I asked Margaret Rappold to tell the jury how she had learned of his addiction.

"It was July of that year and he called me at work and told me he had a very serious problem and he had to talk to me, and I asked him what the problem was. I asked him on the phone and he told me he was addicted to painkillers and needed help." Margaret Rappold said she had noticed changes—Nick looked like "a derelict"; he had lost interest in his appearance, dropped a lot of weight, and yelled at Margaret. The day after Nick's call, Margaret Rappold took him to see their family doctor. They made an appointment for Nick in a "detox" center affiliated with a local hospital, and Margaret Rappold accompanied Nick for his first visit. Nick began taking Suboxone to treat his opioid addiction.

"He went through a terrible withdrawal," Margaret told the jury. "He said he was in a lot of pain and one time he wanted me to take him to the emergency room because he felt he needed some more medication and the doctor from the detox—"

The defense attorney objected. The judge reminded Margaret that she could not testify about what anyone else had said.

"Oh," she said, and stopped talking.

"Did you or someone else call the doctor from the detox center?" I asked. She called, but there was nothing to be done. It took two weeks for Nick to start being himself again. She thought he was "getting on with his life."

"He was back to sports, back to going out with his friends. He was back to his old Nicholas." In August, she said, Nick seemed fine. He was no longer on the Suboxone but was still going to meetings at the detox center.

On the night of September 12, 2010, Margaret had been in bed when a car alarm went off. "I looked out the window," she said, "and it was my son Nicholas's car. He was with his friend in the car and I ran outside and they shut the car off and he said, 'Mom, let's not go in. I want to talk for a while.' So we sat outside on the stoop and then we went to Dunkin' Donuts for coffee. And we came back and was sitting on the stoop until five o'clock and he was telling me about his dreams."

That was too much for the defense counsel.

"Objection," said Mr. Belair.

"Overruled," said the judge. "Please continue."

"He was telling me what he wanted to do with his life," said Marga-ret. "He wasn't going to school that semester. He decided not to go and he told me that morning that he was sorry—"

The judge interrupted her, but Margaret Rappold didn't understand why, so she kept going. My co-counsel, Peter Kougasian, stood up. His pants were cinched up at the waist by a belt; his suit jacket hung loose. He had lost so much weight during this trial.

"Your Honor," he said, "it's a statement of future intent under *Hill-mon*." Peter was referring to a landmark Supreme Court ruling, *Mutual Life Insurance Co. of New York v. Hillmon*, which established an excep-tion to the hearsay rule. We wanted to make sure the jury understood that Nicholas had not committed suicide.

The judge allowed the question. Nicholas wanted to be a history teacher, Margaret Rappold explained.

They continued talking into the morning, she said.

It was clear that she cherished the memory of this conversation: her voice grew softer and the words seemed familiar to her, as though the memory were well-worn by frequent retellings. "He told me that he missed me, and I said, 'I'm right here; how could you miss me?' And he said he remembered when he was small how he wanted, you know, he used to curl into bed with me. And that morning for some reason I said, 'Nicky,' I said, 'you want to crawl into bed today?' and he said yes. So, yeah, he wound up sleeping with me for a couple of hours that morning."

I couldn't shake the image of this tall, tired young man crawling into bed with his gray-haired mother.

JUNE 2011: APPROXIMATELY 1,023 DAYS UNTIL TRIAL

A tall, straight-backed woman entered the office, where Joe, Buddy, and I were waiting. It was Margaret Rappold. Her face seemed stern, but her bloodshot eyes gleamed with tears. We shook hands. She was shaking.

I have no memory of what was said in the first minutes of that meeting. I have a physical memory of the tension, the uncertainty, the expectations.

If the case was going to proceed, she would be a witness. That meant I could not pollute her recollections with any outside facts or any speculations or conclusions. As I spoke to her, introducing ourselves and explaining our presence, I vetted every word and phrase before uttering it out loud, thinking about what Dr. Li's future defense attorney would say if he could hear me. It took a long time to get full sentences out. Margaret, meanwhile, spoke with animation, her skin flushing, her composure breaking. She pressed a crumpled tissue to her eyes, but there seemed to be no end to the tears. "Nicky was no angel," she repeated often, as though she needed to convince us that she wasn't just out to "get" anyone, or as though she was pleading with us to see the value of his life and her love even if he hadn't been "perfect." She told us about Nicholas's athleticism, his friends, his pill bottles, his final days, and his death. She told us about that feeling she'd had in the middle of the night that something was wrong.

I thought about my children's absences, that feeling of beaming signals out into the void. Nicholas was twenty-one years old when he died. He had his own car. I tried to imagine how it must have felt to her not to know where he could be in the big city. To look for someone and to realize that he was already gone. To have invested so many minutes, days, weeks, months, years, so much love and time and effort, all into this child who is then gone forever, invisible, never again to be touched or heard or seen or hugged. How could this happen?

"Do you have kids?" Margaret Rappold asked me. Yes, I answered. "Ride them," she said, with ferocity. "Be *on* them, every day." But everyone's telling me to do the opposite, I thought, remembering my ex-husband's complaints that I was overprotective and the advice coming from all quarters to allow the children to develop more autonomy and privacy. Her admonition—and the gravity of her expression—seared into my brain. Walking back to Joe's car at the end of the meeting, I felt like I had two new sensitive and urgent lists: one composed of investigative tasks for Nicholas and another of how to keep my children alive.

MAY 16, 2014: DAY 58 OF TRIAL

In the courtroom, I directed Margaret's attention back to the night of her talk with her son. Nick had placed a vial of Xanax pills on Margaret's end table. When she asked him about it, he said they weren't his, they were for someone else. He said, "Please don't throw them away," and she didn't.

The day of their pre-dawn conversation turned into their last day together. Margaret Rappold went to see Nick at the restaurant where he worked, to give him a receipt he needed. She saw him again at six o'clock, when he came home, ran upstairs, showered, and kissed his grandmother good-bye—"I love you, Grams."

"He blew me a kiss," Margaret Rappold told the jury, "and he ran out. He said he had a date and that was it."

She went to bed but woke up at midnight to go into Nick's bedroom. Realizing it might be too early for him to be home, she went back to bed. She woke up again at four o'clock.

As we proceeded with the questions, she and I both knew that we had crossed that boundary of time where Nicholas was already dead, or near death, but she had not known it and had not been able to help him. The helplessness was horrific. But we had to keep going.

She couldn't get the words out fast enough and choked on her tears.

"I shot up. I just had a feeling something was wrong and I ran downstairs and put on my sneakers and ran outside in my pajamas and started to drive round the neighborhood looking for him. I didn't find him, and I got back home about ten after five."

"What did you do when you got home?" I asked.

"What did I do? I stayed awake until about six o'clock and I got up, showered, and went to work and I abruptly left at twelve o'clock because my boss happened to be in the kitchen that day and I said, 'I have to leave; something is wrong with my son,' and I left."

Nicholas was already dead when she went home and called six or eight of his friends, asking if they knew where he was.

"And what did you do next?" I asked.

"I waited. One of his friends called back and said they found his car and a friend of his father came, picked me up, and we went to the place where they found the car."

It was time for the court reporter shift change. With a jangle of keys and the clickety-clack of their machines getting lifted up and folded and put down and unfolded, one court reporter switched with the other. When the new reporter was ready, she nodded.

But during those few minutes, Margaret Rappold had lost her momentum and the hold she had been exerting over her emotions gave out. Tears rolled down her cheeks. I asked her a few more questions, but I knew it was time to stop. I knew she couldn't describe what happened next. That there were police officers surrounding Nicholas's car when she arrived on the scene. That some of his friends were there, one of them hysterical. That Margaret couldn't go near the car. That her brother met her there and took care of everything, because she could not.

A random cell phone rang out in the courtroom. The judge asked Margaret if she was okay.

We ran through a few questions about a back injury that Nick sustained when he was working for an air-conditioning and refrigeration company. He had hurt himself lifting an air-conditioner, but he was not hospitalized and continued playing sports, though he sometimes wore a special magnetic belt for pain. And that was it.

Belair promised the judge—and, implicitly, Margaret Rappold—that he had just a "couple" of questions on cross-examination. The mood in the courtroom was wary. Belair followed up on the back injury, then asked some questions about the friends with whom Nicholas had spent his last evening. In one of his questions, Belair slipped and asked about her husband rather than her son. On that note—with a correction from the judge and an apology to the witness—cross-examination ended. Margaret Rappold stood up and walked out of the courtroom with her broken heart.

Next came Michael Rappold's turn. We had spoken to Rappold many times, of course, before trial, and I thought I knew what he was going to say. I had not anticipated, however, the confessional force of the witness stand.

When Rappold took the stand, the jury seemed relieved at first. Everyone had been frozen during Margaret's testimony. I could feel them relaxing just a touch now—sitting back, breathing, moving in their seats. How could it be worse than what they had just heard? Rappold had planned to become a physician's assistant, he said, and confirmed that his brother's behavior and appearance had changed in the months before the overdose.

We had called him to the stand primarily to establish a chain of custody for two important pieces of evidence: a set of empty pill bottles that he'd found while cleaning out Nicholas's room and the bottle of Xanax pills recovered from Nicholas's car. The police officers on the scene of Nicholas's death had found that Xanax bottle, still containing medication, in the center console of the car under Nicholas's body. They bundled the bottle, along with Nicholas's other belongings, into a plastic bag and gave it to a family friend, who then gave it to Michael Rappold. When Michael told his uncle, Margaret's brother, about the bottles (the ones from Nicholas's room as well as the one from the car), Michael's uncle made contact with the FBI and turned them over, without knowing quite what to expect but hoping for some sort of investigation. We obtained the pill bottles from the FBI, but still needed Rappold's testimony to authenticate them.

I asked Rappold to tell us how the day of Nicholas's death had unfolded for him. He was working, he said, and saw that he had been receiving calls from family members as well as Nicholas's friends. He was not allowed to answer his phone on the job, however, so he ignored the calls at first.

As Rappold spoke, he seemed to be breaking open.

"At one p.m.," he said, "I received a phone call from my mom saying to please come home and she sounded quite upset and something sounded urgent. I asked her, what was the problem? And she told me a story over the phone saying something happened with my grandmother."

With this detail, we learned that Margaret had been trying to protect Rappold, because she knew he still had to drive home.

"I quickly gathered up my belongings and proceeded to leave and stopped myself and said, I can't travel home knowing that something is wrong. So, I proceeded to call her at the house again. She answered the phone and she just asked me in a crying voice, 'Please come home.' Then someone else answered the phone and which sounded to me like my brother said, 'You know, Michael, please come home.' So I said okay. In this case, I'm coming home now. Got in my car. And as I was driving, I received a phone call from my cousin who resides in Texas and she said, 'Is everything okay? What's going on?' I said to her, 'I don't know. I think something happened with Grandma.' She said, 'Grandma? I thought something happened with Nicholas.'"

Rappold paused. Caught his breath. "So now I'm in the car. I have two—two stories that I don't know what to do. So, I called my aunt and uncle who would be the next clarification as I'm driving home. My aunt who answered the phone told me my brother passed away. Um, I am in front of North Shore Hospital on Community Drive.

"I don't know how I got home," Rappold stammered. "I got home."

Those three words covered a long drive, from Long Island to Queens. They described a young man on autopilot, pulling himself from point A to point B. They described a young man doing something even though he did not have the strength to do it and because he had no choice.

"And the whole time," Rappold explained, with raw honesty, "thinking just let me see my brother and my mom there, and not wish my grandmother died, but it would be a lot more comfortable with me. And I pulled up to the house. There was people, of course, all around.

And as soon as I got home, I just see my grandmother and my mom sitting there and I collapse on the living room floor."

The whole way home, he'd been sending up irrational prayers for the crisis to be something he could accept. When he saw his grandmother alive in the house, he understood. When he understood, he collapsed.

I needed to stop and process this young man's grief. I could not stop, could not process. I took him through the rest of my questions, sat through his short cross-examination, then watched him leave the courtroom.

Dr. Li sat there and listened to Margaret and Michael Rappold testify. I looked at him and wondered what he was thinking, what on earth he had been thinking—would he ever take responsibility? Was his conscience even burdened by this death? Did he still think of himself as "one of the good ones" or, worse yet, a scapegoat?

I was glad Margaret hadn't watched her eldest son's testimony. I thought about the feeling of having my children cuddled up in bed with me, when they were sick or sad or just needed to talk or for no reason at all. Their warmth, their bulk, the sound of their breathing. I couldn't fathom what it would feel like to have those memories without any possibility of ever holding them again. I also found it unbearable to think that this family was not alone—that Nicholas was not alone.

In fact, Nicholas was far from alone. He was one of 541 unintentional opioid overdose deaths reported by the New York City Office of the Chief Medical Examiner for the year 2010 in New York City alone. Multiply his family's pain 541 times. He was one of 16,651 overdose deaths involving opioid painkillers in the United States in 2010. Multiply his family's pain 16,651 times. That left too many parents counting the days since their child's disappearance.

EARLY JUNE 2011: APPROXIMATELY 1,023 DAYS UNTIL TRIAL

Joe and I were aware of these grim numbers when we first confirmed Nicholas Rappold's death in 2011. After we visited his grave and met his mother, though, we could no longer see numbers: we saw human beings, tragedies, mysteries. We knew the reality behind those bare statistics. Every death was someone's child. Every death had a story. Each one of those stories revealed that these losses left survivors and the deaths broke the survivors' lives as well. Each one of those death stories also contained details, like Michael Rappold's story, that revealed the extent to which humans and families tried to accommodate tragedy, by softening the blow for one another or trying to make sense of it or making deals with the universe about what they could or could not handle. Each story related countless small gestures of compassion or effort or kindness toward others or toward themselves to reduce the pain.

Once we knew about Nicholas, we wondered about all the other points on the graph: What if they were not isolated incidents? Could any more of them be connected to Dr. Li's practice? If so, how could we find out? There was no way to track deaths from pills resold by Dr. Li's patients on the illegal market, but we could at least find out if any of his patients were dead—and we needed an overdose alert system going forward.

Fortunately, the New York City Office of the Chief Medical Examiner (OCME) had long been concerned about the increase in overdose deaths, so they were ready to help.

When OCME was called upon to conduct an autopsy, it was the medical examiner's job to determine the cause and manner of death. The "cause" referred to the illness or injury that resulted in death. The "manner" referred to the homicidal, suicidal, accidental, natural, or undetermined means of death. There were two key staff members assigned to each case: a Medical Legal Investigator (MLI), who documented the location and condition of the body at the scene and collected any available evidence related to the cause of death; and an ME, who conducted the autopsy and made the final determinations. In addition to paper records maintained on-site for several years, the OCME maintained their own internal, searchable database.

Given Dr. Li's patient population, we sent requests not just to the New York City office, covering all five boroughs, but also to the Nassau and Suffolk County medical examiners' offices. We wanted the names of every single person who had died of an overdose involving any of the controlled substances prescribed by Dr. Li: oxycodone, fentanyl, hydrocodone, morphine, Xanax. Once we had the names, we compared them to the list of patients in the Department of Health's controlled-substance prescription database. We began doing this every three months and continued for years.

That pit in my stomach, from the trial days? It was a familiar feeling. It was the fear of discovering that someone else had died—or, worse yet, that someone had died on our watch. It was a fear that came to pass too many times. It was a fear to which some people seemed to be immune.

APRIL 23, 2014: DAY 35 OF TRIAL

Yitong Li* was twenty-three years old and had been in the United States for less than a year when she became Dr. Li's receptionist. It was 2007, and she'd found the job listing in the *World Journal*, the dominant Chinese-language newspaper in the United States. Dr. Li's wife, Anna Guo, whom Yitong Li also knew as the office manager, conducted the interview. Once hired, the young woman worked one day a week, either Saturday or Sunday, earning a flat fee of seventy dollars a day and sharing the work with another young woman.

When the receptionist testified at trial, seven years later, she didn't look at Dr. Li—her former employer who now stood accused of multiple felonies.

I conducted the direct examination with trepidation, watching for any slight shifts in her body language and expression; when her closed lips formed a half smile, or she paused a little longer before answering, it signaled discomfort. She seemed to be indicating to me that there may or may not be a giant hole between us, into which she would let

---

* No relation to Dr. Li.

my questions fall. Of course, I asked anyway: we had to get the facts out, through either verbal testimony or physical exhibits, and the jury would have to determine whether she was being truthful or not. The key was to ask direct, simple questions in the right order and never, ever assume anything. Through it all, I ran a parallel thought process: To what extent was she responsible? Not enough to prosecute in a court of law, clearly, but what about in the privacy of my own mind and heart? Was I even allowed or eligible to judge her—or anyone else?

The young receptionist spoke softly, clearly, simply. She almost made it all sound normal.

She testified that patients were already waiting outside when she arrived at the clinic at 8:15 a.m. on its weekend "open days." She never knew how many patients would show up—no one did. There were no appointments for a specific day or time: each patient was supposed to come every four weeks, so it was first come, first served every weekend. The two receptionists kept a handwritten list of patients in order of their arrival until August 2009, when Dr. Li instructed them to print up a set of small white laminated cards, each pair numbered from 1 to 100. After that date, the staff handed out the cards in addition to keeping a list, "so we know who is the first and who is the second." The receptionists would attach the matching number card to the patient's file, each one kept in a stack for the doctor. On days when more than one hundred patients arrived, they started again with card number one. The numbered tickets changed everything: When she first began working in the office, Dr. Li had called the patients into the examination room by their names. After August 2009, he called them only by number.

Before walking to the lectern, I'd pulled a few folders from the cart and kept them stacked under my right hand. After Yitong Li mentioned the numbered cards, I pulled one of them out and introduced it into evidence. We were going from story to fact, proving the existence of this practice, but would it be enough?

Yitong Li said that the clinic was open from 8:30 a.m. until 5:30 p.m. Dr. Li and Dr. Guo arrived between 8:30 and 9:00 a.m. Sometimes the clinic stayed open until 6:00 or 6:30 p.m., whenever Dr. Li had seen every patient. The two young women were entitled to one ten- to fifteen-minute lunch break. Dr. Li's break lasted ten minutes.

Most patients received prescriptions, but sometimes Dr. Li administered injections. Yitong Li did not have any medical training, but she helped by holding the medication bottle. By her account, Dr. Li spent approximately fifteen minutes with the patients who received injections and approximately ten minutes with the patients who did not receive injections. She also confirmed that there were days when Dr. Li saw more than one hundred patients.

Now it was time to ask the key question. I wasn't sure the wording was good enough—but "good enough" would have to do. "On the days when Dr. Li saw one hundred or more patients, did he spend ten minutes with each one of those patients?"

"I'm not sure."

Frustration got the better of me.

"Did you ever multiply the number of patients by the number of minutes?"

The defense attorney looked at the judge. "Objection."

"Sustained," said the judge.

You can't impeach your own witness. If your witness's testimony contradicts a statement they made under oath, on a material topic that tends to disprove your position, you can confront them with their previous sworn statement. But you can only do that to signal to the jury that your witness is not credible—you can't do it to "correct" their testimony.

I ruminated on my error all day and into the next. Sometimes witnesses will not state the facts as you know they know them to be. Sometimes a witness may not have consciously acknowledged a fact, however indisputable it may seem. It doesn't matter: prosecutors are rightly held to a high standard. I should have moved on.

The other receptionist was more at ease on the stand, but she hadn't worked in the clinic as long. She also avoided looking at Dr. Li while she testified but seemed less protective of him. She was, however, embarrassed to admit what she had not known. For instance, she testified that when Dr. Li began to require urine tests for patients in June 2011 she tested the urine but didn't know what the results meant. Same thing with blood pressure measurements, which they started taking around the same time.

They were young. They were untrained. The job was part of their initiation into the American culture and workforce: Did they perhaps fail to realize that this was an unusual practice? How much did they really know? How much did they care? What did Dr. Li and his wife tell them? Were they naive or confused or indifferent or complicit? Would I ever understand?

After Dr. Li had seen the last patient, the two young women cleaned the office before going home: the floors, the bathroom, and the tables. During this time, Dr. Li rested. I imagined him lying down on one of the exam tables and falling asleep while the two young women scurried around the office with mops and brooms and his last patients rushed to fill their prescriptions. Did the two young women know how much money Dr. Li made in one day? How did they feel about working there? None of this was admissible at trial, so we couldn't ask.

At the end of Yitong Li's testimony in court, a brouhaha alarmed the jury as well as the witness.

"Your Honor," I said, "there are some loud screams." The shrieks were coming from the wall behind the judge's dais, which separated us from the holding cells.

"There is not much I can do about that," the judge answered. "We have neighbors who don't work for the court system. We will leave it there." He turned toward the jury. "You are not to speculate why there is noise. That's why we keep the door closed."

I remember thinking how fitting it seemed for this testimony to be interrupted by piercing screams of unknown cause and origin. We were in the midst of talking about the mechanics of a job in which two young women had enabled a crime and a human disaster, yet their testimony avoided any description of the carnage. These women were no "hothouse flowers," as Belair had charged during one of our sidebar conferences. If anything, they had not been sensitive enough. Had they understood that instead of curing diseases, Dr. Li fueled the disease of addiction? Had they understood that these patients were people? Had they understood that people were dying? The work certainly hadn't left them with the best impression of our country and its citizens, but had it never occurred to them that they were part of the problem? They had been right there. They had done nothing to stop it.

Anna Guo, Dr. Li's wife and office manager, didn't testify at trial. In fact, she never appeared in court during eighteen weeks of trial, until the day the jury rendered its verdict. Was it really for her that he'd opened the clinic? Did she know that's what he was planning to tell the jury? Couldn't he have run the clinic in a legitimate, legal manner regardless of the reason for its existence? Was she complicit in the crimes he committed? We debated the facts and her culpability for hours, over weeks and months. Was it antifeminist not to ask the grand jury to consider charges against her, if she was the office manager and aware of the patients' conditions? Was it legally appropriate or possible to charge her if she wasn't a licensed physician? Through imperfect consensus we reached a decision: Anna Guo remained a witness to the prosecution, just as she had been to the crimes.

Were any of these young women different, I wondered, from all the "good" people who worked in the corporate offices of the pharmacy chains and pharmaceutical distributors across America, those who had played small, indirect, administrative roles in the unfolding opioid crisis? Were they so different from the employees of the pharmaceutical companies who developed the marketing materials for doctors, trained the sales reps, or visited doctors' offices to close the deal, going to work each day with good intentions and an honest work ethic? All of whom, through putting in their hours and advancing their careers and doing what they were told to do, had laid a foundation for a national catastrophe—and for Margaret Rappold's personal catastrophe.

CHAPTER 5

Who's with Me?

The changes to the OxyContin formulation appear to provide some degree of increased resistance to manipulation of the controlled-release features making the new product less easy to chew, crush, or dissolve. These incremental improvements in the formulation will, hopefully, reduce the incidence of overdose due to abuse and misuse by ingestion or administration [. . .] of crushed or chewed OxyContin, which, due to the manipulation, would act as an immediate-release, high-dose oxycodone formulation. [. . .] Nevertheless, the product is not completely tamper-resistant and those intent on abusing this new formulation will likely find a means to do so. In addition, the product can still be misused or abused and result in overdose by simply administering or ingesting larger than recommended oral doses.

—SUMMARY REVIEW FOR REGULATORY
ACTION ON NDA 22-272 (OXYCONTIN),
FDA CENTER FOR DRUG EVALUATION
AND RESEARCH, APRIL 5, 2010

JANUARY 3, 2009: 1,902 DAYS UNTIL TRIAL

It was Joe Haeg's first visit to Dr. Li. He was a tall young man in his late thirties, reporting seventeen years of chronic back pain. He said he'd been taking OxyContin, eighty milligrams, six pills a day, and Roxicodone, thirty milligrams, twelve pills a day. He'd brought a Roxicodone pill bottle with him. Haeg did not provide any medical records or test results. Dr. Li noted a diagnosis of "low back pain" and prescribed Roxicodone, thirty milligrams, six pills per day.

Three weeks later, Joe Haeg was back. Dr. Li modified the prescription, reducing the Roxicodone to five per day and adding one Percocet to the daily regimen. During Haeg's next visit, on March 1, 2009, Dr. Li decided to replace the Percocet with a fentanyl patch, dosed at 100 micrograms/hour. On March 28, the patient complained of increased pain—as well as the excessive cost of the fentanyl patch. Dr. Li went back up to six Roxicodone pills a day, adding a month's supply of Xanax, 1 mg pills.

On April 18, 2009, Haeg asked for OxyContin, the brand-name pill. Dr. Li refused and also declined to increase the quantities of Roxicodone: the patient's current dosage represented Dr. Li's upper limit for this practice. The patient said he'd find another doctor, so Dr. Li discharged the patient from his care—with the same prescriptions.

Haeg nevertheless returned on May 27, 2009. He told Dr. Li that he'd found another doctor but hadn't been able to book an appointment before June 16. Dr. Li prescribed more Roxicodone and Xanax.

On June 16, Haeg returned to Dr. Li's office. He'd been unable to see the doctor, he said, without explanation. Dr. Li prescribed the same dose of oxycodone and increased the daily dose of Xanax: it was now two pills a day, two milligrams each. Dr. Li issued the same prescription again a few weeks later, on July 11, 2009. On that day, Joseph Haeg was Dr. Li's thirty-fifth patient out of sixty-one: Dawn Tamasi had been the fourth and Nicholas Rappold would be the sixty-first and last.

On August 9, 2009, Haeg complained of increased pain. Dr. Li prescribed the same amount of oxycodone but increased the Xanax to two milligrams, three times a day, and added three Percocet pills to the daily regimen. He issued the same prescription again twenty-seven days later, on September 5, 2009. Haeg returned one week early for his next visit, on September 26, 2009. He complained of chest pain and severe pain in his left hand. Dr. Li recommended that he see a cardiologist and wrote three more prescriptions: Roxicodone, Percocet, and Xanax. Haeg returned on October 17 to receive his usual, full prescriptions: 120 Roxicodone 30 mg pills, 90 Percocet, 90 Xanax. And then again on November 14, 2009—and, as always, with cash with hand.

On Monday, November 23, 2009, Haeg presented at Brookhaven Memorial Hospital Emergency Room with an injury to his ankle. He'd tripped and fallen at home, he told the physician assistant (PA).

The PA examined Joe Haeg. The patient's ankle was swollen and he had trouble walking, but there were no exterior injuries or internal fractures. Haeg's blood pressure, however, was elevated: normal blood pressure is 120 over 80; Haeg's was 232 over 96. The PA told Haeg that he needed to see a primary care doctor for his blood pressure. He said he had a doctor but admitted to not having taken his blood pressure medication. The PA kept him under observation until his blood pressure returned to a normal range, at which point she wrapped Haeg's ankle and dispensed two Percocet pills for the pain, at 5/325 mg strength. She didn't order crutches, because Haeg was able to walk unassisted.

One week later, on December 1, he was back—but he didn't see the same person. Haeg told the ER physician that he had injured his leg hiking, three weeks earlier. He indicated a different location for his pain, this time above the ankle. He left the hospital with more pills—and a pair of crutches.

On December 5, Joe Haeg returned to Dr. Li's clinic for his fourth early visit in a row, complaining of increased pain and a swollen foot. Dr. Li wrote prescriptions for Roxicodone, Percocet, and Xanax. Haeg wasn't supposed to return to the clinic until the month of January, but he would not wind up living that long.

LATE SPRING 2011: APPROXIMATELY 1,023 DAYS UNTIL TRIAL

ADA Joe Tesoriero, the Chief of Investigations, rubbed his hands together, gripping and turning his fists under his fingers with a soft, sandpapery scrub. He was deep in thought. This was a familiar gesture. This was productive. I waited, glancing through the window toward Foley Square.

Joe—whom we all called Joe T., to distinguish him from the other Joes in the office—recently had become involved in the case. With the letter from Seth Grant's father and confirmation of Nicholas Rappold's overdose death, the Li case raised Tesoriero-level issues: jurisdiction, agency coordination, investigative methods, forensic accounting, ethics—and death.

Joe T. had entered into public service decades earlier, as a lateral from a private law firm. His office was one of the neatest and most civilized in Special Narcotics: he had a penholder containing *pens that worked*; he had a framed *New Yorker* cartoon on his desk of Superman taking a call from a poolside chair ("*Listen, pal, they're all emergencies*"); the desk surface was clear, except for a few smooth stones from his family's Mediterranean homeland; he'd even managed to squeeze a diminutive conference table with clean, matching chairs into his office.

During the late spring of 2011, in between my assignments on other cases—court shifts, grand jury presentations, phone calls, and witness interviews—and my work on the Li case, I spent hours in Joe T.'s office, learning its details by heart and discussing the building blocks of our prosecution.

Joe T. leaned his head back and wiped a hand down his face like a windshield wiper—this was an escalation. Once again, the Li case had driven me into Joe T.'s office, and, once again, it had driven Joe T. to the brink. The issues were new. There were so many relevant areas of law and all were complex. And, of course, the stakes were high: a man's reputation, livelihood, and freedom were at risk, but so, it appeared, were human lives.

Joe picked up the phone. A few minutes later, ADA Peter Kougasian bounded into the office, already cracking jokes. We relocated to Joe's miniature conference table, Peter folding his long legs in rumpled suit pants around the chair legs, and thus began another round of debates.

Peter was a former Special Narcotics Bureau Chief, senior adviser to Bridget Brennan, and a close friend of Joe T.'s. Peter had worked as an ADA since his graduation from Yale Law School in 1979, and he also moonlighted as a magician on New York City stages. Peter always came into Joe T.'s office for these meetings for a simple reason: you couldn't get more than twelve inches past Peter's office door without encountering a treacherous pile of cardboard boxes, plastic cups, and old newspapers. Peter seemed to have preserved every obscure biography, *Law Journal* copy, napkin, report, memo, and random lost shoe from the past thirty-odd years. These collections were piled and stratified like a geological formation, not only between the door and Peter's desk but also along the walls, behind the desk, under the computer table, and on the desk surface itself. In this cavern of questionable treasures, where autobiographies of famous magicians abutted legal treatises, Peter worked to a bossa nova rhythm. From a lopsided computer desk placed at a right angle to his overburdened wooden desk, he generated long, erudite emails, speeches for office executives, Bar Association reports, and other mysterious high-level projects for legal luminaries.

Peter's office was, in many ways, reflective of his mind and manner of thinking. He had an intellectual, encyclopedic, digressive, and Socratic approach to case discussions—or any conversation. As usual, his arrival put me on the defensive.

But this was the debate team. Confronted with a new threat to public health and safety, the two veteran prosecutors didn't hesitate to dig into the trenches with me, the relative rookie, calling upon their decades of experience, their knowledge of case law, and their extensive networks for comparison, information, and inspiration to make sure every possible position, viewpoint, and argument would be aired. It wasn't an easy process: only acts of God could bring an end to these meetings. The meetings were an exercise in collective anticipatory anxiety, with a side of statutory review and a fair share of digressive stories, courtesy of Peter, about the Armenian people—his beloved countrymen. Our discussions then bled into uneasy, sleepless nights. I had never imagined there were so many ways we could ruin an innocent physician's life, deprive legitimate patients of their medication, violate our ethical code, or violate a witness's constitutional rights, and we wouldn't be able to live with ourselves if any mistakes led to such unjust consequences.

DECEMBER 2009: APPROXIMATELY 1,570 DAYS UNTIL TRIAL

Officer Kevin Wustenhoff, of the Suffolk County Police Department, was making a car stop. The driver hobbled out of his seat, pulling a pair of crutches with him, before slumping against the side of his vehicle, unable to stand straight. Wustenhoff couldn't smell any alcohol on Haeg's breath, yet Haeg's speech was slurred and he couldn't seem to keep his eyes open. Wustenhoff told Haeg there'd be no more driving that day and asked him to call a family member. They waited together until Haeg was able to get a ride home.

DECEMBER 2010: APPROXIMATELY 1,205 DAYS UNTIL TRIAL

The name Joseph Haeg was unfamiliar to Bridget Brennan, Joe T., and Peter Kougasian, but prescription drug cases were not new to the OSNP. "An alarming trend has emerged across New York City," Bridget had written in the 2009 Annual Report, "as the number of people using illegal prescription drugs and heroin escalates. Opiate addiction often begins in the medicine cabinet with abuse of painkillers, sedatives, and tranquilizers."

In fact, the office's annual reports had reflected a growing sense of unease since 2006: not only was prescription drug abuse more common, but crimes involving the diversion of those drugs were on the rise and there was an alarming and related increase in the availability of high-purity heroin, marketed as a cheaper alternative to prescription opioids. There was also a lot of money in this business.

As early as 2006, the office had noticed a sharp increase in oxy-codone seizures and noted the trend of diversion crimes. That year, Special Narcotics had broken up a drug ring that sent fake patients to fill forged prescriptions, paying $250 for 240 Dilaudid pills at the phar-macy, then reselling the pills at $20 apiece in Alabama. In 2007, the office wrapped up another large diversion investigation where metha-done, oxycodone, and Xanax pills gathered through forged prescrip-tions were shipped to other states for resale.

Between 2007 and 2008, heroin seizures doubled, with our agency alone nabbing 270 pounds, the equivalent of hundreds of thousands of single-dose glassines. In her introduction to the 2009 Annual Report, Bridget Brennan remarked that the seizures that year, still at a high, represented "more heroin in user-ready form than during any single year in recent memory" and that dealers were targeting young clients who were already hooked on opioids but seeking a cheaper alternative to pills. Indeed, the office also apprehended a doctor that year from Amagansett, New York, who supplied OxyContin and other narcotic prescriptions to a co-conspirator in the Bronx and shared in the profits of those pills being resold on the black market for the astounding price of $30 per pill.

Those cases were followed, in 2011, by my Russian supermodel case and the Lickety-Split prosecution, which nabbed a prescription drug ring operating out of a Staten Island ice-cream truck. Several forces had combined to create both an overwhelming supply and a growing demand: an increase in prescriptions; the increased nonmedical use of prescription drugs; and the influx of cheap, pure heroin.

According to the New York City Department of Health and Mental Hygiene, there had been a 22 percent increase in prescriptions of opioid painkillers between 2008 and 2010, from 1,661,465 in 2008 to 2,029,156 in 2010.[1] There were just over 8 million people living in New York City in 2010, so this was the equivalent of one in every four New Yorkers receiving a prescription. But, in actuality, those 2 million prescriptions had been filled by only 722,000 New Yorkers.[2] In addition, the medications were often misused: in 2010, more than 4 percent of New Yorkers over the age of twelve used these painkillers without a prescription or other than as prescribed.[3] In New York City, 4 percent of the population over the age of twelve in 2010 represented more than 300,000 people—a number approaching the total population of Tampa, Florida. Meanwhile, street dealers hawked pure, branded heroin to a younger, whiter crowd of drug abusers.

The result of these converging trends, on a national scale, was catastrophic. The abuse or misuse of opioid painkillers, specifically, caused 474,133 emergency visits in the U.S. in 2010, up 174 percent from 2004.[4] The increase in ER visits for other drugs, such as Xanax, was also stunning: a 168 percent increase in six years, from 46,526 visits in 2004 to 124,902 in 2010.[5] Meanwhile, the legal distribution of prescription medications to retailers reached 14 billion pills in 2010 and headed toward a peak of 17.2 billion pills by 2011.[6] In 2010, over 12 billion of those 14 billion pills were hydrocodone or oxycodone.

Admissions to substance abuse treatment for pharmaceutical opioid addicts began to catch up to heroin admissions. Opiates other than heroin increased from 1 percent of admissions among patients aged twelve and older in 1999, to 7 percent in 2009. Opiates other than heroin represented 8 percent of all opiate admissions in 1999, but rose to 33 percent in 2009.[7] At the same time, substance abuse treatment providers began seeing a deep shift in the demographics of heroin addiction: while the overall number of patients admitted for a primary addiction to heroin had remained more or less stable between 1999 and 2009, heroin abuse was on the rise among young, non-Hispanic white adults—the same demographic group that made up 88 percent of non-heroin opiate addiction patients.[8]

And then there were the deaths. As the rates of prescription painkiller sales and treatment admissions increased, so did the rate of overdose deaths.[9] It was a close correspondence. The numbers varied depending on whether you counted deaths resulting only from pharmaceutical painkiller overdoses or combinations of prescription opioids with illicit drugs or alcohol, but the toll was shocking: tens of thousands of human beings. It seemed as bad as it possibly could get.

DECEMBER 26, 2009: 1,545 DAYS UNTIL TRIAL

Joe Haeg's friend Lyle Park was a placid man with dark hair. They were close enough for Haeg to pepper Park with requests for small favors, like small amounts of money, duct-taping the side-view mirror of Haeg's car, or even buying toilet paper. Park helped him out, but not without teasing Haeg that the requests needed to stop.

On December 26, 2009, Park agreed to do Haeg another favor: drive him to the doctor's office. Haeg was in bad shape, Park said, with a bandaged foot, crutches, and "a very sloppy appearance": "his clothes were a mess; his hair was a mess." They drove to Queens.

That day, Dr. Li issued Haeg's usual prescriptions for Roxicodone, Percocet, and Xanax—as well as a prescription for five hundred milligrams of naproxen, to be taken three times a day. He'd noticed that Haeg's foot was swollen and red.

Before Park had time to find a spot, Haeg was ready to go. "That was one of my concerns," he later said about Haeg's visit to the doctor. "It wasn't very long."

After they left the doctor's office, Park drove Haeg to a nearby pharmacy. The pharmacist knew of Dr. Li's practice: she filled at least ten prescriptions written by Dr. Li every Saturday and always called Dr. Li's office to verify the prescriptions when, as in Haeg's case, both oxycodone and Percocet were ordered, because she wanted to make sure that the doctor intended to prescribe two opioids together. She called; Li's office confirmed the prescriptions; she dispensed the medications for Haeg at 12:22 p.m.

Haeg began taking pills as soon as he got back into the car. Park drove him home. And that was it.

EARLY SUMMER 2011: APPROXIMATELY 1,023 DAYS UNTIL TRIAL

"Are we really going to get into the business of telling a doctor what he can or cannot prescribe?" Joe would argue. "Isn't it someone else's job to investigate doctors?"

Doctors—especially those licensed to prescribe controlled substances—operated in a special territory, and if we were to pursue a criminal case against Dr. Li, we needed to be able to prove that he had stepped outside the boundaries of legitimate medical care and even further beyond, into illegality. But where, exactly, were those boundaries? Who was in charge of policing them?

New York Education Law, Article 131, Section 6521, defined the practice of medicine as "diagnosing, treating, operating or prescribing for any human disease, pain, injury, deformity or physical condition." The state licensed and allowed qualified physicians to exercise the profession.

With respect to prescribing, the federal government respected and deferred to physicians by licensing them to serve as gatekeepers for otherwise illegal substances. Prescription narcotics, such as oxycodone and fentanyl, were classified as Schedule II Controlled Substances, which meant they had an accepted medical use despite a high potential for abuse and could be obtained with a prescription. Xanax was a Schedule IV Controlled Substance, based on a lower risk of dependence and abuse, which also had an accepted medical use but could only be obtained with a prescription.

In New York State, the standard for prescribing such substances was both subjective and deferential, requiring only that the practitioner act in good faith, in the course of his or her professional practice, for legitimate medical purposes or treatment, and in quantities "ordinarily recognized by members of his profession as sufficient for proper treatment."[10]

Peter, Joe, and I read these statutes aloud to one another, in whole or in part, picking apart every word. What constituted "good faith"? What was a "professional practice"? Was it enough to be in a medical office, wearing a white coat? Wasn't a physician always "in the course of their professional practice" if they were treating a patient, whether they were doing it from home, by telephone, or in a clinic? What constituted a "legitimate medical purpose"? What was "ordinarily recognized" by members of the medical profession as "sufficient for proper treatment"? Could there be exceptions based on the specific facts of a unique case? There seemed to be a tremendous amount of discretion allowed for physicians: the rule referred to an accepted standard of care within the profession, set by the profession, but also allowed for case-by-case determinations.

We looked to definitions of professional misconduct to define the outer borders to the physicians' haven of discretion and autonomy but found little clarity there, either.

We knew that doctors are often constrained by economic forces to practice medicine in a manner other than their education or conscience would dictate—but bad medicine could not be automatic grounds for misconduct, let alone prosecution. What was the next worse thing—negligence? Incompetence? Both might qualify as misconduct, but neither was necessarily a crime, especially if Dr. Li was operating "in good faith," whatever that meant.

The first line of defense against medical misconduct in New York State was not the District Attorney's Office but rather the Office of Professional Medical Conduct (OPMC), which was empowered by the state legislature to monitor physicians and impose disciplinary consequences. The categories of possible misconduct falling under the OPMC's exclusive jurisdiction included negligence, incompetence, exploiting patients for financial gain, and filing false reports, with penalties ranging from monetary fines to the loss of medical licenses.

Meanwhile, the laws designed to draw the line between good faith and greed, misconduct and crime, required interpretation and inquiry.

New York State doctors were not allowed to prescribe controlled substances to addicted persons or habitual users. Section 80.65 of the *New York Codes, Rules and Regulations*, pertaining to controlled substances, warned that "[a]n order purporting to be a prescription, issued to an addict or habitual user of controlled substances, not in the course of professional treatment but for the purpose of providing the user with narcotics or other controlled substances sufficient to keep him comfortable by maintaining his customary use, is not a prescription [. . .] and the person knowingly filling such an order, as well as the person issuing it, shall be subject to the penalties provided for violation of the provisions of law relating to controlled substances."[11]

Section 80.76 of the same statute stated that "[c]ontrolled substances shall not be prescribed for, administered or dispensed to addicts or habitual users of controlled substances" but referred back to the Public Health Law for exceptions, which include "emergency medical treatment unrelated to substance abuse," "the treatment of incurable and fatal diseases," or "to relieve acute withdrawal symptoms."[12]

We asked ourselves whether the exception to relieve withdrawal symptoms applied if the doctor had created and enabled the addiction. Or what if a patient was obtaining the prescriptions under false pretenses? After all, New York's *Codes, Rules and Regulations* also prohibited patients from obtaining or attempting to obtain a controlled-substance prescription by fraud, deceit, concealment, or forgery.[13] But what if the doctor *knew* that the patient was lying and still wrote the prescriptions?

Somewhere, beyond the zones governed by the OPMC and the Public Health Law, lay criminal conduct and criminal penalties: Where was that boundary? At what point and with what kind of behavior was a doctor committing a crime—a felony narcotics crime—fit for prosecution?

Looking back, I wonder why it was so hard, for so long, for us to accept that a doctor might be driven simply and only by greed. We didn't want to believe it until we had solid proof.

As the investigation advanced, every new piece of information raised the stakes. In May 2011, I had received a large white envelope from the Office of the Chief Medical Examiner, containing the autopsy report for Nicholas Rappold. In the photo, he was pale, stubbled, still-faced, neither smiling nor alive. Reading about his organs and bones, I considered the detachment of this anatomical inventory: in this report, Nicholas was more a puzzle than a person. The autopsy's conclusion was clear: the cause of death was "acute intoxication due to the combined effects of alprazolam and oxycodone."

Joe T., Joe Hall, Peter, and I had been careful with the word "homicide," but that possibility was beginning to weigh on us. Homicide, or "conduct which causes the death of a person," came in several forms under New York State law: it could be Criminally Negligent Homicide, the result of a failure to perceive a risk; it could be Manslaughter in the Second Degree, requiring proof of awareness and conscious disregard of risk; it could be Manslaughter in the First Degree, or an intentional killing. The different types of homicide charges depended upon the intent driving the deed—which was hard enough to determine. In our case, we didn't even have physical contact or a murder weapon: all we had was a doctor, a bunch of prescriptions, cash payments, and a young man in his grave.

Or maybe two young men, in two solitary graves.

DECEMBER 29, 2009: 1,542 DAYS UNTIL TRIAL

Police Officer Maureen Bourguignon, from the Suffolk County Police, was on patrol by herself when she was dispatched to respond to a 911 call. She walked up the stairs of a town-house condominium building in Moriches and found a distressed woman waiting for her in the living room. The woman's name was Kathleen Haeg* and this was her son's apartment, she explained. Shaking, she directed Officer Bourguignon to the bedroom.

---

* Kathleen Haeg died of pancreatic cancer in 2013, one month after her diagnosis and several months before the trial. May she rest in love.

There Officer Bourguignon found a male body slumped, facedown, over the bed, wearing white underwear and a gauze bandage on his ankle. A pair of crutches rested nearby. She walked around the room, looking for anything that didn't seem right or didn't belong. She did not need to check for vital signs: the body was bloated with fluids, blood had pooled in response to the pull of gravity, and she noticed bleeding from its orifices. The unattended death of a young man for some unknown cause led Officer Bourguignon to call in the homicide squad.

When Police Officer Kevin Wustenhoff arrived, he noticed a prescription pill bottle on the bed. He recognized the young man.

Wustenhoff didn't move anything in the room but reached out to touch Joseph Haeg's arm, just to be sure. Nothing could be done.

Detective Vincent Stephan, from the Suffolk County Police Homicide Squad, made his own rounds of the apartment and found the decedent's cell phone. The last outgoing call had been made on December 26 at 7:05 p.m.† Detective Stephan noticed prescription pill bottles in the kitchen, all in the name of Haeg. Stephan left the pill bottles untouched; it would be the responsibility of another professional, the Medical Legal Investigator, to document their location and preserve them.

David Reed worked for the Suffolk County Office of the Chief Medical Examiner. He was the Medical Legal Investigator assigned to the Haeg case. When he later testified at trial, he described his job as "investigating death." Reed then told the jury what he had seen and done inside Haeg's apartment.

When David Reed first arrived at the Moriches condominium on December 29, 2009, he noticed that the air in the apartment was warm, which would be relevant to his analysis of the death scene. There was no weapon, no alcohol, no suicide note. Just several prescription bottles and a prescription for an MRI issued by a Dr. Stan X. Li. Reed sealed these items into plastic evidence bags. Now it was time for the examina-

---

† We never knew to which number Haeg had made his last call and the phone was no longer available by the time we met his family. When it is your job to reconstruct past events, it is sometimes hard to accept gaps.

tion. He pulled the comforter off the body and felt Haeg's skull, spine, back, and extremities, looking for any signs of trauma and taking photos. He turned the body over and conducted the same examination. Rigor mortis, the stiffening of the body's muscles that occurs within nine to twelve hours of death and lasts anywhere from twenty-four to thirty-six hours, had begun to dissipate. The state of Haeg's capillaries and skin also indicated moderate decomposition.

Back at his office, Reed counted the pills in the bottles, all dated December 26, 2009 (three days prior) and bearing Dr. Li's name. A bottle of naproxen remained untouched, and from a bottle of gabapentin, also prescribed by Dr. Li to Joseph Haeg, only two pills were missing. But out of the 90 Percocet pills prescribed, only 67 now remained. The bottle of 120 oxycodone pills now contained only 85. And the Xanax bottle was empty—all 90 pills were missing.

Reed dialed Dr. Li's number, informing him that his patient was dead. Without revealing any further details, he asked Dr. Li to fax him a copy of the patient file.

Later that day, Reed received a fax from Dr. Li. He accepted the chart without question or suspicion and forwarded the Haeg case to Dr. Odette Hall, the medical examiner to whom it had been assigned.

More than one thousand days later, the entire case file, including Dr. Li's fax, would end up on our evidence cart. It was stored just a few inches away from Dr. Li's original patient chart for Joseph Haeg, of which the fax purported to be an exact copy.

MID-AUGUST 2011: APPROXIMATELY 948 DAYS UNTIL TRIAL

It was the worst possible news: we had a match. From the Suffolk County Office of the Chief Medical Examiner's list of overdose decedents: Joseph Haeg. From our database of Dr. Li's controlled-substance prescriptions: Joseph Haeg. The addresses and dates of birth matched up. And only three days had elapsed between Joe Haeg's last prescriptions from Dr. Li and his death.

After hearing from Joe Hall and our analyst about the data, I called Joe T. It was time for another meeting. A decision had to be made. Were we investigating these deaths as potential homicides?

APRIL 3, 2014: DAY 15 OF TRIAL

Dr. Odette Hall testified without incident.

As the medical examiner she'd been charged with performing Haeg's autopsy to identify the cause of death, referred to as the "physiologic derangement" that caused the person to die, otherwise known as "what went wrong." She'd reviewed Reed's file, including the patient file faxed by Dr. Li. Other than the bandage on Haeg's right ankle, there was no external sign of injury.

After having reviewed the toxicology report from the blood samples she'd taken, Dr. Hall determined that the manner of death was accidental. She identified the *cause* of death as an acute oxycodone intoxication with a contributory cause of probable pulmonary sarcoidosis, hypertensive and atherosclerotic cardiovascular disease. In plain English, the level of oxycodone in his body was high enough to cause death and he had other conditions—the contributory causes—that may have aggravated the situation but were otherwise unrelated. Although the levels of oxycodone in Haeg's blood were within a toxic range, Dr. Hall could not tell how many oxycodone pills he had taken. She couldn't tell whether the drug was on the "upswing" or "downswing," meaning that she could not say whether the detected levels represented the peak concentrations of oxycodone in Haeg's blood or misleadingly low levels because his body already had begun to metabolize the medicine. Dr. Hall did not consider the role of Xanax, because in her reading of the report Xanax was not a factor.

A few days after Dr. Hall's testimony, Chief Toxicologist for the Suffolk County Office of the Chief Medical Examiner Dr. Michael Lehrer took the stand. Dr. Hall's colleague, he'd overseen and verified Haeg's toxicology testing.

From his usual seat at the defense table, Belair listened to the testimony motionless, attuned, unknowable—and well armed.

Dr. Lehrer confirmed the highly toxic levels of oxycodone in Haeg's blood, small intestine, and gastric contents. The tests detected the presence of oxymorphone, a substance produced by the body as oxycodone is being metabolized, which indicated that Haeg's organs had been working overtime, for some time, to try to get rid of the drug. According to Dr. Lehrer, the toxicology report also indicated the presence of Xanax, however, in a "moderately high therapeutic concentration." While the levels of Xanax had not been sufficient to merit specific quantification in the toxicology report, it was a sufficient concentration to have been noted—and to have had an effect on the body.

"Death doesn't happen instantly when you take a lot of depressants," Dr. Lehrer told the jury. "You fall asleep, and then you are drifting in and out of a coma, and then you are in a coma; and all during that time the body is metabolizing or chewing up the drug. Then at some point your breathing becomes so shallow that you are not getting enough oxygen over a period of time to support the essential functions of the body. Your heart basically just doesn't get any fuel to pump, and it slows down. It slows down and stops. Because you are so sedated you don't even feel it. So, you just go to sleep, and you don't wake up essentially. So, the presence of things like Xanax or alprazolam are [sic] that they are also depressants and they are also pulling in the same direction of the oxycodone. Plus, the level at death is usually much lower than it was when the person was still alive. He died over hours, and the body meanwhile is chewing up the material and breaking it down, so it's no longer alprazolam."

"So," I asked, "even if a person is unconscious, is their body still processing the drug?"

"Oh, yeah."

"At what point does that stop?"

"Once the heart stops," Dr. Lehrer said.

We may have been discussing bodies in general, but we were talking about Joseph Haeg in particular: He fell asleep. He slipped into a coma. His body kept trying, but his heart slowed down until it stopped. He didn't feel a thing. He just went to sleep and never woke up.

We were reviewing concentration levels and metabolization in general, but we were talking, specifically, about a toxicology report that Dr. Lehrer and Dr. Hall had interpreted—or testified about—differently. Did Dr. Hall make a mistake during her testimony? Was the toxicology report unclear? Was Dr. Lehrer placing undue emphasis on a low-level finding?

When Belair took over the lectern for his cross-examination, he proposed another theory: Dr. Lehrer was being dishonest and responding to prosecutorial pressure (meaning from me and Peter and our entire office) to talk about the Xanax when it hadn't actually appeared in the report.

"You have to know how to read the report," Dr. Lehrer responded.

The inconsistency between the two witnesses could have been seen as proof that we had not coordinated their stories. We told Dr. Hall and Dr. Lehrer to tell the truth: we had to let the chips fall where they would. The report was in evidence for the jury to see, should they wish to do so during deliberations. We would just have to wait and see.

After Dr. Lehrer, a forensic chemist testified about the pills found in Haeg's apartment. This testimony was long, technical, and essential: it was our burden to prove that the pills in the prescription bottles did, in fact, contain oxycodone and Xanax.

During the chemist's cross-examination, Belair riffed one of his frequent lines of attack: this case wasn't a homicide until Special Narcotics made it so. Little did he know that we were proud of this fact. These deaths had just been accepted as unfortunate by-products of the opioid epidemic, but we had questioned them.

FALL 2011: APPROXIMATELY 931 DAYS UNTIL TRIAL

The meetings in Joe T.'s office had given way to shorter but bigger meetings in the office's formal conference room, just across the hall. Through the big windows framed with carved wood, we could see . . . a brick wall, and the dirt-fogged windows of the units on the other side of the courtyard. Still, it was an intimidating and stately setting, especially with Bridget Brennan herself and her top executives, including Joe T. and Peter, sitting beside her.

Joe Hall and I gave our report: over the last few months, our over-dose alert system had identified ten people who had died of opioid-related overdoses while under Dr. Li's "care" or within a year of leaving his practice. Of those ten deaths, we proposed to investigate two—the deaths of Nicholas Rappold and Joseph Haeg—as possible homicides.

The mood in the room was somber, to say the least. For a grand jury to charge a doctor with the overdose death of a patient would be a first in New York State—and yet here we were, slowly and carefully following the facts to what seemed like the worst possible conclusion and a high bur-den of proof: we were beginning to see evidence that a licensed physician might have caused the death of at least one patient, if not more.

We looked at similar federal and state prosecutions for guidance. In Georgia, prosecutors had charged a doctor with felony murder for his patient's fatal overdose. "Felony murder" is a special kind of homicide law that doesn't exist in every jurisdiction. It means that whether or not a defendant had the intent to kill, they are liable for the death when it occurs during the commission of a felony crime. New York State had a felony murder statute (Penal Law §125.25[3]), but only certain felonies were eligible: robbery, burglary, kidnapping, arson, rape in the first degree, criminal sexual act in the first degree, sexual abuse in the first degree, aggravated sexual abuse, escape in the first degree, and escape in the second degree. Illegal sales of prescriptions didn't qualify.

Under federal law, the overdose death of a patient could lead to a sentencing enhancement. For individuals convicted of certain drug offenses, including the possession of painkillers with intent to distrib-ute, unlawful distribution, and conspiracy to commit those crimes, homicide was an aggravating factor that could result in the addition of twenty years to the defendant's prison sentence.[14]

Of course, federal prosecutors couldn't just say that someone died and expect the judge to add twenty years to the sentence. Until 2014, the standard was contributory causation, meaning that the prosecution had to prove that the drug contributed to the death. In 2014, however, the Supreme Court ruled that in cases where the drug illegally distributed by the defendant was not an "independently sufficient cause of the victim's death or serious bodily injury," the penalty enhancement could not apply. In those cases, where death was the result of more than one drug and the drug traced back to the defendant would not have killed the victim on its own, the prosecution had to prove that it was a "but-for cause of the death or injury."[15] In other words, the jury had to find that without that drug in the mix, the victim would not have died.

Under New York law, there was no such sentence enhancement for narcotics crimes: if there was a death, prosecutors had to ask the grand jury to consider that charge as a separate crime and meet their burden of proof in the grand jury and then at trial.

Whether or not our team could meet the burden of proof for any homicide count in the Li case, in either forum, was a later discussion. One thing was clear: because we were dealing with a doctor who was writing prescriptions for medications that were taken—and abused—at a later time by patients who subsequently died, whatever approach we took would be novel, and we were certain to have many more debates in Joe T.'s office, the conference room—and, ultimately, one or more New York State courtrooms.

One question always resurfaced during these debates: What did the doctor know? Did he know that his patients were abusing the medications? Did he know about any of the overdoses, fatal or nonfatal? What if he continued prescribing medications to addicted patients despite that knowledge? Notice was tied to intent. Intent distinguished reckless criminal conduct from mere incompetence or negligence. A doctor without a clue, or who didn't even know to check for a risk, did not have the same level of culpability as a doctor who knew the risks, received clear warnings, and nevertheless disregarded them. But was that the case, and if so, could we prove it?

Joe Hall and I pulled the discussions back to money. We'd been gathering evidence about Dr. Li's cash fees and insurance claims. His was a volume business. We'd even begun talking to the folks who investigated Medicare fraud about evidence that Dr. Li forced beneficiaries to pay cash for visits and submitted false claims. If we believed this doctor was behaving as a drug dealer, then why not prosecute him the same way, by pointing to the profit? Why get lost in the nuances?

Peter pushed back. He told us about a friend of his who had managed to ship vast quantities of expired medications to Armenia as part of a relief effort. "What's to say Dr. Li is not a humanitarian," Peter challenged us, with a hypothetical defense argument, "and you're going after him when he may be the only one providing pain relief to an underserved, suffering population?" I had little patience for it: we would present proof that Dr. Li sought profit at any cost, and he'd respond by playing the martyr? At the time, it seemed absurd.

APRIL 2, 2014: DAY 14 OF TRIAL

"He was so funny, and he was so smart," Haeg's sister, Kristin, told the jury. "Probably more than I gave him credit for. Loved his family.

"Joey was so good at so many things and he, he loved his nephews and, you know, he loved outside, and he loved, you know—he was very good with kids and animals and good with nature and he loved being around his friends and he was just, he was a people person, my brother, you know."

As I asked my questions and listened to her responses, I thought about all the people who had been there for Haeg on the other side of life, checking his room, examining his body, testing his blood, counting his pills, analyzing their contents, interviewing his family, tracking down his doctors, reading his medical records, reconstructing his last movements, questioning witnesses, cross-examining, making rulings, bickering over evidence in sidebar discussions, sitting in judgment of the facts in a grand jury chamber and again in a courtroom, writing about him, thinking about him.

Kristin, Kathleen, Kristen's husband, Haeg's father—they had been all on their own trying to help him when he was alive, fighting against powerful, unseen forces. What an indictment of our world when we have better systems in place to protect people after death, rather than in life.

When Haeg moved to the town-house apartment, in the summer of 2009, Kristin saw him almost every day for a few months as she was studying to receive a graduate degree. "He would come over and at the time I was finishing my master's so he would play with the kids and I would do homework or we would cook together or ride bikes with my kids or, you know, we just kind of hung out, watched TV." In October, Kristin began noticing changes in her brother's appearance and demeanor. She noticed that he wasn't sleeping, that he seemed very confused, sluggish, and tired. He called her four or five times a day, they talked, but then he would have no recollection of their conversation the next time he called. Kristin took pictures of her caller ID screen, thinking she could use the photos to show him what he was doing. She videotaped him one night, as she wanted to show him what he looked like.

"I wanted him to see the way he was acting because I thought it was strange," she explained. "I wanted him to see, you know, what he looked like through my eyes and I thought, you know, maybe if he saw it then he would, you know, say, well, maybe I am acting strange."

"Did you ever show him that video?" I asked.

"No," Kristin admitted, "I never got to show it to him."

In early November, Kristin received a frantic and confused call from her brother one morning: he had been pulled over and needed someone to pick him up. Kristin sent her husband, Jim. The next time Kristin saw her brother, she noticed that his leg was swollen. His eyes were dark, she said, and sunken into his head. His car had unexplained damage. Toward the end of November, his state of mind degenerated. "He was, he was very confused, you know," Kristin told the jury. "Especially as it got into December. He would call me, he would say he was with imaginary friends or that he was working at two o'clock in the morning. Very bizarre."

On November 21, 2009, Kristin's birthday, she walked into the kitchen and didn't recognize the man sitting at the table.

He had flowers.

It was her brother.

Four and a half years later, on the witness stand, Kristin Delumen started crying as she remembered that day. "I looked at him and I just said, you know, you are gonna die, there is something really wrong with you, you have to get help." Within just a few days, he had changed so much, she said. He looked terrible—scary. Her son was home and wanted to see his uncle, but she kept him away from Joe. "His whole, the whole shape of his faced changed," she described. "You know, his eyes were dark, he was, like his skin was sort of clammy a little bit. He didn't look like my brother."

Kristin had seen her brother taking pills and heard him talking about his back pain. She also had taken him to a pharmacy once to fill prescriptions, driving all the way to Westbury because he told her he couldn't go to the CVS or Walgreens nearby. She thought this was weird but did what her brother asked, and he was going to see a doctor, so it was okay. He did not have enough money to pay for the prescriptions, so she gave him money.

As her brother became less able to take care of himself, Kristin brought him meals, tidied up his apartment, and gave him money. She emailed her mother, who was on a cruise, and told Kathleen that Joe was "acting crazy," that she couldn't handle it on her own anymore, she needed help to take care of him. Kathleen was coming home in December and promised to help.

On December 24, Kristin spoke to her brother on the telephone. He had said something hurtful about her and she was angry. "I said things that really weren't—" She interrupted herself, choking back a sob. "I yelled at him," she admitted.

It was the last time they spoke. Their last time seeing each other already had passed.

Joseph Haeg spoke for himself twice during the trial.

Kristin found a small notebook in her brother's apartment after he died. It contained one thing: a letter to her. She'd kept the notebook with her in her purse ever since. Poor Kristin—once she mentioned it to us and we looked at it, we knew that it was important evidence. The words were written in large, uncontrolled script that spread over one page, continued on the next, and ended in a downward scrawl, like a pen dragged across paper. Not only did we want to borrow it, we said, but we would need to store it indefinitely with the rest of the evidence in order to ensure its integrity. She held it close, then handed it over. It became People's Exhibit 5 and found a home on the evidence cart, our repository for the most precious, painful, and persuasive relics of so many lives.

As Peter described it to the judge during a sidebar conference about admissibility, it was an "antisuicide note." Belair made a forceful objection. His client would be prejudiced by the notebook's admission, Belair said, because "it is dripping with emotionalism and how he [Haeg] treated her so badly and all of this. It is a distraction; it is just modeling; it doesn't prove anything."

The jury did not see the pages themselves. They just heard the words, read out loud across the courtroom, in Kristin's voice.

"Dear Jim and Krissy. I want you to know that I am so sorry about the way I acted and all the grief that I caused you." Kristin struggled to form the words as her mouth filled with sobs. "Jim, what you did went above the call of duty. I want you to know that what you did for me saved my life and I am going to do the best I can to live it to the fullest, a clean, honest, hard-working, productive person. You gave me a second chance on life and I am so thankful. As far as the drugs, I haven't done illegal drugs in years. When I went to the hospital my blood pressure was 284 *above 182. The ER doctor told me I had to get a doc right away because I could have a stroke. When I did, the doctor gave me a Xanax. Prior to this I hadn't slept in almost four days or eaten a decent meal.*" The last few words were illegible, so Kristin just stopped reading and looked up. The jury couldn't see that the pen marks straggled and fell off the page—they wouldn't know unless they asked to see the exhibit later, during their deliberations.

And then there in his sister's ten-second video was Haeg himself, sitting at a table in front of a pizza. "I'm so hungry," he mumbled, lifting a piece. His hair was mussed and you could see what Kristin meant when she said his eyes were dark and sunken in—they looked like cartoon circles of darkness within the shadowed orb of his eye sockets. He was still handsome, but he looked and sounded hollow. His voice strained to reach a normal tone and speed, like a record player losing power. But he was there.

Haeg had family and friends willing to help with so much for so long, but they were no match for a doctor with a prescription pad. Stan Li was Joseph Haeg's doctor, but Joseph Haeg was the doctor's victim.

At the end of that day, we packed up the remains of Joe Haeg's life—the video recording and his tender, incomplete message to his sister—into the evidence cart and rolled it all back to our office, where it remained under lock and key until the next morning.

CHAPTER 6

The Fruits of Our Labor

Misuse of prescription opioids, which are used to treat both acute and chronic pain, has become a serious public health problem for the U.S. population, including Medicare beneficiaries. The Centers for Disease Control and Prevention (CDC) reported that from 1999 to 2013 the rate of drug poisoning deaths from prescription opioids nearly quadrupled from 1.4 to 5.1 per 100,000 people. In addition, the Department of Health and Human Services (HHS) Office of Inspector General (HHS-OIG) reported that 14.4 million people (about one-third) who participate in Medicare Part D received at least one prescription for opioids in 2016, and that Part D spending for opioids in 2016 was almost $4.1 billion.

—GOVERNMENT ACCOUNTABILITY OFFICE, OCTOBER 6, 2017[1]

MAY 1, 2014: DAY 43 OF TRIAL

She was the only witness with a fashion blog. Jean Stone, recipient of one of the federal government's highest civil service awards, wore her hair in a crisp white bob. An array of graphic bangles and rings decorated her arms and fingers, echoing the graphic black-and-white designs of her outfits. She wasn't there to advise on style, however: she was there to teach the jury about the rules that Dr. Li had broken. She provided her full formal title: Director of the Northeastern Program Integrity Field Office in the Medicare Program Integrity Enforcement Group. She worked within the U.S. Department of Health and Human Services, in the Centers for Medicare & Medicaid Services' Center for Program Integrity. After hearing her qualifications, the judge recognized that she would be testifying with expert knowledge about an issue that was beyond the understanding of a "typical juror,"* and allowed Stone to offer her opinion as an expert in Medicare program structures, Medicare enrollment policies, and Medicare claims processing.

Ms. Stone taught the jury that Medicare paid physicians according to the time and labor they invested in a patient's care. Physicians communicated this information to Medicare through numeric codes, which described the nature of the care performed. A long, new-patient visit, for instance, involving extensive medical history and a physical examination, would pay more than a short repeat visit from a familiar patient that involved only limited medical work. Stone explained the codes to the jury and told them about the different "levels" of patient visits and how much time the doctor would be expected to spend with the patient at each level. It may not have been a view of medicine with which every doctor agreed, but it was one they had to accept if they wanted to participate in the Medicare program.

"Ms. Stone," I asked, "are you familiar with the term 'upcoding'?"

"Yes."

---

* "As a general rule the admissibility of expert testimony on a particular point is addressed to the discretion of the trial court. The guiding principle is that expert opinion is proper when it would help to clarify an issue calling for professional or technical knowledge, possessed by the expert and beyond the ken of the typical juror." *De Long v. County of Erie*, 60 N.Y.2d 296, 307 (1983) (citations omitted); "Ken: the range of perception, understanding, or knowledge," *Merriam-Webster Dictionary*.

"What does that mean?"

"That's a term we use when a provider bills a higher level of service than was rendered to the patient."

I needed the jury to know the term "upcoding" because they would hear it from the Medicare auditor, who, even without knowing how many patients Dr. Li had seen in one day, could tell from his patient records that he had not spent anywhere close to the amount of time he'd claimed to have engaged in the medical treatment of his patients. I needed them to remember Jean Stone's explanation when they saw Dr. Li's claim forms, all featuring the codes that stood for the longest, most complex visits.

Jean Stone also explained the "global surgery rule." This was a fancy way to say that a doctor could only charge Medicare once for a procedure. Everything was included in the procedure fee: the underlying visit as well as the operation itself. You couldn't charge Medicare for a visit and procedure on the same day unless an exception to the "global surgery rule" applied. If a doctor performed a visit on one day and a procedure on the next day, however, they could avoid the global surgery rule—and get paid for each service separately, which meant *more*.

The jury needed to hold this information in their minds long enough to hear from the Medicare auditor. She would tell them that Dr. Li billed Medicare for visits and injection procedures on two consecutive days, even though his own records indicated that he never saw patients two days in a row. The jury just needed to hold the testimony in their minds long enough to see the claim forms themselves, see the patient records themselves, and remember that this lie, repeated in claim form after claim form, meant more money for Dr. Li. They needed to connect this information back to the receptionists, who had testified earlier during the trial that they were instructed by Dr. Li's wife to write false, consecutive dates on the claim forms.

I was so focused on the witness and keeping the jury awake that I had little clue that the judge, of all people, was absorbing this testimony with great interest.

A doctor enrolled in the Medicare program, Jean Stone explained, could not refuse to bill Medicare for patient visits—not if Medicare had been slow to pay claims, or if the Medicare beneficiary agreed, not even if Medicare was paying too little by the doctor's standards. The doctor could not charge a cash fee other than co-insurance or deductible.

"Now," I asked, presenting a hypothetical situation, "may a doctor make an agreement with a Medicare beneficiary that the beneficiary will pay cash up front, the doctor will bill Medicare, and when Medicare pays, the doctor will pay the patient back?"

Stone was firm.

"No," she said, then added, "We would consider that a kickback."

I hoped the jury would remember her answer.

Of course, Medicare wasn't just paying for doctors' visits. They—or rather, *we the taxpayers*—were also paying for many of the medications that Dr. Li prescribed. While many of Dr. Li's Medicare and health insurance patients paid cash at the pharmacy to elude scrutiny or avoid limits on monthly doses when they were getting extra, they always used up their monthly medication allowances, at great taxpayer expense. Dr. Li may have felt underpaid, but he was racking up significant societal costs without meeting even a minimum standard for care—and that wasn't even taking into account the cost of medical intervention when patients overdosed.

I tried to ask Stone whether Medicare set higher standards for medical visits when doctors were prescribing opioids. "It seems to be a silly question," the judge rebuked me. He turned to the witness. "There are no differences based upon what the prescriptions are for, are they [*sic*]?"

"Generally, no," answered Stone, "but for controlled substances there is a stronger expectation that the patient is under the care of a physician and would be documented in a medical record."

I recalled my prep sessions with Stone, in a conference room on a high floor of the federal building near Foley Square. She had betrayed a workaholic's knowledge of the rooftops around the building, pointing out the loveliest gardens. If she, like the judge, had deemed some of my questions to be "silly," she never let on. Instead, she took the time to teach me about her work. We'd combed through document after document, policy after policy, in satisfying and productive conversations where not a word went to waste and she held specific, enlightening answers to every single question I could conjure—a direct correlation between effort and understanding.

On cross-examination, Belair attacked Stone—and the Medicare program—for not having given Dr. Li a second chance with his claims. They should have sent him a warning, Belair suggested, instead of ratcheting up the case to criminal charges.

With Ms. Stone, however, Belair pushed on to a criticism of Medicare's cheapness with physicians and an overt attack on the prosecution, challenging Stone to admit that, but for the pressure from our office, Dr. Li's fraud would have remained undetected or unaddressed.

There wasn't much more he could do with her—though he did try.

"Yes, sir," Stone answered at one point during her cross-examination.

"Okay," Belair responded, exasperated, "please drop the 'sir.'"

Peter objected.

The judge turned to Belair. "If Ms. Stone wants to call you 'sir,' Mr. Belair, I won't stop her."

"All right," Belair gave up. "Okay."

I sat through the cross-examination of my Medicare expert, fuming over Belair's tactics: they were both effective and maddening. He drew the jury's attention away from the falsified claim forms, confirming instead that the Medicare payments were small and that a similar case, under different circumstances, might have resulted simply in a warning letter. He also asked questions based upon premises that the witness could not accept, but then restricted the witness to "yes" or "no" responses; when she tried to question the premise, she seemed combative. I reminded myself that if Belair was not quibbling over the existence of the fraud but rather trying to enlist the jury's sympathy for the doctor or frustrate the witness, it meant that our proof was compelling.

Cross-examination is about control as much as it is about substance. I knew Stone would be fine and I knew that Belair's role required him to deny Stone her due, but it was confounding to hear them tussle. What she was saying seemed so clear to me. I remained bewildered, and angry, that our system of justice created situations where a lawyer could blur meaning and dangle red herrings and *just be doing his job*. Nevertheless, I barely allowed myself to move, other than to take notes, and worked hard to maintain a neutral stance and expression. Belair was demonstrating his skill—and I needed to control my own reactions.

MAY 11, 2011: 1,044 DAYS UNTIL TRIAL

The title was printed on the cover, in large penciled letters: "Nina's Book of Drawing + Witing [*sic*]." How cute! Inside, I found colorful sketches of kids doing gymnastics under the benevolent supervision of a long-legged teacher, followed by a list of eight children, including her little brother (*aww!*), whom Nina wished to invite to her birthday party.

Nina pointed me to another page—to the drawing meant for me. It was a cartoon. In the first frame, a brown-haired woman with a drawn-out, downturned mouth pointed an oversized arm toward a girl in a school uniform. Blue polka-dot tears fell from the girl's eyes down to the floor. In the next frame, the girl lay on her bed, crying the same blue tears. Her sheets featured a red design—just like Nina's. In case the drawing wasn't clear enough, there was a purple crying sad face in the upper left corner. "You do this to me," read the caption.

In the final frame, a little boy (labeled "Charles") and a woman (labeled "you") sat cross-legged together on the floor, smiling and playing under the caption: "You do this to Charlie." In the upper left corner: a purple smiley face and a crossed-out girl.

It took a lot of effort not to cry. I wasn't with them all the time, so it was always so hard to draw the line between just enjoying their presence and doing my job as a parent. And what *was* my job as a parent?

How are you supposed to discipline or help or teach your child if you can't follow through?

Parenting was my hardest and most important job. I worked at it—but I just couldn't seem to get it right, no matter how many books I read or counselors I consulted.

I received little comfort from my co-parent, who never seemed to experience the challenges of bedtime or sibling rivalry and lived, more than ever before, at a different rhythm. We didn't just have different visions of what a family should be, we now had different *experiences* of family—but with the same children. Far from supporting each other, we were always in conflict or competition.

My email in-box turned into a minefield. I held my breath as I scanned the messages: Would there be another grenade hidden in there? If there was, I read it and fumed, then fired off my own responses, scathing or disappointed or self-righteous or trying in vain to set boundaries. Even after more than a year of separation and a signed, mediated agreement, there was no respite and no predictability. Despite my best efforts to set up a stable structure, I felt unable to protect my children from a jagged and confusing new life between two very different homes. And I certainly never had thought to put on the armor before looking at my own child's drawings.

It was so hard to know what to attribute to normal friction between parents and children, to the divorce, to "normal" sibling dynamics, or to my own shortcomings. Yes, I was frazzled, angry, sad at times—not usually at the kids, but of course it sometimes came out with or at them. Was this just a normal parenting pitfall? How the heck was I supposed to know? What was the standard for "normal parenting"? Was the standard set by "intact" families, however dysfunctional? My own parents? Other divorced parents? Some idealized movie mom, always able to acknowledge, validate, support, and comfort?

"You're so lucky," some friends would say, envious of my "free" evenings and weekends when the children were with their father, or of my ability to make decisions for myself, without compromise. If only it were so simple. In reality, just at the moment when the kids and I settled into a routine together and I'd finally had an opportunity to set parental expectations about bedtime, homework, respect for each other, and the daily brushing of teeth, they would be whisked away to their other home, with its own set of rules, where everything seemed to be easier, better, freer, and fairer. Of course, I did not know those rules and I had no say in them. Each time the children came back, it felt like we started again from scratch. Was anything sinking in?

I may have succeeded only in making them feel inadequate. While I played the role of perpetual "bad cop," we still seemed to be landing on the lowest common denominator. Could it be enough that they were safe and alive? Was it even in my power, under the circumstances, to make them feel safe, let alone happy?

I also sometimes wasn't sure of the right course and felt the need for a trusted partner with whom to discuss and decide. Someone to whom I could say, "I'm not sure what to do about this, what do you think?" and then talk it out. Some people looked to prayer for such guidance, others to their own internal compass. I had neither, apparently. I was fortunate enough to be able to pay a therapist to hear me out and give me advice, but then I'd still find myself on Wednesday mornings hugging the kids good-bye, taking in a big breath of them to hold out until the next time we'd see each other before letting them go. They were just going to their dad's, but for me they were disappearing into an unknown. Of course, I also knew that I was lucky to expect them home again: I felt guilty about the divorce, guilty about the transitions, and guilty for not appreciating the simple, precious fact of their aliveness and safety. I couldn't help but miss them desperately.

Only work could interrupt the downward spiral. If I worked long enough to feel okay again, on topics complex and precise enough to occupy my brain circuits, I could take myself home and coast into a night of sleep, however uneasy. I preferred to toss and turn over professional challenges rather than revisit the usual nightmares about losing my children, or the children whom others had lost.

OCTOBER 2010: APPROXIMATELY 1,266 DAYS UNTIL TRIAL

Eddie Valora always had suspected that the doctor was getting paid, but now he had proof. It was right there, in black and white, in the Explanation of Benefits letters and the Medicare Summary. It was a fact that Medicare was paying the doctor. Always had paid the doctor. When the doctor had told Valora that he hadn't received any payment, that had been a lie. When the doctor had forced Valora to pay cash for the visits and promised to pay Valora back when Medicare paid, that had been a scam. You know what else had been a scam? This whole thing. All of it. He should have known on the first day, when he brought the doctor that pile of medical records, everything to explain his illness, and the doctor didn't seem to care. And then the doctor didn't even remember him the next time. What a waste of time and money, and now he wasn't even better. He couldn't do without the meds anymore—*and* he was still in pain. Actually, he'd added another layer of pain because in addition to the tightening and trembling and endless aching of his muscles, there was the craving and the shaking and the soreness of the withdrawals. He rode the waves of craving and pain until he couldn't anymore, but when he took the meds—especially the Xanax—he just dropped out, knocked out, blacked out, for hours and hours, just *lost*.

How many times had he told the doctor, for nothing. For *nothing*.

"You look anxious," the doctor had said.

"Just keep taking it," the doctor had said. "You'll get used to it."

Was he used to it now because he needed it all the time? But if he were used to it, would it still knock him out the way it did? Now he had to stop—he had to—because this guy was ripping him off and Valora was pissed.

He had to be careful. He couldn't let anger get the better of him. He had the law on his side, though; he was pretty sure about that. And he had the proof: the official statements from Medicare. The doctor would have nothing to say to that. Just one last time, to get his money and make his point—and get one last set of prescriptions to tide him over until he could find someone else, a real doctor this time, someone who'd understand his medical records and learn about his illness and treat him.

He didn't even bother to go early. There were already forty or fifty people there already, between the people waiting outside the drab brick building in Flushing, the people in the basement hallway, and those already in the office. Valora blew right past them, past the reception desk, cutting the line without hesitation. He used to have confidence in his body. He walked like he used to walk, strong and fast, right up to the room the doctor always used. He banged on the door. That got everyone's attention.

"You have to wait!" The receptionists and other patients tried to stop him. They didn't know him, clearly.

"I'm not waiting," he said, and banged some more. "I want to talk to the doctor right now!"

The door opened and as the patient came out, Valora pushed right past him. The doctor was sitting at his desk. "We have to have a talk right now, Doc," Valora insisted. "I want my money back." He didn't want to be aggressive. He wanted to be treated right. He wanted things to be set straight. He suspected there was a storm brewing outside the door, in the office, because he'd cut so many people, so this had to be quick.

The doctor shook his head. "No, you're not getting your money back."

Maybe the doctor hadn't understood, Valora thought. He told the doctor about the Medicare summaries. He reminded the doctor about that promise, that if Valora paid cash up front for the visit, the doctor would pay him back when Medicare paid. He wanted his money back—and he wanted another prescription. Maybe he should ask for that now. He didn't have much time. He didn't like the fact that he was asking for a prescription at the same time that he was asking for his money back, but he needed that medication; he couldn't go without it anymore. It's the last time, he promised himself, and the doctor. "The last time. Never again. I need my prescription."

The doctor started writing. "That's one hundred fifty dollars," the doctor said.

Valora's voice strained with anger. "I don't have money. You owe me money. Give me my prescriptions. I'm going to go and I'm not going to see you no more. That's it."

Was he yelling? He was yelling. The door opened, bringing in trouble: two big guys who looked like bouncers from a bar. Where'd they come from? Did they work here? They lunged at Valora, who tussled his way out of their grasp and ran out. This is it, he thought. He'd fought people before, but he was alone and he wasn't that strong anymore—actually, it had been a long time since he'd felt strong. They were catching up to him—he stumbled and there they were, in his face, yelling, "Shut up! Shut up!"

Valora hollered, but they were bigger and louder, one screaming, "Shut up! Get out of here!" and the other yelling at him, "Sit down! What are you doing?"

"I don't care about any of you!" Valora yelled back. "I want my money! I'm going to call the cops on him for this!"

Wrong thing to say? The two guys went nuts. "We're gonna fucking kill you," they growled, and Valora believed them and ran away, ran down the hallway and up the stairs and panicked: where to go, where to turn, because he didn't want to die right then, not now, not by these guys—

And then he saw someone he knew. A tall, dark-haired, tattooed man, the longtime neighborhood "businessman," who always seemed to be hanging out in front of the doctor's office these days, buying prescriptions and pills from the patients. The very person who had referred Valora to this doctor, as if that shouldn't have tipped Valora off that maybe it wasn't a good idea.

The two guys—well, they stopped. Maybe it was Valora's friend's face or his size or his reputation or just something about him that made it clear that he was capable of inflicting more pain than them—things got so quiet that Valora wondered if maybe there was still a chance.

"Hey," he asked his friend.

"What?"

"You got a hundred fifty dollars I can borrow?"

They'd known each other for a long time. Valora wouldn't have a choice but to be good for it. His friend unfolded a fat roll of money and peeled off a few bills. Valora walked right back down those stairs and right back in that office and right by those meatheads, the bouncer-looking guys, right up to the doctor's door, and knocked. It wasn't pleasant, you can say that, but he did what he had to do.

"I got the hundred fifty dollars right here," he said through the door. "I need my pills and I'll never see you again," he added, looking around, careful, watchful.

The doctor opened the door. Valora showed him the cash. The doctor walked past Valora and gave one of the girls in the front a prescription form, with Valora's medication already written out. Valora handed over the money. He'd stop soon, but not now.

Dr. Li took the money and put it right into the pocket of his white coat.

APRIL 24, 2014: DAY 36 OF TRIAL

Special Agent Cindy Hearn, of the United States Internal Revenue Service, was poised to tell the jury how much money Dr. Li had earned from his cash-only, weekend-only pain management practice. She'd just told them that he had several bank accounts: two accounts at the Bank of America, including one personal account for his private practice in anesthesiology (which received automatic payroll deposits amounting to more than $10,000 every other week, indicating a net salary of approximately $240,000 a year), and one for insurance payments related to the pain management practice (totaling more than $140,000 between May 2009 and December 2011); he had another account at PNC Bank, also in New Jersey, where he'd purchased certificates of deposit worth thirty-five thousand dollars with a check from his personal account at the Bank of America; he and his wife shared an account at a small community bank, Roma, in New Jersey, which received cash deposits; and another account at the Bank of Princeton, which also received cash deposits. The cash deposits were always made on Mondays or occasionally Tuesdays, and almost always signed by Dr. Li's wife, Anna Guo.

I was ready to ask Special Agent Hearn for the grand total of cash deposits. I put the question to the witness: "What was the total value of the cash deposits in just Roma Bank and the Bank of Princeton between 2008 and 2011?"

It was a moment of high drama, just like in the movies. Cinematic courtroom dramas, however, often fail to capture the complete lack of suspense at trial: that's the cost of fairness and procedural integrity.

The judge stopped Agent Hearn as she was reaching for her folder. "Do you need to look at a document to refresh your recollection?"

"Yes."

"Agent Hearn," I said, trying to be helpful and professional and move things along, "next time just ask the Court's permission or let me know."

"We are there already," the judge said to me with a snap. My inner critic piled on—*there you go again, being redundant and looking like a fool.* The judge then turned to the witness. "If you need to look at a document, you need to let us know that that's what you are doing."

"Yes, Judge," responded Agent Hearn. "I'd like to look at a document."

"You can look at it if you need to refresh your recollection," the judge reminded her. "You can't read from it because it's not in evidence."

"Correct," acknowledged Agent Hearn, before perusing the document, raising her head, and speaking into the microphone.

The total value of cash deposits in just the Roma Bank account, between 2008 and 2011, was $462,860. The Bank of Princeton account, during the same time period, accumulated more than $80,000 in cash deposits. Together, Agent Hearn told the jury, the cash deposits in those two accounts amounted to approximately $542,000. Additionally, the cash deposits in the PNC account, made over a period of just eight months, amounted to $42,000.

Later in the trial, the jury heard examples of a few weeks' worth of cash deposits into the Roma account.

"February 2, 2010: seven thousand dollars.

"February 8, 2010: seven thousand dollars.

"April 26, 2010: eight thousand, five hundred dollars.

"June 28, 2010: eight thousand dollars.

"July 7, 2010: seven thousand, five hundred dollars."

I hoped the jury, considering all this evidence at the end of the trial, would make the connection to a set of statistical charts prepared by our analyst, Stefani Miotto. I hoped the jury would see, as we had, the direct correlation between the number of patients and the amounts of money collected.

Of course, since most of Dr. Li's proceeds from the weekend clinic had been in cash, we had no way of knowing if the amounts in these various accounts and financial instruments represented his total gains.

MAY 1, 2014: DAY 43 OF TRIAL

In the middle of my direct examination, during key trial testimony, a class of middle schoolers entered the courtroom. The children's faces revealed excitement and reverence: A homicide trial?! A judge in a long black robe!? A jury?! A big cart full of crime evidence?! A prosecutor questioning a witness!? *This was going to be awesome!*

"Sir," the judge said to their chaperone, "why don't you put them on that side of the courtroom. Folks, please. Yeah. Thank you. We're being visited by a class."

I continued asking my questions, one after another for a full fifteen minutes. Once I'd executed the necessary tasks, I ended with a dramatic salvo:

"Do you recognize the type of information that's contained in these spreadsheets?"

"Yes, I do."

"What do you recognize it to be?"

"These data elements are unique items that are reported on the Medicare claim and these would be the record in our system as a Medicare claim is processed for all of the different information that we use to process the Medicare claim."

"And did National Government Services inherit all of the data that was maintained by GHI for Queens County?"

"Yes, we did."

"At this time, Your Honor, we offer One Fifty-Three A and B subject to connection."

The students filed out, dejected.

"I've had lots of school classes come visit," the judge quipped, "and none of the times have been particularly interesting. Sorry, Ms. Fishman."

Cue: giggles, laughter, smiles.

There were many times when I wondered whether the strategy to focus on the money and the insurance fraud was more of a gamble than I had anticipated. This was one of them. This witness had been necessary to set our jurisdiction over the Medicare fraud crime, establish the chain of command for the subcontractors who performed the Medicare audit, and lay a foundation for the introduction of a crucial piece of evidence: the spreadsheets containing claim records. Her testimony was long, dense, and dry, but it was also indispensable.

I had come into this case as a Medicare novice, numbed by the technical jargon and with a vague but overwhelming sense of the program's complexity, importance, controversy, and bureaucracy. Having moved to the U.S. in the mid-eighties and having reached voting age in the early nineties, I'd watched many rounds of presidential debates, and I cringed at even the word "Medicare." But I knew fraud—and suspected that this side of Dr. Li's business would reveal his true intentions.

Under the thoughtful and clear guidance of my Medicare experts—a whip-smart data investigator, a former secret service agent, and the formidable Jean Stone—I came to understand and love the program. I didn't need the jury to share my love of the subject, but I needed them to understand the basics: taxpayers funded Medicare; Medicare served the elderly and disabled; Dr. Li participated in Medicare; Dr. Li cheated Medicare; Dr. Li cheated Medicare no matter the race or age of the patient, almost from day one of his private pain management practice.

If the jury understood that, I argued in our strategy sessions, they will see his true motive: they will see his greed. But would they be able to keep their eyes and ears open long enough? We'll pare it down to a minimum, I promised. We'll make it interesting!

"Why are we taking all this time to go through this?" the judge interrupted as I was asking a witness about the process by which Dr. Li could have opted out of the Medicare system.

"Your Honor—" I started to answer.

"You're losing the jury," the judge warned. "They're falling asleep."

There was no easy pep talk for this dilemma. "You can't care what they think" didn't apply here. Neither did "do one thing a day that scares you." This trial wasn't "scary": it triggered the brainless, chilling anxiety of stepping out into a void. The judge had authority to make rulings on what we could and could not present to the jury. We were also sure that the defense would move for a "trial order of dismissal" at the close of the People's case, which meant that Belair would ask the judge to dismiss some or all of the charges for lack of legally sufficient evidence. If the judge granted that motion in part or in whole, we were done: the jury never would get to deliberate on those charges. Entering seventy-two witnesses and hundreds of exhibits into the courtroom and onto the record was the first hurdle; surviving eighteen weeks without a mistrial or trial order of dismissal was another. Retaining the jury's attention may have seemed like the least of our worries, but it was also paramount. We couldn't afford to have them fall asleep or feel like we were wasting their time. We couldn't hold back or go too far—and there was no way to know, at any given time, how close we were to the edge.

OCTOBER 16, 2012: 520 DAYS UNTIL TRIAL

He'd had months to think about it, I fumed. So many meetings and discussions. So why did everything have to happen at the last minute and feel like such a jumble? Peter and I had to make decisions about which victims' cases to pursue and time was running out, yet the digressions, jokes, and delays never ended.

And then suddenly—boom—the hammer came down. He was the senior trial attorney, so he had the final say and held on to it so long that by the time he decided, it was too late to re-argue.

You'd think I would have learned to be strategic—I hadn't. I picked *every* battle and failed to conceal my outrage.

Our different styles bred tension: I didn't let him take original documents back into his messy office for fear that they would be lost; he rolled his eyes at my protectiveness; I thought about this case night and day; he refused to reveal what else was occupying his time, out of deference to the luminaries who relied on him.

How did he do it? He could make intellectual leaps, in our debates or when questioning a witness, between high-priority topics without fretting about laying exhaustive foundations for each subject, closing out a topic, or losing his audience. If you tested his underlying knowledge of the law, it was flawless and profound. Was this the payoff of experience, memory, diligent study, instinct honed into habit? Was it confidence? There was no question that Peter knew more about the law than anyone else in the room and had a way with words: Was that why everyone had such patience for the extra stuff? Did Peter have more freedom to be himself and let loose his messy genius in this case because he was paired with me, his polar opposite in terms of neatness and predictability? Would a woman ever be able to get away with the "messy genius" approach?

My anticipatory anxiety, my need for preparation, organization, clarity, and my relentlessness made much of my work possible—it also made much of my life impossible. I thought of the filing cabinets in my office, filled with labeled manila folders, broken down by witness, patient, date, or topic. Those were helpful and necessary—at work. I thought about my task-tracker spreadsheets, compiling assignments for the entire team—also helpful, also necessary, given the scope of the case and the monumental trial prep still ahead. But what did spreadsheets and folders contribute to my parenting? Nothing. To my divorce negotiations? Nothing. I didn't need to be a messy genius, but I would have liked to feel like I could be myself, trust myself, learn how to be better, build a strong team, take care of the things and people I cared about and execute a plan. The lack of self-confidence, the impostor syndrome, my reflexive protectiveness for the kids and my case—they limited me. They blurred reality. They made progress impossible.

Whether or not the prescription data, the bank records, or the Medicare case seemed boring to others, they were a joy for me. There were rules. There were promises. There was data. There were experts. There were answers. There were direct correlations between effort and understanding.

MAY 5, 2014: DAY 47 OF TRIAL

Jean Stone's testimony spilled over onto a second day. When she finished on May 5, Valora was in the hallway, waiting his turn with apprehension. Did he see Stone pass by, the stylish woman with a commanding posture and a confident walk? Either way, he had no idea who she was or why she was there. Nor did she know him or his purpose. Nevertheless, together they constituted a dynamic duo of civic superheroes: the expert and the young man, both coming forward to say that they wouldn't stand for Dr. Li's fraud.

After Mr. Valora told his story, Belair hit hard. His aim was to reveal Valora's flaws and then let the jury sit with the implications. *This is the person the prosecutor's siding with*, he was telling the jury. *This is the person they want you to believe over a hardworking, well-qualified, licensed physician.* It was an explicit attack on the witness and an implicit attack on the integrity of the prosecution.

Belair struck a rich vein probing for the details of Valora's criminal record. So rich, in fact, that he was unprepared for the witness's candor on that subject. Just tell the truth, we'd told Valora. Be as helpful to Belair as you are to us, we had instructed him.

"Okay," Valora started, without hesitation. "I was involved in an altercation where I just came out of the hospital with bacterial meningitis. . . ." He told a long story of an altercation involving thirty-five fighters "on the other side," "people with bats, knives," himself weakened after an extended stay in an isolation chamber and significant weight loss, and a violent Marine who was "killing" someone with a chokehold. When Valora reached the part where he admitted to striking the Marine in the eye socket twice with a bat, inflicting critical injuries, Belair stopped him. "I think that's sufficient," he said, in a tone both smug and surprised. "Thank you."

"And then it got broken up," Valora volunteered, undeterred.

"That's okay," Belair checked him. "Thank you."

The jury seemed shell-shocked. We weren't handing them a neat package. Every witness came with baggage. We were asking them to see past Valora's history. We couldn't control the outcome and they couldn't control the input.

I, for one, could relate to Valora, our intensely self-critical tipster, who could not seem to find a peaceful path through life. He seemed to be short-circuiting from one thought to the next, getting ahead of himself and yet never catching up, always doubting and second-guessing . . . it was all so familiar. It was something I knew.

APRIL 9, 2014: DAY 21 OF TRIAL

She had pie charts. She had graphs. She had numbers. She had percentages and she had maps. Everything was ready, in a neat folder on the evidence cart. Most important, Stefani Miotto, our investigative analyst, was ready, despite her initial trepidation about any form of public speaking. In fact, she'd been ready for many months, but the rest of the case had needed time to catch up to her. She was better than an expert: she was a miracle. Stefani sweated to get the work done right and no one—other than Joe Hall—worked harder.

That effort paid off. There was a direct correlation between the intensity of her work and our understanding of the facts. We couldn't change the data, but by the time Stefani was done with it we could *see* and *read* it.

The same logic applied to our partnership: we saw each other's strengths and weaknesses and had much to teach each other. She always was a fearless wiz with Excel, but when she started, she was too shy to make "cold" calls. She taught me how to sort, filter, calculate, and—most important—verify the data; I put her to work making phone calls to hospitals and banks to gather addresses and fax numbers for our document requests. "Don't worry about how you sound," I told her. "You're not asking for any favors; you're just doing your job." I quoted Eleanor Roosevelt: "'You must do the thing you think you cannot do.'" It's all about preparation, I told her: disregard the inner critic; get in, get out; do one thing every day that scares you. I rolled out every cliché, giving her all the advice that I struggled to follow myself.

By the time Stefani took the stand, we'd long since stopped working so closely. She was assigned to other cases and I prepped her like any other witness, turning over all our notes and emails to the defense. Still, I knew her well enough to know she was nervous. Of course, I was nervous, too.

The rules of evidence required that we stick to the facts. Only in the summation could we weave all the facts together into a compelling argument for the jury—and that would be Peter's job, not mine. I could ask only narrow, direct questions, which Stefani could answer only with numbers and percentages and distances. There were no guarantees that the jury would listen, understand, care, or believe the testimony, but that uncertainty didn't mean we could prepare less.

Dr. Li had written 21,837 controlled-substance prescriptions since January 2008, until the closing of his pain management practice. Stefani had reviewed them all.

Fifty-six percent of the prescriptions Dr. Li had written were for oxycodone, in any strength or formulation. Twenty-seven percent were for Xanax, followed by 5 percent for hydrocodone (including Vicodin or Norco).

Of the 21,837 controlled-substance prescriptions, opioid-based medications accounted for 14,811. Among the opioid medications, oxycodone took the lead by far, representing 82 percent of the prescriptions. By comparison—not that Stefani could furnish such a comparison to the jury, because she was not deemed qualified to do so—oxycodone represented only 49 percent of all the opioid painkiller prescriptions issued in New York City in 2010. Oxycodone was Dr. Li's "go-to"—his bread and butter.

Xanax held the same position among the non-opioid medications, representing 81 percent of the prescriptions in that category.

In 2008, Dr. Li had written 1,947 controlled-substance prescriptions. In 2009, he wrote 5,454. In 2010, he wrote 7,740. In 2011, he wrote 6,694 between January and November—but we'd interrupted him before the end of the year.†

Some of Dr. Li's patients had traveled from out of state, she added—Florida, Georgia, and Pennsylvania—but there were also Long Islanders who lived up to sixty-two miles away from the small basement clinic. As Stefani responded to my questions, I projected the charts she'd prepared to illustrate the findings. For instance, Stefani showed the jury that patients between the ages of thirty and thirty-nine received more than 33 percent of the prescriptions Dr. Li issued—a

† These were the numbers recorded in the transcript, based on the testimony and evidence at trial. Since I did not have access to the original exhibits, I could not verify them and therefore cannot, unfortunately, explain why there is a discrepancy of two units between 21,837 (the total number of controlled substance prescriptions) and the sum of these numbers.

total of 7,282—by far the greatest portion for any age group. Among those were 4,482 controlled-substance prescriptions that Dr. Li had written for patients between the ages of twenty and twenty-nine years old, including Nicholas Rappold. Dr. Li had even written controlled-substance prescriptions for patients *under* the age of twenty—there were only fifty-eight, but among those, as the jury would later learn, were the prescriptions he'd written for Alli Walton, who started seeing him when she was just nineteen and who'd busted into his lunchroom, on November 27, 2010, begging for more pills.

There were so many hot spots like that in the data. In fact, every data point was a hot spot for one family.

Judge Sonberg looked concerned. His eyes scanned the jurors' faces. I wondered what he was thinking, and I didn't have to wait long to find out.

"While I understand to some people statistics are not exciting," he said, breaking my heart, "I'm going to ask all of our jurors to try to keep their focus. I'm seeing some eyes look like they were starting to close. If you need a break, we will take one in a few minutes, so you can get up and walk around. For some people this is fairly dense and less than exciting."

I took a breath before picking up again. This wasn't even the most dry or technical testimony the jury would need to sit through and digest—not by a long, long stretch. In time, they would learn what each little dot in the charts represented: money and lives; overdose cocktails and fatal doses; children, husbands, girlfriends.

They never would hear that one of those dots represented a mass murderer, but he was in there, too.

CHAPTER 7

Soft Targets

JUNE 18, 2011: 1,006 DAYS UNTIL TRIAL

My children sat at their play table and messed around with face paints while I struggled to remain upright and coughed into my elbow. Nina, who was seven years old and missing a few teeth, asked me to paint a pink butterfly on her face. I stretched the butterfly's neon orange body from Nina's forehead all the way down the nose and drew a pink wing on each cheek decorated with blue polka dots. Charlie, then four years old, asked Nina to paint his face. He giggled and wriggled as she dragged the paintbrush over his round cheeks, ending up with an abstract attempt at a horse's head in pink and yellow. They smiled for a photo, then left to spend a week with their dad. The flu had knocked me out—so much that I'd asked their father to take them one day earlier.

My ex-husband picked them up and I went back to bed. Our cat, Higgins, relocated from the kids' room into mine, as was his habit whenever they left. His presence offered some small comfort in the empty silence of the apartment whenever the children were away. Within a couple of hours, my ex-husband sent me photos of the children playing at the beach near his parents' home on Long Island. They looked happy. I knew I had done the right thing but dreaded the week ahead without them.

My fever broke that night. The next morning was Sunday, June 19, 2011: Father's Day. Everything was far too empty in my corner of the world, so I sought refuge in the quiet familiarity of my office and my long, detailed to-do list. Afterward I went straight to a movie theater to avoid being in my apartment alone. I felt sorry for myself all day, blindly taking for granted my bubble of security and good fortune.

Not until I returned to the office early the next morning did I see the headlines: four innocent people had been shot inside Haven Drugs, a pharmacy in Medford, Long Island.

Raymond Ferguson, forty-five.
Jennifer Mejia, seventeen.
Bryon Sheffield, seventy-one.
Jaime Taccetta, thirty-three.

News reports said the shooter had stolen prescription drugs after executing his victims. Two images from a surveillance camera recording showed an emaciated young man in his late twenties or early thirties, with a white baseball cap, a gray hoodie, a prominent Adam's apple, dark-framed glasses, and a beard.

I moved from sadness to anger and then began thinking like a prosecutor again: Why a pharmacy? Was the theft of the prescription drugs an afterthought or a motive? Which drugs were stolen? I was willing to bet it was an opioid. What if—

At 9:00 a.m., Stefani Miotto, our investigative analyst, walked into our office.

"Have you seen the news?" I asked.

She began reviewing news reports about the shooting. Bridget walked in, surprising both of us. She got right to the point: Hadn't we told her that some of Dr. Li's patients traveled quite far to see him? As Stefani and I both launched our Excel spreadsheets containing Dr. Li's prescription data, Bridget voiced the question on all our minds: "Did any of his patients fill prescriptions in that pharmacy?"

In an urgent rush, we sorted and scanned and checked. We never voiced the possibility that we might be looking for the killer, but we were all wondering whether addiction might have driven one of Dr. Li's patients to murder. We found two patients—a married couple—who had filled prescriptions in that pharmacy, within the last month. It was near their home. We googled their names and found their wedding announcement. They were young. He didn't look quite like the man in the surveillance video, but there were no clear disqualifiers, either: both he and the shooter were slim white males with a narrow face, and the beard could have been fake.

We divided up the work: Stefani was assigned to collect as many images as possible from the Internet and put together a summary of the prescriptions the couple had filled at Haven Drugs; meanwhile, I ran the young man's rap sheet to see if he had a criminal record. "No convictions," I said, speaking as I read—and then my eyes landed on the little black box at the bottom. "Wait," I said. "He has a gun license."

We printed everything except the prescription data (which we could not disclose at the time) and slipped the papers into a manila folder. Bridget ran the folder down to the fifth floor, where she gave them to Bill Cook, the Chief Investigator, who knew everyone in law enforcement in the tristate area, with the instruction to pass the information along to the Suffolk County Police. In our office, Stefani and I kept looking at the young man's photos and comparing them to the surveillance video. Maybe. Maybe not. Couldn't be. *Please no.*

JUNE 22, 2011: 1,002 DAYS UNTIL TRIAL

I was in a meeting in the office's large conference room when Bridget walked in. She said she needed to talk to me. *Immediately. Outside.*

The conference room fell silent. I excused myself and followed her out. A few steps down the hall, she stopped and turned to face me. I couldn't decipher her expression and wondered if I'd done something wrong.

"They arrested him," she said.

"Who?" I asked.

"David Laffer. They arrested him."

My eyes flooded with tears, despite my rule about never crying at the office. I struggled to compose myself. I really had wanted to be wrong about this one.

I knew addiction could trigger criminal behavior, including murder. But three factors made the killings—and the connection to our case—surreal and troubling. First, hydrocodone was supposed to be a *medication.* As a substance, it was legal and regulated: nevertheless, it had triggered an unfathomable level of addiction, craving, and violence. In stealing eleven thousand hydrocodone pills from the pharmacy, for himself and his wife, Melinda Brady, Laffer had exchanged four lives for pills.

Second, the murderer's addiction had been fueled by a doctor's prescriptions. A doctor who seemed to be acting with either complete indifference to the consequences or conscious intent to cause harm. A doctor who, at this moment, was still out there, writing prescriptions. A doctor whom we needed to stop as soon as possible.

Finally: this had happened on our watch.

In fact, the Laffer shooting marked and precipitated the most dramatic, wrenching phase of our investigation. We learned about the shooting during the same time period that we began receiving responses from the Offices of the Chief Medical Examiners in New York City and Long Island about overdose deaths. We matched up name after name after name after name after name . . . sixteen names in total. Sixteen patients of Dr. Li had died of overdoses involving a controlled substance either while under his "care" or within a year of leaving his practice. *Sixteen.*

Most of the names never made it into the public record—and can never make it into the public record—because the grand jury did not charge Dr. Li with any crimes relating to their treatment or their death. Still, I remember each of them and think of them and their families often.

How could our team sleep knowing this? How could we work on anything else? How could we look at our kids and not grab them and hang on tight? How could we have any normal conversations with friends, colleagues, spouses?

Some of the names—Tara Palamar, Alexander Mitzner, Giovanni Manzella—made it into the public record because Dr. Li was charged with selling them prescriptions. The jury learned only that these three patients were dead, without explanation or detail.

Why? Why couldn't the jury hear more? For a reason similar to the hush around the murders committed by David Laffer: basic fairness. The jury was there to decide Dr. Li's guilt or innocence on the crimes with which he was accused. If they heard about other events, such as overdose deaths or a gruesome killing, we could not expect them to be impartial or fair in their decision, as they might begin speculating about Dr. Li's possible connection to the events or apply a bias.

In our trial, Dr. Li was not accused of having played a role in David Laffer's murder of four innocents. Rather, Dr. Li stood accused of having sold seven prescriptions to David Laffer without a medical basis, in exchange for money. Whether the jury—or anyone else, for that matter—might think the two events were related was far beyond the scope of our trial and would leave an indelible stain on the proceedings. Nor was Dr. Li accused of having caused the deaths of sixteen patients. The grand jury only had charged him with two counts of manslaughter, for Nicholas Rappold and Joseph Haeg, while two additional overdose victims, Kevin Kingsley and Michael Cornetta, became the subjects of reckless endangerment charges.

All those charges—and decisions not to ask a grand jury to consider other charges—had come as the result of a long, deliberate winnowing process.

For each of the sixteen individuals, we went through a cold but necessary balancing test. Were they still one of Dr. Li's patients when they died? If so, how much time had passed between their last visit and their fatal overdose? Was Dr. Li aware that they were abusing the prescribed medication? Had he received any warnings from loved ones or other doctors about abuse, concurrent drug use, or overdoses? If they were no longer a patient of Dr. Li's at the time of their death, what was their condition while they were a patient? Was he one among many prescribers, or did he play a distinct and significant role in exacerbating their addiction or placing them at risk of death? For all the overdose victims, we examined the cause of death: Did the overdose involve any substances not prescribed by Dr. Li? Did the overdose involve any illegal drugs?

The Laffer murders made it clear that we needed to move fast. We needed to move faster. We needed to shut down Dr. Li's clinic. He was a one-man epidemic. The stakes were so high.

But we needed to get it right—also because the stakes were so high.

Our first step was to settle on a strategy. At the time, of course, we didn't have the patient charts. Back in June 2011, our investigation was only six months old. All we had were witness accounts and records from other medical facilities where Dr. Li's patients had been treated. We couldn't get the charts without tipping Dr. Li off to our investigation. To shut down his clinic, we needed to identify a crime that we could prove, based on the evidence we had or could obtain. What conduct could we prove without access to his patient files? Joe, Stefani, and I discussed it on our own; I discussed it with Joe T. and Peter; we all debated it together, under Bridget's watchful eye, in the conference room. The Nicholas Rappold and Joseph Haeg cases were off the table for the moment: since those involved potential homicide charges, we were going to take more time to investigate and we needed the patient files to understand Dr. Li's state of mind and the progression of events. Valora, our tipster, presented a case that involved Medicare fraud, a topic that we were just beginning to understand at the time. Since he had a legitimate medical condition, we did not believe it was appropriate to ask a grand jury to charge Dr. Li with crimes related to the prescription sales. There was Seth Grant, the young man whose father had faxed Dr. Li an angry letter—but he'd stopped seeing Dr. Li after his overdose.

That left one possibility: Michael Cornetta. We had learned of his death through our overdose alert system. His autopsy report contained jarring photos of a young man's interrupted life: a strong jawline, young skin, prolific hair, body unremarkable except for the unnatural congestion of the lungs and the forced stoppage of the heart. Cornetta's cause of death was acute intoxication due to the combined effects of fentanyl, cocaine, and benzodiazepines. He died in the hospital on November 18, 2010, after a week on life support, and a few months after his last visit to Dr. Li in August 2010. The time lapse and the presence of an illegal drug in Cornetta's system precluded consideration of any homicide charges. However, there had been indications from his relatives and medical records that we should consider reckless endangerment charges against Dr. Li, even without access to his medical file. Between June and October 2011, our team ran down every lead.

Thanks to Joe's extraordinary detective work and piles of medical records, we sketched out a picture of Michael Cornetta's last year of life, which he spent in pursuit of fentanyl and in narrow avoidance of death, with multiple overdoses. Joe had tracked down Cornetta's brother and girlfriend, Sybil Stearns, a childlike young woman ravaged by grief, anxiety, and anorexia.

As I read the records, I checked the dates against Dr. Li's prescription data for Cornetta. At least once a month starting in May 2009, Dr. Li prescribed him fentanyl, oxycodone, and Xanax. During the other days of his life, Cornetta attended substance abuse treatment, visited emergency rooms in an attempt to obtain more medication, or ended up there, unconscious. His drug addiction was a full-time job. His life seemed dedicated to the pursuit of and recovery from pharmaceutical drug abuse, and while the ER doctors had figured out that he was addicted, there was nothing to indicate that they knew where he was getting his medication or that they tried to intervene. And then I hit upon the notes of a psychiatrist in a local hospital, Dr. Shushan Hovanesian, dated January 17, 2010.

Now we had it.

We pulled together our proposal for the case and after exhaustive examinations of our proof and theories by supervisor after supervisor we received the green light. The plan to shut down Dr. Li was a go.

Yet even as we focused on the Cornetta case and our goal of protecting the public, we had to keep other fires burning. We knew we needed to secure an indictment against Dr. Li and obtain a search warrant for his patient files, but then, while the Cornetta case moved into the post-arrest phase of defense motions and discovery, we would need to review the files and push forward on the rest of the investigation. Enormous pressure weighed on us and we knew it was just the beginning.

JUNE 20, 2014: DAY 93 OF TRIAL

On the tenth day of Dr. Li's direct examination, Belair asked him about David Laffer.

To address David Laffer's initial complaint of knee and jaw pain during the first visit, on October 17, 2009, Dr. Li prescribed opioids. His plan, according to his own records, was to do so for just three months, but then Vicodin Extra Strength (7.5 mg hydrocodone to 325 mg of acetaminophen) three times a day escalated to Norco. The patient had requested Norco by name, and with the switch Dr. Li increased the opioid dose by 33 percent. A few months later, when the patient complained of neck pain, Dr. Li increased the quantity of pills prescribed to 120 a month, billing insurance for every visit.

On November 19, 2010, Dr. Li discovered through the Controlled Substance Information (CSI) database that Laffer was obtaining Norco from other prescribers, giving him access to a total of 540 pills within the span of just three months. With David Laffer, as with other patients named in the indictment, the records of Dr. Li's CSI database use played a key role: we presented the records as proof of notice that Dr. Li knew his patients were multi-sourcing and taking far more than what was prescribed by any one doctor; the defense, as in the case of David Laffer, used the records to argue that Dr. Li checked on his patients and counseled them.

It was a compelling argument. At the time, CSI was voluntary: physicians were not obligated to sign up for access or consult it. The New York State Department of Health kept track of which doctors had signed up, as well as all the searches those doctors conducted *and* the results of those searches. The defense made much of the fact that Dr. Li had been an early adopter and frequent user: his files were full of printed search results showing the stunning quantities of controlled-substance prescriptions that his patients were obtaining from other providers. There was just one problem: he marshaled this information not for the benefit of his patients, but for his own profit. Even after discovering David Laffer's doctor shopping, Dr. Li continued to prescribe—and to charge. Dr. Li had figured out a way to monetize the state's controlled substance physician alert system.

On November 27, 2010, Laffer returned early for his next visit and nevertheless received his usual prescription from Dr. Li. Dr. Li billed the insurance. Two early visits and a supply for two months' worth of prescriptions later, on January 2, 2011, the patient came back early again and said he had dropped his prescription in the toilet. It was unclear whether he meant the paper or the pills. This time Dr. Li did not bill insurance. Instead, he charged the patient a cash fee—$150—for two new prescriptions: a full month's supply of Norco, and Soma, a Schedule IV controlled-substance muscle relaxer. When Dr. Li saw the patient for the last time on June 11, 2011, he prescribed a full month's supply of Norco, doubled the Soma prescription, and sent the patient, David Laffer, on his way.

All the testimony about Laffer, ranging from the expert opinions to Dr. Li's testimony on direct and cross-examinations, was discrete and unremarkable, to the extent any testimony about any of Dr. Li's patients could be unremarkable. The Laffer charges may have seemed almost like an afterthought at trial, to the jury. Just another name among twenty different names, just 7 counts out of 211. That was quite intentional. The jury didn't know it, but we were treading on delicate ground: one misstep and many months' worth of work could tumble into the void. Any reference to the horrific crime this patient had committed could prejudice the jury against Dr. Li. The damage would be uncontrollable, irreversible—and cause for a mistrial. That would mean dismissal of the jury, and back to the drawing board.

The grand jury had charged Dr. Li with seven counts of Criminal Sale of a Prescription for a Controlled Substance with respect to Laffer, each count covering one medication. Our evidence, therefore, was necessarily limited: it was restricted to proving beyond a reasonable doubt that, on the relevant dates, Dr. Li knowingly had sold those prescriptions in something other than good faith.

Laffer was still alive—but there was no way we would call him as a witness. If it meant that the judge would have to instruct the jury about a missing witness, allowing them to draw a negative inference from the fact that we hadn't produced an individual who was under our control (by virtue of the fact that he was incarcerated), so be it. We would not align ourselves with a murderer or ask the jury to believe anything he might say. We suspected that Belair did not want him to testify, either.

As a result, no one called the shooter to the stand, and Dr. Li's own records and words told the story.

NOVEMBER 17, 2011: 854 DAYS UNTIL TRIAL

"A grand jury," reads the New York Criminal Procedure Law, Section 190.05, "is a body consisting of not less than sixteen nor more than twenty-three persons, impaneled by a superior court and constituting a part of such court, the functions of which are to hear and examine evidence concerning offenses and concerning misconduct, nonfeasance and neglect in public office, whether criminal or otherwise, and to take action with respect to such evidence [. . .]." The grand jury's loyalty is to the Court—not the prosecution. Their job is to hear the evidence and vote on proposed charges. "After hearing and examining evidence [. . .] a grand jury may [. . .] indict a person for an offense," the statute continues.

Prosecutors may not charge individuals with felonies: only the grand jury can decide whether the evidence supports such a step. In New York State, "a grand jury may indict a person for an offense when (a) the evidence before it is legally sufficient to establish that such person committed such offense [. . .] and (b) competent and admissible evidence before it provides reasonable cause to believe that such person committed such offense."[2] The standard is lower than the trial burden of "beyond a reasonable doubt," but contrary to the cliché, no ham sandwich ever would pass muster. I would have no pity for the New York City prosecutor who attempted to secure an indictment for a ham sandwich, on any kind of bread and with any assortment of condiments. The grand jurors I met were, thank goodness, still New Yorkers in their chamber: feisty, skeptical, intolerant of time wasting or bullshit. Of course, the statute provides for a check even upon the grand jury's power: upon a motion of the defense, the Court may dismiss any or all charges after examining the grand jury minutes.

At trial, the charges in the indictment set the boundaries of relevance for evidence and testimony. The trial jury, ultimately, deliberates upon the indictment charges in the privacy of their chamber and votes on each count of the indictment. Our goal was, therefore, to assemble an accurate, fair, and thorough set of proposed charges that captured the full range and scope of the criminal conduct. We wanted the future trial jury, if they had to be left just with the bare indictment, to be able to read it and understand how all the pieces fit together in Dr. Li's lucrative practice.

The first grand jury to hear evidence against Dr. Stan Xuhui Li returned an indictment related to Michael Cornetta in November 2011, charging the doctor with fifteen counts of Criminal Sale of a Prescription for a Controlled Substance and five counts of Reckless Endangerment in the Second Degree in connection with illegal sales of prescriptions between May 2009 and August 2010. The indictment itself was a signed and stamped document, printed on special paper with a red margin line on the left: beyond the substantive angst of a grand jury preparation, there was the frantic pursuit of the precious paper, the struggles with cantankerous printers ("Which one is working? *Which one is working?!*"), and the inevitable misprinting of the indictment with the line on the wrong side.

On November 18, 2011, I made the last of several appearances in a large, ornate courtroom on a high floor of the New York State Supreme Court building at 100 Centre Street, in connection with our application for a search warrant for Dr. Li's Flushing clinic. The courtroom was one of the largest and most stunning in the building—it felt as spacious and formal as a cathedral, with untouchable ceilings and carved benches, but smelled of dust and paper rather than incense. Until the last moment, I agonized over the application: my four years at a law firm had left me with document-perfection PTSD. Layered upon this familiar anxiety, however, was the anticipation of a unique moment in which, for the first time, someone outside our office—a judge, and one with a reputation as a thoughtful, impartial jurist—would evaluate the merits of our investigation.

The judge ultimately signed the search warrant and handed it to the court clerk, who apposed the official stamp. Joe Hall and I walked out of the courtroom and looked at each other when we reached the hallway, weighing the gravity of the moment. With every step forward, we felt a greater obligation to get it right.

The same day, I received a copy of the filed indictment, along with a blank warrant for Dr. Li's arrest. My hand shook as I filled out the warrant form. One year after the civilian tip, we were finally ready to go: we had an indictment, a warrant for Dr. Li's arrest, a search warrant for his clinic, and a team ready to execute both warrants on Saturday, November 19, 2011. There was no turning back and there could be no mistakes.

Dr. Li's life changed that day—we burst his bubble and he spent the night in jail. The case also took a big turn: after we announced the indictment, we undertook a deeper investigation, delving into Dr. Li's patient files. By early spring of 2012, we were ready to present evidence to a Special Grand Jury to apply for a second indictment that would supersede the first and capture all of Dr. Li's criminal conduct, spanning from 2004 until 2011. A few weeks into that Special Grand Jury presentation, which began in May 2012 and was expected to last six months, Bridget appointed Peter Kougasian as senior trial counsel, given his experience prosecuting homicide cases. Around the same time, Belair came on as Dr. Li's defense attorney and began sending us acerbic letters and submitting motions on the case.

We had our work mapped out for us and there was nothing to do but execute. One foot in front of the other, I kept moving forward. With the bodies piling up, however, as well as the pressure that came from the novelty of the case and the urgency of action, I needed endurance, discipline, and focus.

APRIL 1, 2012: 718 DAYS UNTIL TRIAL

"Read the statute." It was the mantra of every good lawyer, it had been the mantra of Mr. Robert Morgenthau, and it was the advice of Nancy Ryan, our newly deputized consultant who'd served as Chief of the Trial Division under the legendary "Boss."

We had spent our first of many remarkable marathon days together reviewing the facts. Now it was time to hit the books, review the law, and think about the charges we might propose.

I had a lot to do to understand—let alone try to catch up on—Nancy's and Peter's erudite, experiential understanding of the law.

To trick my brain, I moved from my desk to my chipped "conference" table, moved the boxes and folders to the floor, and laid out my notebook and blue Penal Law book. No emails—no calls—no texts—no distractions.

I cracked the book and started at the beginning of the Penal Law, with Section 1.05: "General Purposes." These familiar words always revealed new meaning. They reminded us of our purpose, priorities, and the limits on our authority.

"1. To proscribe conduct which unjustifiably and inexcusably causes or threatens substantial harm to individual or public interests; 2. To give fair warning of the nature of the conduct proscribed and of the sentences authorized upon conviction; 3. To define the act or omission and the accompanying mental state which constitute each offense; 4. To differentiate on reasonable grounds between serious and minor offenses and to prescribe proportionate penalties therefor; 5. To provide for an appropriate public response to particular offenses, including consideration of the consequences of the offense for the victim, including the victim's family, and the community [. . .]."

I paged through the book, alternately reading and skimming as I fell upon relevant sections. Alone in my office, I read the statutes over and over again on so many days, sometimes several times a day; then we repeated the readings with Joe Hall, with Joe T., with Peter and Bridget, with Nancy Ryan, in subsets or all together, in individual offices or in our large, formal conference room. Each of my team partners also read and reread the statutes and all the related judicial decisions on their own, and together we explored the meaning of every provision, precedent, and word.

The definitions of culpability were crucial: as I read through the Penal Law, I mentally categorized Dr. Li's crimes. If we knew which definitions of culpability fit our case, it would help us decide which crimes—or which degrees of a crime—were the right and just choice.

Most crimes in the New York State Penal Law require proof of a particular culpable state of mind or "intent."

Certain crimes require proof of intentional conduct, but there's also "knowing" conduct, recklessness, and criminal negligence. When a person acts according to their "conscious objective" to cause a certain result, they have acted "intentionally." Just one step down the ladder, a person who is aware of their conduct or circumstances acts "knowingly."

By contrast, a person "acts recklessly" when they are "aware of and consciously disregard [. . .] a substantial and unjustifiable risk that such result will occur or that such circumstance exists." The statute calls attention not only to the person's state of mind, but also to the risk itself: it must be "of such nature and degree" that to disregard it "constitutes a gross deviation from the standard of conduct that a reasonable person would observe in the situation."

Criminal negligence, by contrast, occurs when a person *fails* to perceive a risk. I remembered my conversations with a former executive in our office about criminal negligence. She had referred me to a line of cases in which unlicensed providers of colonics—folks with apartments, a couple of plastic tubes, and a colon-cleansing business—had been prosecuted following the accidental deaths of their patients. In those cases, prosecutors had proposed to charge criminally negligent homicide, because the defendants were not medical professionals and therefore failed to see or understand the risks of their conduct. In our case, Dr. Li was a highly trained, well-credentialed medical professional. His education alone may have been sufficient to prove awareness of the risks—and we believed we could prove, in addition to this general knowledge, that he had received specific and particularized warnings about his population of patients, their abuse of the prescribed medication, and the dangerous consequences of such misuse.

There also was the overall context of the conduct: Dr. Li ran a business, a pain management clinic, which seemed to rely upon and consist of cash transactions for controlled-substance prescriptions. Each of those transactions was a crime, to the extent we could prove that the prescriptions were not issued in good faith. But was the entire business a crime? Could we prove that it was a criminal enterprise? We checked the Penal Law entry for enterprise corruption: that statute required proof of three or more acts, from a list of eligible crimes, related to one another through a common scheme and committed within a span of ten years. It was a dead end: Criminal Sale of a Prescription for a Controlled Substance was not one of the eligible crimes. Nor was Conspiracy an option.

What if we reframed the case as being about money, in any form, rather than prescription sales? I thought about the fraudulent claims submitted to Medicare and the health insurance companies: those went back to the early days of the clinic, in 2004. Even before Dr. Li struck gold with his prescription sale business, he was already committing crimes for profit. I flipped through my Penal Law: Scheme to Defraud in the First Degree—a "systematic, ongoing course of conduct" with "intent to defraud." Could that work?

Scheme to Defraud was the overarching crime, even if it wasn't the most serious felony on the indictment. The larceny charges and criminal sales of prescriptions were the specific, repetitive acts that advanced and characterized the scheme.

What about those patients whose lives had been severely affected and damaged by the repeated prescriptions? We thought about Dr. Li's patients and considered the crimes of Reckless Endangerment.

Reckless Endangerment in the First Degree would require proof that, under circumstances evincing a depraved indifference to human life," Dr. Li recklessly had engaged in conduct that created "a grave risk of death" to his patients. The case law for depraved indifference was tough: previous judicial decisions in New York State had set a high standard. Not all patients would qualify, based on the element of "grave risk of death," and even within that group we would have to filter down to those where we could prove the existence of circumstances revealing a depraved indifference to human life. A grim task indeed.

JUNE 2012: APPROXIMATELY 640 DAYS UNTIL TRIAL

Maybe I should have realized that I needed help that Sunday in 2012, in the Unitarian Church of All Souls, when I felt them all sitting next to me in the empty pew: Nicholas Rappold, Joseph Haeg, Tara Palamar, Kevin Kingsley, and Michael Cornetta. I will not say that I *saw* them there, because this was not a hallucination. I *felt* them there: their physical presence; their silence. Waiting, voiceless. They were as I had heard them described or as I had seen them in their last photos: heavy limbed, dull eyed, tired, with just a little bit of life left deep inside, far out of reach.

I had been raised in a culturally and religiously diverse family, so my presence at a church service was a surprise and a relief. I'd loved the All Souls building since I'd moved to the neighborhood and had noticed their activity in the community: a preschool, a soup kitchen, open meetings. The name All Souls, on its own, did much to draw me in, for its limitless acceptance. On this random Sunday without my children, I just needed to be around life and souls.

The church was bright and airy, with a high ceiling, white walls, and windows decorated by creeping ivy. I sat in a long wooden pew, just me and my sad ghosts. We were comfortable together. I promised to take care of them. They promised to stay with me until it was over. I croaked my way through some of the hymns, sat and listened and absorbed the feeling of being in a caring community. It wasn't the first or the last time I felt their presence: Nicholas Rappold and Joseph Haeg, especially, stuck close to me. Perhaps because I thought so much about their mothers, too. Perhaps because I missed my own boy so much and had the luxury of knowing he was safe somewhere, even if not always with me: How could any parent survive the permanent disappearance of their child? I felt so guilty wanting more—always more—of my chil-

SOFT TARGETS • 141

dren, always fighting for those extra nights, when other parents would give anything just to know their child was alive.

I had weaned myself off antidepressants in 2009 and, for a while, I was operating within a "normal" range of emotions. There was stress, but there were objective reasons for stress: a tough case, a full docket, a custody tussle, a pending divorce judgment, childcare juggles, parenting dilemmas. Besides, the memories of the "zapping" feeling in my brain as the SSRI wore off was still too fresh. If I could avoid taking medication again, that was my preference. Even though I knew, on a rational level, that SSRIs and opioid painkillers had little in common, the case had made me increasingly wary of any pills. I took up boxing instead and "powered through," stretching myself across multiple futile battlefields.

While the divorce had been finalized in August 2011, my ex-husband continued to press for changes to the custody schedule. I hated the schedule, too, but we both had agreed to it—and couldn't agree on anything else.

Sunday nights, Monday nights, Tuesday nights, and every other weekend. It was—and still is—a shitty schedule that never allows anyone to settle in. My son, who was six years old, complained that being away from either parent felt like he was holding his breath—which meant he was always holding his breath, because he was always missing one parent. "I don't understand why you divorced," he said to me one day. "Can you explain it to me? Why didn't you think about us *before* you did that?"

Wednesday mornings were the worst, with tensions running high over stupid things like getting ready for school, because the three of us anticipated our separation, but we all knew we had no choice, and they were as happy to see their father as they were sad to leave me. My kids got used to filling bags with stuff and carrying them back and forth, and the bags then accumulated in our hallways and their rooms, never emptied.

When it was time to update the custody calendar every few months, my ex-husband and I spent hours on the telephone, revisiting his every grievance and butting heads over our continuing incompatibility. He wanted to leave things "open" and "play it by ear," planning no more than a few months in advance and adapting the schedule as we went along. I wanted to limit future discussions and conflicts and uncertainty by planning in advance and adhering to our agreement. I wanted predictability; he wanted freedom. I wanted routine; he wanted flexibility. He wanted trust; I had no trust. He was cooperative until I said no, and then the hostility revealed itself yet again, as sharp and biting as ever. Where had all the love gone? All to the kids. A desperate push and grab for love, all piled onto and competing for their two little selves.

Our love didn't translate into happiness for them. Nina, age nine, hated nighttime and felt torn between two separate homes. She suffered through night terrors, during which she shrieked and slapped away my hands as I tried to safely guide her back into bed without jolting her awake. The work at school grew harder and teachers expected more autonomy: Nina wanted nothing to change ever again, but everyone was asking her to adapt, to grow, to take risks.

Charlie had entered the golden age of school viruses, and we spent countless hours in steamy bathrooms, the two of us, as he coughed and snurfled through the night. For the first time, I began wondering whether his chronic ear infections might be affecting his hearing. Nina and I often kidded him about not answering to his name, or responding to instructions with an innocent "What . . . ?" What if he actually couldn't hear us? What if he only seemed to get sick with me? What if I had such a reputation for overprotectiveness that I couldn't help Charlie when he needed help, because no one believed me? What if I needed help?

Thanks to my city employee health insurance company's sparse list of in-network providers and low reimbursements, psychological help came in fits and spurts, through a rotating cast of occasional therapists. While depression had manifested itself in different ways through my life, it always managed to camouflage itself as a "normal feeling," until I was in such a deep pit that I could no longer climb out—and no longer cared. I could neither smile nor cry. I was locked into a mind that raced with task lists, recriminations, worries, longings, feelings, and ideas but was unable and unwilling to verbalize them beyond what was necessary for minimal functioning. When I tried to open up, I felt like my words spilled and reached too far, revealed too much, confused everything, and I promised myself not to do it again—but I did again and again, hating myself even more each time, and the cycle continued.

Sitting in the pew of All Souls on that bright late spring morning, I realized that the only children who were with me all the time were other people's children—and they were dead. Some—like Tara Palamar—haunted me because I felt so helpless. Her face had imprinted itself into my mind from an old photo we had found, taken during her struggle with addiction: a heart shape worn and weighted by sleeplessness, with sunken, tired eyes and hair pulled around to one side, forehead wrinkled and eyebrows tilted almost as though she were shocked to be in such bad shape. She was a difficult ghost, because there was not much we could do for her.

Others, like Rappold, Haeg, and Kingsley, presented thorny issues of law and fact. I couldn't even begin to think of all the other ghosts who had died of the same causes, the tens of thousands of other Americans whose last years of life were tangled up with doctors, prescriptions, dealers, pills and more pills, always more pills—for whom medicine, the law, and the government offered no explanation, no justice, no remedy.

The Special Grand Jury was impaneled in May and sat for six months, three mornings a week. Three days a week I arrived suited up, binders up, witnessed up and ready to go at the opening bell, on the spot for three to four hours, then dazed at my desk scarfing down a salad before meeting with my team or more witnesses. Two days a week, when the jury was not working, I went out into the field with Joe or prepped in the office. I kept track of everything at work: every piece of paper, every appointment, every theory, every charge, every day that Dr. Li had seen any one of our twenty patients, every prescription he had written, every payment he received, every bank account, every subpoena, every set of records received. The stenographers typed up transcripts in record time.

There were some tough decisions: immunity agreements that needed to be consistent with the office's values and that we would not be ashamed to disclose to the jury at trial; whether or not to ask the grand jury to charge Dr. Li's wife with any crimes, given her limited command of the English language and lack of a medical license; whether to allow Dr. Li to turn himself in or arrest him at his home. Since we were contemplating felony charges, we would have to work with the local police in his New Jersey township and go through extradition proceedings if we decided to go forward with the arrest.

My anxiety and stress snowballed with every passing week.

By late October, we were wrapping up the grand jury presentation. It was coming time to instruct the jury on the law and ask them to vote on the proposed charges. We were just a little worried about the weather: there was a storm brewing in the Atlantic Ocean.

OCTOBER 29, 2012: 507 DAYS UNTIL TRIAL

President Obama had declared a state of emergency in New York, so my office and the children's school were closed. It was my custody night with the kids, but we were staying with my parents while our apartment was under construction. We stayed home, waiting. As the air turned gray and wet, I drew the curtains in the room the three of us shared and hoped for the best. I pushed the children's beds far from the windows. It was a long night, listening to the wind, attentive to any unusual sounds that might indicate flying objects approaching the glass.

By the time we woke up the next morning, there was no power. We played board games and ate, and I bickered with my parents, teenage-style. They decided to leave for their house on Long Island, and I called my ex-husband to find out if he had power: he did. When the storm died down, I bundled up the kids and we went looking for a cab. Cars moved across intersections according to a tenuous honor system. Streetlights swayed from their cables, dark and useless. I dropped off the children uptown with their father so that they could be more comfortable, visited a friend, and then headed back downtown on foot to the strange world of powerless Manhattan. As I walked toward Union Square, I noticed a group of people standing around on the sidewalk. "What happened?" I asked a young woman. "Someone just jumped out of a window," she said.

In my parents' dark building stairwell, I passed several families who were heading down and out, toward safety and light and groups. I tried to buck myself up, reminding myself that I was lucky to be in a dry neighborhood. That I had friends if I needed to go elsewhere. This felt like a preview of the end of the world. When an invitation came to stay with a friend in Brooklyn, I leapt at the chance. The next morning, I visited another friend and held her baby's little hand. Less than a mile from my empty, dark apartment, there was life and love. Okay, so everything was fine . . . right? I went back to Manhattan and climbed the seven flights.

I walked around the dusky apartment, telling myself that this was my chance to take a break from my phone, read books, maybe light a candle, kick it nineteenth-century style. I couldn't stop thinking about all the empty apartments over and under me. After a few hours, I went back down the stairs and across the street to an Italian restaurant, where they were serving candlelit family-style meals for a minimal, set price, to empty their freezers. I ate pasta and drank a glass of wine, soaked in the beauty and safety of people huddling together over food and candles, and then climbed back upstairs, wearing a head lamp. This time, I encountered no one.

I opened the door and closed myself in the apartment. I wandered around, then checked my messages and fell into my phone. I felt the pull to text, email, call—but who? And why? Why was it so hard to just be alone? And when I thought of the possibilities, only the toxic memories rose to the surface: the friends with whom I had lost touch; all the times I had suddenly broken away from people I loved because I was afraid they would leave me; all the times I'd been left; my recent breakup with my long-distance boyfriend; the brother with whom I seemed unable to communicate; my inability to untwist myself out of the conflict with my ex-husband. I dropped my phone on a table and tried to read a mystery novel, but the memories, regrets, and recriminations swelled and spiraled and won. I curled up in one of the kids' beds and time seemed to stop in the darkness. The city was silent. Everything around me was lifeless: concrete, glass, metal, paper. I couldn't get away from myself—I'd never be able to get away from myself. I'd never be able to forget all the things I needed to forget. There was an evidence cart in my mind, loaded with memories, always available to provide proof of my guilt. I'd never be able to forgive myself for all my mistakes or acts of inconsiderate selfishness. If I tried to reach out to all those people to apologize, they would think I was a crazy narcissist— and they would be right. It is just so messed up that you can't learn how to live until you live. I had expected better from myself. It was time to give up and see things as they were.

Over the next few days, my internal power went out. I fell into a dead zone. There was no horizon—just the thick walls of my brain and endless, choking tears. The worst moments were when I wasn't crying, when I felt blank and dry on the inside, lifeless and finished and hurting at the thought of continuing to live another day. I revisited every situation in which I had done wrong—and there were many. There were real, actual emergencies and losses happening everywhere around me in the city, so in addition to the shame and guilt of past unkindness, there was also shame and guilt at the thought that I could feel this unhappy when, actually, I was safe and fortunate in the aftermath of the storm. I went to see the woman who was serving as my ersatz therapist, but she just stared at me as I sat, as dead and dry as a broken shell, talking in circles. I didn't dare tell her that I wanted to die. I wore my sunglasses during the entire session. I never heard from her again.

NOVEMBER 4, 2012: 501 DAYS UNTIL TRIAL

The minister of the Unitarian Church of All Souls opened with a poem by Emily Dickinson:

There came a wind like a bugle,
It quivered through the grass,
And a green chill upon the heat
So ominous did pass

We barred the window and the doors
As from an emerald ghost
The doom's electric moccasin
That very instant passed.

On a strange mob of planting trees,
And fences fled away,
And rivers where the houses ran
The living looked that day,

The bell within the steeple wild,
The flying tidings whirled.
How much can come and much can go,
And yet abide the world!

And yet abide the world, indeed. I just had to go on. At the end of the service, I walked past the minister as he stood by the door and thanked him, like everyone else. He looked at me and asked if I was okay. "I don't know," I said, tearing up. "I'm not sure what's happening to me." He invited me to come by for a chat.

A few days later, I sat on the edge of a prim upholstered settee in a small office overlooking Lexington Avenue, trying to keep from crying. The reverend sat in a chair. It was strange to see him in a suit, without his robe. We talked for an hour as other church employees and volunteers milled around in the hallway and worked quietly in the reception area. At first, I didn't know what to say. I wasn't religious—was I even allowed to be there? But he asked simple questions and I answered. He absorbed the nonconfidential account of my case: so many dead people; so many grieving families; so many documents; so much uncertainty. I struggled to express how much I missed my kids without crying, even though I knew that just having them out there in the world, alive and healthy, was a gift. He offered a list of church meeting groups and books that might help, but it was his presence, patience, and steadiness that got me through that day. And that was enough.

From that moment, I learned to hang on to one thing each day. It did not occur to me to seek medical help. There were objective circumstances to explain my feelings, I thought. It was normal to have feelings, right? Normal people just pushed through. That's what I always had been taught to do and I didn't want to need medication again.

On Thursday, November 8, the kids went back to school and our office reopened. I suited up and bindered up. Joe Hall walked into my office early in the morning and took one look at me. "What's wrong?" I told him that I was not in great shape but would be fine. We talked about the hurricane recovery efforts in his neighborhood.

It was a grand jury day—would anyone show up? The city was still in shambles. Peter and I walked over to the grand jury chamber, not knowing what to expect, not knowing if everyone was okay or if everything that had been presented over the past few months would have to be done all over again.

Every single grand juror came in that day.

People from all across the city. People with day jobs, intense jobs, no jobs, medical conditions, elderly parents, and children. We were so relieved that everyone was safe—and so grateful that their civic duty had prevailed over the difficult conditions that many of them were facing. I never learned any of their names or stories—that would not have been authorized or appropriate—but I remain so grateful for their service.

The grand jury voted a 219-count indictment against Dr. Li a couple of weeks later, including two counts of homicide for Nicholas Rappold and Joseph Haeg.*

We decided not to offer Dr. Li an opportunity to turn himself in, as there was a risk of flight. We also decided to wait until after Thanksgiving.

On Thursday, November 22, 2012, the children and I scooped out three small acorn squash. We roasted the exteriors and then filled them with a bright beet soup. The children were proud of their handiwork and posed for photos with big smiles. I stuffed a turkey breast and the three of us ate together at the table in the middle of the day, then watched movies and ate some more. The meal was delicious and so were my children.

After they went to bed, I sat down in front of my laptop. The children would be with me for Christmas week, as usual, but they spent the second week of their winter break with their father. I was thinking of taking the second week off as well—I needed to rest before the next phase of the case but knew it would not be a good idea to be alone and idle in the city. I browsed workshops and locations. I thought about the place that always blew the rust out my mind: California. I remembered being in the back of the car as a kid, as my dad drove us from our home in the Bay Area down to Big Sur, the car following the curve of the steep cliffs along Highway 1, my mother crouching down in the front seat every time he took a turn along the narrow curves. There was a sign I remembered, along one of the stretches, a driveway that angled

---

* The judge later struck eight counts as duplicative, leaving us with a 211-count indictment for trial.

down. I knew it was some sort of retreat. I imagined little houses nestled in the cliffs, lanterns shining a warm light. I couldn't remember the name. I pulled up a map of Highway 1, zoomed in, and flew over the map.

A wooden sign. One word. A driveway. Between the highway and the ocean.

Esalen.

I booked a one-week meditation retreat for the New Year. I closed my laptop. That day, I hung on to two things: my beautiful children and a future plan, just five crazed weeks away.

NOVEMBER 29, 2012: 476 DAYS UNTIL TRIAL

Shortly after dawn, Joe and his team drove to Hamilton Township in New Jersey. The OSNP investigators occupied two cars: Joe and his boss in one car; Buddy and a partner in the other. The Hamilton County Police Department sent two patrol cars: the local police would make the arrest. They waited around the corner from Dr. Li's house. It was a cold and bright day. A yellow school bus pulled up and stopped. Dr. Li and his daughter, who had been warming themselves in the family's car, went out to meet the bus. The little girl said good-bye to her father and got on. The bus closed its doors and drove away.

The team waited for Joe's signal. Joe waited for the bus to be out of sight.

It was time—

The two cars blocked in Dr. Li's vehicle. An officer from the Hamilton Township Police placed him under arrest. The police transported Dr. Li to the Mercer County Correction Center. Joe walked up to Dr. Li's blue house and rang the doorbell, to inform Anna Guo of her husband's arrest. She answered the door and took in the news, flustered. While they spoke, Joe's eyes drifted around: on a little table near the door he saw a small Dixie cup containing orange juice and a paper plate holding a slice of cold pizza. There was a child-size bite missing from the pizza. It was their daughter's breakfast. When Joe called me from the car a few minutes later, that's all he could talk about. It broke his heart.

Dr. Li spent a week in a suburban New Jersey county jail. On December 5, 2012, Joe and his partner drove him to Manhattan, pulling up to the grungy sally port behind the Criminal Courts Building on Baxter Street. When the gates opened, Dr. Li blanched. As Joe and Dr. Li waited in a hallway, they were startled by a deafening, buzzing, strident alarm. They heard and felt the pounding approach of a horde of correctional SWAT team officers dressed in black, bearing hard shields, helmets, and weapons. The officers rammed into the facility, pushing Joe and Dr. Li aside. Dr. Li was shaking: a few minutes later, he was in the custody of the Department of Corrections.

DECEMBER 6, 2012: 469 DAYS UNTIL TRIAL

Judge Sonberg arraigned Dr. Li on the new indictment, which superseded the 2011 indictment. As part of the arraignment proceeding, I made a new bail application based on the gravity of the new charges. Belair was outraged at the arrest, the indignity, the delay, the homicide counts; he, too, spoke on the record on behalf of Dr. Li. After the arraignment, I stood next to Joe and behind Bridget during her short press conference. The next day, I left work early and drove my children out to my parents' house on Long Island. We had dinner; I put the children to bed and took a shower. I was alone in a room, in a house, in the dark, in safety, and a phase of the case had just finished. The year was almost finished.

And then it happened again: rising, suffocating panic; tears; emptiness; a feeling of exposure, humiliation, loneliness, worthlessness. The tides flowed in and flooded me.

Depression never feels to me like depression. It's a whorl of heaviness to which someone has given that name, but the name doesn't fit when you feel it. Maybe that's why it's so hard to admit to and recognize. Especially when you hate yourself so much that the the feeling of being mismatched with life feels justified.

I felt like a big, slow fish in deep, dark waters. Every day, it was all I could do to pull myself through the routine: getting up, getting dressed, taking the subway, saying hello to co-workers, having meetings, writing, answering the phone, cooking dinner, putting the kids to bed or calling them to say good night, going to bed, having bad dreams, repeat. The only things that kept me going were my kids, the thought of California just a few weeks away, and the team of colleagues and families who were pushing the case forward, together.

I drew comfort from the fact that we were taking action in the midst of the opioid crisis and prayed that what we were doing would help. I would have been crushed to know that it was about to get so much worse. A sickening number of lives already had been lost to prescription painkiller overdoses, but I'll be honest, I thought we were at the peak of the epidemic in 2012. I was hopeful that a recent wave of "dirty doctor" prosecutions, including ours, had raised awareness— and that criminal doctors who sold prescriptions would be deterred by the threat of homicide charges such as the ones the grand jury had just brought against Dr. Li. I was hopeful that well-intentioned physicians would be horrified to realize they had been misled by pharmaceutical companies as to the risks of addiction, and even more horrified that some among their midst had exploited the addiction of their patients for profit. I was wrong—so wrong.

There were so many thousands of people still alive then who died soon thereafter of opioid overdoses. The number of dead—and our tolerance for those numbers—had kept going up after the year 2000. Each life that ended was a travesty and a crime, but our collective response to the opioid epidemic was similar, in many respects, to a body's response to opioids. We grew so accustomed to the deaths that the numbers need to keep getting higher in order to set off the alarms. And overdoses were but one indication of a larger problem affecting tens of thousands more people: opioid addiction. There were parents, siblings, children, partners waking up every day with constant worry and uncertainty. The lives of addicted persons and their loved ones were being hijacked daily—hourly.

More than forty-seven thousand humans died of drug overdoses involving opioids in 2017.[3] It is horrific beyond words. It was a war launched by folks with advanced degrees and executive positions, which they were fighting in unspoken alliance with drug cartels, street dealers, and overseas drug shippers. Their lies were avoidable. The overprescribing was avoidable. The overdose deaths were avoidable. Drug marketing was the result of conscious choices. Those who knew about the risk of addiction and had the power to alter the trend—but declined to do so—are responsible. Will they ever be held accountable?

CHAPTER 8

Modern Medicine

It is our aim in this little booklet to present the busy practitioner brief descriptions of Bayer Pharmaceutical products, comprising their physical and chemical properties, their physiological action and therapeutic effect, together with a number of formulae which have proved serviceable in the practice of prominent physicians. [...]

Heroin: [...] If administered properly, Heroin is completely devoid of the unpleasant and toxic effects of opium derivates, such as digestive disturbances, constipation, etc. [...] To be taken with a cupful of hot fluid before retiring.

—"BAYER" PHARMACEUTICAL PRODUCTS AND TECHNICAL
PREPARATIONS, CIRCA 1900S[1]

OCTOBER 10, 2003: 3,814 DAYS UNTIL TRIAL

My first child was born by emergency cesarean section, a full two weeks after her due date. "If I'd lived in the Middle Ages," I asked a midwife in the recovery room, "what would have happened?" "Oh," she said, "you'd probably both be dead." My body didn't "do" labor in 2003—or again in 2006, when Charlie was born.

That C-section was my first encounter with an opioid analgesic. In that case, it was morphine, a natural derivative of the same poppy plant that is used to produce heroin.

I never had smoked pot. Never smoked a cigarette. Never even had a cup of coffee. I'd taken a mini-dose of Valium a couple of times on airplanes to prevent panic attacks, but otherwise reality was as much as I could handle. Until now. I tapped the small white button on the patient-controlled analgesia (PCA) IV pump, heard the soft *beep-beep-beep* that meant morphine was about to be delivered right into my veins, and a few moments later I was *flying*. Those twenty-four hours after surgery with my PCA pump felt like ten days *and* they felt like ten minutes. The morphine didn't just take away the pain—it lightened my mind and brushed me to sleep, killing the post-surgical pain as well as every other physical and emotional pain I carried. I joked about looking forward to my next C-section but swore to myself that I never, ever, could allow myself to seek out this feeling.

Depending on how it is administered, heroin is between two to five times more potent than morphine, but there is a synthetic, or manmade, opioid even stronger than both morphine and heroin: fentanyl.

I remembered my post-surgical oblivion when I learned about Michael Cornetta's use and misuse of fentanyl.

Fentanyl is listed as a Schedule II controlled substance because it combines a "high potential for abuse" with "a currently accepted medical use in treatment in the United States or a currently accepted medical use with severe restrictions."[2] Fentanyl is fifty times more potent than heroin and one hundred times more potent than morphine.[3]

Fentanyl is manufactured and distributed legally, by pharmaceutical companies. It is available by prescription. It is absorbable, though only after prolonged, targeted exposure through skin and mucous membranes. It is legally sold in lollipop, tablet, and patch form. Duragesic is a brand-name fentanyl patch: a squishy, Band-Aid–like adhesive pouch containing a reservoir of painkilling gel.

The indication for Duragesic is "the management of pain in opioid-tolerant patients, severe enough to require daily, around-the-clock, long-term opioid treatment and for which alternative treatment options are inadequate," though doctors have had the discretion to prescribe it "off-label," meaning even for conditions for which it was not specifically approved by the FDA.*

The lowest strength and dose for Duragesic patches is twelve micrograms per hour, according to the package insert. If used as intended, the patch delivery mechanism for fentanyl delivers the prescribed dose to the body every hour. Once the patch is applied, it takes twelve to sixteen hours to reach "therapeutic levels," meaning that the patch can be trusted to release its intended dose continuously only after that time.[4]

The package insert anticipates a dosing interval of seventy-two hours for pharmaceutical fentanyl patches. That means you can wear the patch for three days and it will continue to release the prescribed dose during that time. After the twelve-to-sixteen-hour ramp-up to patch effectiveness, you then have more than forty-eight hours of efficacy. Fentanyl persists in the body for another sixteen to twenty-two hours after the patch is removed.[5]

Fentanyl is the ultimate modern medicine. It is a miracle drug that lifts the human body out of the realm of pain. It is not just a substance: it's a hero and the villain; it's legal and illegal; it's lifesaving and potentially fatal; it's a blessing and a temptation; it is praised and defamed; it is medically prescribed, yet it may be dangerously misused.

---

* Pharmaceutical companies, however, are not allowed to market a drug beyond its indication.

MAY 14, 2014: DAY 56 OF TRIAL

The court building was a dark, contemporary rectangle with all of its luster long lost. A chain-link fence separated it from the small public park with its small, dirty pond. It was an odd little park that never felt restful or natural but at least allowed for airspace and views on the upper courthouse floors. As our witnesses waited around the corner from the courtroom, to avoid the jury members on their breaks or other folks milling around the doors, they stood in the streaks of sunlight that streamed through the windows. When I went out into the hallway to greet them and exchange a final few words before their testimony, if I had time to do so, we had to shield our eyes. It was a sterile building but for that sunlight, and a place I don't think anyone would have imagined would become a memorial for so many deceased victims. And yet through this trial, we were bringing them back into the world for just a few hours.

Dr. Shushan Hovanesian was nervous as she waited. She came accompanied by one of her colleagues, for moral support. Dr. Hovanesian's short, fluffy black hair framed a round face, with lips tight and tense. She had a soft voice and soft accent. Her beautifully penned notes about Michael Cornetta, in a careful cursive script, waited for her on the evidence cart if she needed them. Peter conducted the direct examination, of course. When we had drawn up the list of trial witnesses, he had laid immediate claim to all those with Armenian ancestry.

Dr. Hovanesian explained to the jury that she had attended medical school in Armenia, obtained a PhD in Moscow, done a residency in the United States, and also passed American medical board exams.

Dr. Hovanesian was a psychiatrist. In fact, she was *the* psychiatrist who had penned a report on January 17, 2010, after meeting Cornetta. That report made its way into his medical record, and then to my office in 2011. When I read it, I knew we had a case.

Dr. Hovanesian met Cornetta on January 17, 2010, after he walked into the Flushing Hospital Emergency Room, seeking help with pain and depression. Dr. Hovanesian interviewed Cornetta for nearly forty-five minutes. Having spoken to him, she was concerned that he had no safe plan for discharge. He was thirty-nine years old and he wanted to die.

"He felt hopeless and helpless," she said.

As the doctor testified from the witness stand, she turned toward the court reporter, out of a need to tell her story to another human being or perhaps because she thought it would make the stenographer's task easier. The court reporter smiled at the witness, but she was a pro, so she did not take offense when the judge, who was always concerned about the acoustics in the room, intervened.

"Ma'am," he interrupted, "you really can't have a conversation with the court reporter. We all need to be able to hear what you are saying."

Cornetta's girlfriend had just broken up with him and he was on the street, the doctor told the jury. Cornetta was skinny. He had not eaten or slept much since his girlfriend had kicked him out. He felt low. He felt anxious. He suffered from bipolar disorder. He took Zyprexa, Paxil, and Remeron, but he had run out of all of them. He also took pain medication, specifically fentanyl and oxycodone, because he'd had some surgeries in the past. He also took Xanax and drank. Dr. Hovanesian worried that she couldn't get Cornetta to name a safe place where he would be welcome.

As I listened to her testimony, I thought about Michael Cornetta's brother and girlfriend, both of whom we knew and who had loved him with all their hearts. I thought about the ravages of addiction on his relationships. The erosion of trust to the point where there was nothing left—until it was replenished again by the power of love, and then destroyed again. A cycle that ended only with his death.

Dr. Hovanesian tried calling Cornetta's girlfriend on January 17, but there was no answer, so the doctor ordered admission to a psychiatric unit and one-to-one observation. Cornetta agreed and signed the papers. He was accompanied out of the emergency room for hospital admission and Dr. Hovanesian got to work on his treatment plan.

First, she tried to figure out his medication. She knew the Paxil would have been prescribed for depression; Remeron for both anxiety and depression; Zyprexa for bipolar disorder. Benzodiazepines were also psychiatric medications, but the patient had mentioned the Xanax in the context of his pain management. And then there were the opioids and the alcohol. As for the combination of the opioids (the oxycodone and fentanyl) with the Xanax, especially such a high dose of Xanax, it seemed very dangerous. She couldn't make sense of it.

She looked at the oxycodone bottle that she'd received from the patient. She read the doctor's name from the label: Stan Li. She wrote down the phone number. She called the doctor's office but didn't expect to reach anyone. When a woman answered the phone, Dr. Hovanesian introduced herself.

When Dr. Li got on the phone, Dr. Hovanesian was surprised to find that he was working on a Sunday. "I am treating one of your patients, Michael Cornetta, for depression and withdrawal," she said, then asked about Cornetta's oxycodone. "Did you prescribe it to him? In what dose?" Dr. Li confirmed that he had prescribed thirty milligrams of oxycodone, four times a day. He did not ask Dr. Hovanesian any questions. She thanked him and ended the call.

Maybe the jury was wondering—as I had the first time I heard this story—why Dr. Hovanesian had not asked more questions of Dr. Li or given him more information. Why hadn't she told him about Cornetta's suicidal ideation? Why hadn't she asked the reason for his prescriptions? Doctors, as Peter and I had come to learn during this investigation and as the jury would learn, trusted one another to make sound medical decisions. Dr. Hovanesian's role was not to question another physician's treatment, but to verify the patient's prescriptions.

Nevertheless, the call she made was enough to put Dr. Li on notice: he learned that Cornetta had gone to an emergency room and that a psychiatrist was now treating him for depression and withdrawal. That information should have been sufficient to cause concern and prompt Dr. Li to ask questions of his patient, at the very least.

After Dr. Hovanesian spoke to Dr. Li on January 17, she told Cornetta that she was comfortable prescribing the oxycodone because she had been able to confirm the dosage with his doctor. What about the fentanyl? he asked. That was also from Dr. Li. Michael obsessed about the fentanyl, but Hovanesian hesitated. She couldn't prescribe it without confirming with Dr. Li first. She decided to call again. This time, Dr. Li was not in the office. Dr. Hovanesian left a message. Dr. Li never called her back, and she never saw Cornetta again.

It was time for the court's lunch break. The judge instructed the jury, as usual, not to discuss the case, but with a new twist.

"Let me just take thirty seconds about this. Trials are not baseball games. There is no one who is ahead or behind at any point along the way, and the People's case isn't finished. [. . .] So, that's why I tell you don't form an opinion even in the privacy of your own mind or express any opinion concerning the guilt or non-guilt of the defendant because you really can't start reaching that issue until you hear all the evidence and until you hear the lawyers' summations, which may help you structure the evidence in a way that you didn't see before, and until you hear my instructions to you on the law because you don't know what it is that the People have to prove beyond a reasonable doubt in order to support a verdict of guilt. [. . .] I realize how difficult it is, how much of a human urge it is to do, but it is an urge that you have to resist until the end."

JUNE 18, 2012: 640 DAYS UNTIL TRIAL

"[B]orn of particularly ill grace"? "Unencumbered by any formal knowledge of the facts"? Mr. Belair's latest letter conveyed his fury at the news that we were presenting additional charges to a second grand jury—it also revealed a talent for personal jabs. I grabbed the letter and strode down three long hallways toward the office of my newly assigned official trial partner, Special Assistant District Attorney, and now Senior Trial Counsel, Peter Kougasian. We needed to discuss the contents of the letter, of course. But also, given Peter's typical banter and familiarity, I figured I might also have the liberty to vent with him about my impatience with Mr. Belair's dismissive tone. How wrong I was.

Peter sat behind his desk, barely visible behind a tidal wave of documents sliding across its surface, a wooden duck perched precariously atop the wave's crest. "Can you believe this letter—" I started, but Peter interrupted me with a sharp tone. "If you can't handle it," he said, "maybe I should take over all calls and correspondence with the defense attorney."

Caught short, I cobbled together some verbal response—something to the effect of "I can handle it; I was just venting; I certainly won't make that mistake again"—and stormed out. Did familiarity, oversharing, and emotion only flow in one direction in our working relationship?

Over the next few months, I marched myself into his office on several more occasions, this time forcing out the words to request a conversation about our communication dynamics, as we called it, and our latest conflict, whatever it had been. I might get a sentence or two of serious conversation before Peter changed the subject, cracking a joke or pulling us back toward a legal debate. It soon became clear to me that my designated role was "bossy detail woman" to his "eccentric idea man." If he displayed anxiety, it was charming and funny, but if I expressed mine, it revealed a lack of competence. Our partnership evolved into predictable instability, or stable unpredictability, where our minds might meld for a few moments over a task list, a witness interview, or a new case we'd discovered, then tensions would flare suddenly, then one of us might try to do something nice for the other, then another breach would follow.

I read books and articles about stress management and workplace tension. I followed scripts for tough conversations and prohibited myself from crying at the office. Every night before sleep I reviewed the day's evidence, pulling moments and memories as exhibits of my successes or failures, running a rough tally of whether I was a "good" or "bad" person, whether I was really trying or just pretending, whether I really wanted to make things better or just needed to be liked. At best, it felt like a draw. At worst, I returned a harsh verdict against myself after hours and came back in the morning to find that even my appearance was working against me.

"You look worried; are you okay?"

"You look so anxious."

"You have to stop obsessing over this case."

"Why are you so stressed?"

"You have to relax."

I'm all for checking in on people. It's important to do that. If someone close to you looks worried, anxious, stressed, it's worth taking a chance to find out if they feel hopeless, if they need help.

This was something different. The alleged concerns about my perceived anxiety were questions about my competence—and appearance. If I had a frown line between my eyebrows (which I did), if I looked worried, if I seemed anxious, it somehow indicated that I was not able to handle what was happening. If I was stressed, if I was working hard, it meant that I should work less hard, distract myself, "relax."

Also—you bet I was worried. We had to rally dozens of witnesses for criminal proceedings in which many of them were not eager to participate. Sixteen people were dead. *I was challenging a man's right to live freely.* Would the taxpayers want me to relax under those circumstances? I don't think so.

Peter was not relaxed. The longer he worked on the case, the more weight he shed, the more rumpled his suits looked. The piles of paper in his office reached skyscraper heights and his tie pointed to four o'clock. He played up his anxiety, though, alternating between a mad professor/ hapless detective persona and that of a hard-hitting, critical prosecutor. But no one ever told Peter to "relax"—and I don't think he would have cared if they had. He certainly kept me on my toes: he mused and teased about the "trial gods" and my complete lack of "mazel" one day, then gave me a stern lecture the next day, shedding all humor and smiles in order to impress upon me the error and danger of my ways. I tried so many times to settle on a course of action for our professional relationship, but that required reaching a conclusion about who he was and what he was doing. Every time I thought I'd accumulated sufficient evidence to support one point of view, new events upended my conclusions.

MAY 14, 2014: DAY 56 OF TRIAL

I would not have been surprised to learn that Dr. Mark Rydzewski, the other doctor whom we called to testify about Cornetta that day, had the lowest blood pressure ever to be recorded. Dr. Rydzewski worked as an attending physician in the Flushing Hospital emergency room. He seemed exhausted and imperturbable. He had something of the late Philip Seymour Hoffman: the pale blond hair, the thoughtful eyes, the low, controlled voice. He'd handled so many emergencies, he had no independent recollection of Cornetta: we retrieved the chart from the evidence cart so that he could flip through the records.

Dr. Rydzewski had seen Cornetta twice: once on March 1, 2010, and once a few months later on May 19. On both occasions, Cornetta arrived by ambulance. On March 1, the EMTs had first found Cornetta lying faceup, unresponsive. They noted that he had "eaten" several fentanyl patches and was taking only six breaths per minute. "That's on the low side," Rydzewski explained. "Normal is anywhere between twelve to fourteen and twenty." The EMTs revived Cornetta with four doses of Narcan, a lifesaving, fast-acting antidote to opioid poisoning, but noted that even after he reached a rate of eighteen breaths per minute he remained unresponsive.†

Once Cornetta was in the emergency room, Dr. Rydzewski ordered

---

† Narcan may be purchased over the counter from pharmacies, may be carried in a purse or briefcase, and may be used to save the life of another person's child. See https://www.narcan.com for instructions and availability.

toxicology tests: "They were positive for opiates, positive for amphet-amines, negative for barbiturates, positive for benzodiazepines, positive for cocaine." In addition to a drug overdose, Rydzewski also diagnosed Cornetta with Tylenol toxicity. Cornetta avoided an ICU admission during that visit, but he was in the hospital for four days, during which time a psychiatrist diagnosed him with bipolar disorder and anxiety disorder.

By May 19 Cornetta had lost approximately twenty pounds. He came by ambulance again, overdosed on Xanax, oxycodone, and fentanyl—again. Dr. Rydzewski had noted that Cornetta looked "thin and wasted." I asked him to explain what he meant by "wasted." "Oh, muscle wasting," the doctor answered, "basically that, you know, he looked less full, if you will." By the end of the day, Cornetta was stable. The ER staff was preparing to discharge him but just needed to remove his heplock—the capped-off intravenous access point into his veins. They never had a chance to remove it because Cornetta ran out of the emergency room.

Why was the heplock a concern? I asked Rydzewski.

"Well, we always like to remove IVs because that could be a source of infection and also a patient could potentially administer something intravenously through that access."

Rydzewski's casual, calm tone was hypnotic. Listening to him, you almost could forget that his eyes had seen the worst of everything. His descriptions and definitions arose from a gruesome reality.

APRIL 12, 2013: 342 DAYS UNTIL TRIAL

Just after 2:30 p.m. my cell phone rang. I hesitated to answer: it was from an unknown number. Always paranoid, I picked up. The woman on the other end of the line was frantic and I recognized her voice: it was Charlie's first-grade teacher. I remembered the staff and first grad-ers from another school, whose names would now forever be burned into my heart,‡ and for a few seconds I couldn't breathe. "It's raining," she said, "and it's so crazy here with everyone pushing each other near the door to get picked up, and I had Charlie and then a woman took him and I realized I didn't recognize her and she wasn't on the list and it happened too quickly—"

"Where is he now?" I asked, relieved that it wasn't what I had first feared but not sure what to think.

"He's gone . . . but I just had a bad feeling—"

"Call security," I said.

"They're already gone; it's too late."

Our after-school sitter at the time was a young man, so I knew it couldn't be him.

"Can you describe the woman?"

"No, I'm so sorry, I'm so sorry . . ."

My brain started running three parallel processes: I tried to figure out who might this person be, and I planned to call Joe Hall to ask for help, and I wondered how the police go about finding a missing kid in New York City.

My first call was to Charlie's dad. "Oh, wait," he interrupted. "I forgot to tell you, I canceled the sitter because my mom wanted to pick up the kids."

"Did you let the teacher know?"

"No."

Oh. Okay.

Okay! Phew. Fine. Great. Moving on. Just another normal day.

I called the teacher back. I apologized to her for not having informed

‡ Rachel D'Avino, 29, Dawn Hochsprung, 47, Anne Marie Murphy, 52, Lauren Rousseau, 30, Mary Sherlach, 56, Victoria Leigh Soto, 27, Charlotte Bacon, 6, Daniel Barden, 7, Olivia Engel, 6, Josephine Gay, 7, Dylan Hockley, 6, Madeleine Hsu, 6, Catherine Hubbard, 6, Chase Kowalski, 7, Jesse Lewis, 6, Ana-Grace Márquez-Greene, 6, James Mattioli, 6, Grace McDonnell, 7, Emilie Parker, 6, Jack Pinto, 6, Noah Pozner, 6, Caroline Previdi, 6, Jessica Rekos, 6, Avielle Richman, 6, Benjamin Wheeler, 6, Allison Wyatt, 6. May they rest in love.

her of the change beforehand. Back to work. I considered it lucky that Charlie hadn't been swept up in the drama.

There's such a fine line between safety and disaster. With anxiety, especially in our incomprehensibly violent world, the line blurs, dissolves, twists and turns. At work, I looked at the world unveiled, raw, and sinister; at home, I could not believe the invisible, inexplicable mercy that kept so many of us on safe paths. It did not feel like a miracle: it felt like just a matter of time.

MAY 14, 2014: DAY 56 OF TRIAL

When Sybil Stearns, Cornetta's girlfriend, took the stand, she talked to us not about the patient, but the *man*. *Her* man. Stearns was tiny—thin and small—and anxious. She repeated her name three times before spelling it.

"Thank you [. . .]," said the judge. "If you could move your chair up a little bit so you're not sitting on the edge of it, it would make me feel more comfortable."

"Sorry," she answered, scooting back.

"And you could pull the microphone down a little bit so it is a little—we need you to be loud and talk into the microphone."

"Okay."

"You may inquire," the judge said to me.

"Thank you, Your Honor—" I said, but he had turned back toward Stearns.

"Not quite that close," he told her, "because I could hear you breathing."

"I'm sorry."

"It's okay. Sometimes people get a little too enthusiastic." He was being kind. Optimistic, maybe, in his choice of the word "enthusiastic," but I could tell he was just trying to put her at ease with some humor.

Stearns told the jury that she had suffered from panic disorder, obsessive-compulsive disorder, severe depression, anorexia, and ADD since childhood. When she met Michael she was sixteen years old and he was nineteen. I asked her to describe him to the jury.

Stearns smiled and her face lit up. "Um, wow," she said in her soft, breathy, still-nervous voice, "he was beautiful, just healthy, handsome. He took such good care of himself. Muscular. He was into athletics, martial arts. Um, he would walk into— Everyone would look at him. He was beautiful, in my eyes, he was beautiful."

"I simply cannot hear," Belair said, from the defense table.

Stearns leaned into the microphone. "Okay," she repeated in her loudest voice. "He was beautiful. He was a beautiful, beautiful, handsome man."

They lived together for a total of seven years. Michael had his own business, a power-washing company. He had a bad motorcycle accident, which left him unable to work, collecting disability payments and in pain. That's when he began using crack cocaine and heroin as well as prescription drugs, including oxycodone, Xanax, and fentanyl.

Stearns noticed that Michael was no longer taking good care of himself, but even though she was living with him (or perhaps because she was and the change was progressive) it took her a while to connect the dots.

"He didn't care if he had dirty clothes on," she told the jury. "He stopped cutting his hair. [. . . I am] not passing judgment on anyone who uses anything and any kind of drugs, but he just looked down-and-out and sick. He looked very sick. A lot of weight loss. Um, he just didn't care about himself, like. He just didn't. It was like he didn't have to brush his teeth anymore."

The truth emerged in a moment of crisis, in August 2009. "How did you become aware that he was using those prescription drugs?" I asked.

"It was— It was—his first overdose when I— It was his first overdose when the EMS was working on him and they gave me his clothes and I went through his pockets."

"He was at my door," she told the jury, "and he was acting, um, bizarre and I knew something was wrong. I—I didn't know what exactly was going on or what he was on and I let him in. Um, and he—he started, um— Immediately, like, I can notice in his face just the down-ness and the discoloration. I kept watching him. I kept an eye on him. I kept talking to him. I then left the room for, I would say, two minutes. And at that point, um, he was purple. Um, I didn't know what to do. It was my first time in this situation. I—um, I remember saying, 'Michael, Michael,' and I'm shaking him and shaking him and I immediately called nine-one-one. Um, I never took a CPR class. I had no idea. They kind of tried to walk me through. The cell phone fell. I lost connection. They had the address and everything and I was— I held his head back and I was trying to give him air. And maybe once or twice he took it. And he didn't—and then he wouldn't take it any more of my air. And I was trying to give him part of CPR."

She was crying.

"[I]f you need to stop and compose yourself," I said, "please, take as much time as you need to do that."

"I'm sorry. I—at that point he was starting to turn—he was purple. He was blue. I just continued to pound on his chest. He was—I would say it was twenty minutes before the EMS came. Um, and when they arrived, I walked. I heard them pulling up and I'm on the fourth-floor walk-up and I ran from him and I started to help them bring their stuff up. Please, please, help him. Please, help him. And they went into the room and they must have worked on him for they were paddling him for twenty minutes to half an hour. He was DOA and he came to. Finally they removed him and they didn't—they told me they had no idea what I doing, not taking a course, but whatever it was, I kept him alive."

Stearns found the pill bottles in Michael's clothing that day and saw Dr. Li's name on the labels. When Michael recovered from the overdose, Stearns encouraged him to treat his addiction.

"I asked him to please leave and go get help, that he needed help. Um, I tried—I tried everything to try to—I didn't know what to do. I tried everything I could to try to help him, get him into facilities. Um, I would tell him to leave and check into programs. Um, he'd listen. He would—he would come back out."

He came back out and kept using. Did she have to make any more calls to 911, I asked, during the time that Michael was still a patient of Dr. Li?

"Several. Um, one being, um, he was in a drug-induced, um, psychosis, um, as much as I know about it, by the grace of God, I was so scared. Um, I know it could go either way. Um, and they become gone to that extent. He was doing rituals. I was scared for my life. I didn't know if he thought I was against him, but he thought people and other things were against him. And then he told me he was protecting me as well. And I was looking for every moment within a couple of hours to have private time to get in that call to EMS. And I finally did. And they showed up and had to remove him. He was talking to the sky. He was incoherent. Um, he was just looking up like he was in a straitjacket like being removed from the apartment. He knew who I was and then he just blanked out. He—he, um—when the cops came in, they had big, big, big guns. And he says, 'Big hockey sticks you have.' And just he'd go in and out and that was it. They said, 'This one's gone.' That was all I remember. And they took him out."

"Please take a moment, if you need to," I said. We waited. "[Let] us know when you are okay."

We still had more ground to cover. She still had to face Belair's cross-examination. It was not my place to tell her what she could and could not bear. Still, I felt a divided loyalty between the case and her well-being.

"I'm okay," she said, wiping her eyes. "I'm sorry. Thank you."

"Did you ever see Mr. Cornetta using the fentanyl patches?"

"I caught him. I caught him a couple of times. One time I say, 'What the heck is this?' They were all over his body. I say, 'What are you doing?' At first I didn't know what it was. 'What is this? What are you doing?' 'Um, oh, it's for my pain. It's for my pain.' I guess that's when he was trying to at that point get one over on me. Um, I witnessed, I walked in. I knew something was going on when he was in that bathroom with the door shut. And I opened it and he was sucking. I witnessed him rip open the package and suck it dry like as if he was hungry for it. And I told him, 'You have to leave. You can't do this. I can't do this anymore. I can't watch you kill yourself.' 'Please, please.' He was begging me to stay. And he—I believed that time he walked out, but then later came back in."

"[Y]ou described a time where he had fentanyl patches on his body. How many did you see?"

"I saw four at that point."

"Now, did you ever see Mr. Cornetta taking Xanax?"

"Yes."

"Could you please tell the jury what you saw?"

"He would open a bottle and just like he would just open the bottle and take—put whatever he could—just put as many as he wanted in his hand and swallow them like he just didn't want to be here. He didn't want to be coherent."

"You mentioned earlier that Mr. Cornetta would complain of pain; is that right?"

"Yes."

"And you mentioned I think you used the words 'he was trying to get over on me'; is that what you said?"

"Yes."

"He had a serious motorcycle accident, right?"

"Yes."

Belair objected. The judge overruled his objection.

Stearns answered with bitterness, "Um, well, Michael, if he knew that there was drugs involved, he moved just fine. If there was nothing— like, 'cause I would search his pockets to see what was going on and I know he would hide things, but you could see there was withdrawal. I felt there was withdrawal going on. He would lay there and say, 'I'm in pain. I'm in pain.' And—and—and I asked him, 'Do you feel pain? Do you really feel pain? Or is it the drug that you want? Is that your pain? Is it mental? Is it? Is this what you need? Is that it?' Because he moved if he could get to some place to get drugs, there was not a pain in that body."

Belair had not taken an aggressive tone or approach with any other bereaved witnesses, so we were not expecting it, especially with this fragile young woman. Perhaps Cornetta's case offered the best material. Perhaps he saw in Stearns a vulnerability he could exploit to his advantage. In any event, he used his cross-examination to make the point that while we were demonizing Dr. Li, many other doctors were prescribing the same drugs, in similar quantities, if not more, to the same patient.

In our prep sessions, we had discussed only what Stearns knew. We did not tell her anything about Michael that she did not know. We did not want to pollute her recollection or cause her to review and adjust her memories based on information that she did not have at the time. We told her to tell the truth and talk only about what she knew.

Belair battered Stearns with new information: specifically, the names of doctors—some of whom she had met, making her feel betrayed—as well as dates and dosages of prescriptions that Cornetta had received. He prefaced his questions with "were you aware that . . . ," to which she responded, through sobs, "I was not aware."

The judge intervened. "Are you okay? Could you answer Mr. Belair's question? He doesn't want to do it while you're crying."

"I'm sorry."

"Don't apologize."

"I'm okay," she said.

"Okay," said the judge, then asked, "It's okay for him to ask you more questions?"

"Yes," she said.

Peter and I sat in helpless silence as the cross-examination continued and intensified.

Belair asked Stearns about her own psychiatrist, Dr. Sciales. "Were you aware," he asked Stearns, "that Dr. Scial[e]s had prescribed something like a thousand pills of oxycodone in the time that he was seeing Mr. Cornetta?"

It was a double blow: surprise and betrayal. Stearns howled with pain and collapsed. Peter objected.

The judge snapped at Mr. Belair, "I think the answer is obvious and all that you are accomplishing is upsetting [the witness]."

Belair had no further questions. The judge excused the jury and asked one of the court officers to help Stearns off the floor. I tried to go to her, but the officers were hustling her out of the courtroom and the judge was reserving us for another purpose. He waited until the courtroom was empty and then blew up. I can't recall his exact words and the stenographer was also gone by that time, but he was outraged at our decision to put Stearns on the stand.

I had been angry at Belair, but I understood why the judge was angry at us. Belair was just doing his job. We were the ones who had exposed her to this. I felt guilty that I had not been able to prepare or protect her for that line of questioning. Perhaps there was a way I could have done so without introducing new information? We had warned her that it would be unpleasant, but none of us had anticipated that it would be so shattering. Truthfully, I still felt like we had been right to call her: she'd brought Cornetta to life for the jury, with all of his contradictions and complexities—turning heads at parties, turning purple on the floor, getting kicked out, sucking on fentanyl patches, performing drug-induced rituals, loving her and needing her, being loved and revived and missed. She'd also gone into this knowing it could be painful and wanting to stand up for her beautiful man.

We left the courtroom. There was a ten-minute break. When we came back, before the jury entered, Peter stood up.

"I have to quickly make a record about one thing," he said. It was our obligation, under New York State law, to disclose any benefits provided to witnesses. "We bought [our next witness] a pastrami sandwich for lunch."

We trudged onward.

APRIL 21, 2011: 1,064 DAYS BEFORE TRIAL

At 5:14 a.m. I'd already micromanaged the day's schedule. "Hi," I wrote to the babysitting service, "Nina's leotard and tights should be delivered by midday today—could [the sitter] please stop by the apartment before picking up the kids and get the package from the doorman? They should be in different packages—one for the footless tights, one for the leotard. Also, Charlie has a birthday party today. One of his friends will take him to the party, and I will pick him up and bring him to [their dad's] apartment. So [the sitter] only needs to pick up Nina at 3 pm and then take her back to [her dad's]. I'll ring up to the apartment shortly after 6 p.m. Thank you!"

I was highly organized—except for the fact that I'd forgotten to order the stuff Nina needed for dance class and didn't have a regular after-school babysitter. My one true partner, our nanny, had left us when Charlie went to school in 2010 and proved hard to replace even into 2011. At ages four and seven, the children were in class much of the day then but still needed care until we came home from work. As a prosecutor, I could neither employ a childcare provider off the books nor afford to pay for a full-time nanny to work part-time hours. Nor could I coordinate the legal employment of a part-time caregiver with my ex-husband, as he wanted maximum flexibility in the schedule and expenses, while I needed maximum predictability. We had, as a result, an arrangement with a babysitting agency that did its best to assign us the same freelance sitters for extended periods of time. Of course, it never held up for long, as those young folks often moved on from their babysitting jobs to bigger and better things, leaving my kids to meet their next new sitter for the first time at school pickup. It was a constant source of guilt and a frequent headache. I couldn't live with my kids every day, and I couldn't even ensure consistent childcare: this was failure.

Every morning, I published the schedule and crossed my fingers that I hadn't forgotten anything. "Hello," I wrote the next day, "Nina

and Charlie will be having playdates at our apartment this afternoon.
This is how it is planned:

- [The sitter] should pick up Charlie and his friend from Charlie's class, then wait for Nina and go home
- [The friend's] sister will arrive around 3:30/4 with their babysitter
- The babysitter [. . .] will stay there with them so [the other sitter] isn't dealing with all four kids until either I or their mom arrives. We expect the kids to have an early dinner, but they can have a substantial snack. I'll do Nina's homework with her tomorrow morning. I expect them to be pretty tired today . . . I kept the playdate because Charlie was really asking for it, but [the sitter] should let me know if it's not going well for any of them. Thank you! Also—what is the plan for the next couple of weeks, please? Can we expect a steady schedule? My preference would be to have one person Mon–Wed, and one Thurs–Fri, if there are going to be two people. Best, Charlotte."

Could they hear my plea for predictability, layered under my proto-professional email with its bullet-pointed list? Do you think they could tell I was a lawyer? How could I advocate for myself and my children without being the most annoying person ever? "Well," I later wrote, in response to the offer of a "floating" schedule, "I would definitely prefer a steady schedule: it's difficult for Charlie not to know who is picking him up, and I frankly have so much going on that I have to keep checking my emails to tell him every day who it will be."

Somehow, asking my little kids to switch between two homes, two parents, and multiple sitters several times a week had become the new normal. Every time I had to write one of those emails, my head exploded with guilt—and then I carried the feeling around, through trials and intake shifts, rushing home by 6:00 p.m. on my custody days and lingering late in the office the rest of the time.

Writing emails became my parenting channel. I wrote emails to run our days, and I wrote emails to try to fix the unfixable. "[Charlie] was asking me about his shoes," I wrote to my ex-husband, "—which ones are 'from daddy,' which ones are from me, to decide which to wear today. I told him not to worry, what matters is that they are all HIS shoes, and he can wear whichever ones he wants to."

"Nina is having a hard time falling asleep and was crying," I wrote to him again another night. "She said it was because she loves me and that you cry because you love them." So much for my aspirations of a peaceful, predictable, happy home. I didn't even know how to start making it better for them. They were so little, so confused, and so sad, yet forced to be both flexible and resilient.

How was I supposed to apply the lessons learned from work? There seemed to be so little in life that we could control, and it was impossible to guarantee any life's joy or safety. If safety couldn't be our objective, what should it be? At work, I was seeing wrong and fighting for justice. At work, though, the deeds had been done—the damage inflicted and so often irreversible. My personal life presented a gridlocked, blessed, bewildering contrast: my kids were still young, still safe. We were molding them every day, preparing them for the future and teaching them through our behavior about the world: that was a privilege and a weighty obligation. As a parent, I was responsible—but of what, to what extent, when, how? As a divorced mother, I shared the responsibility with their father, who did not share my expectations or tolerate my oversight. And as the children grew older, they needed to develop autonomy. I was hunting for the secret ingredient that would protect them later in life, the amulet of care that would shield them from future harm, but for the moment I didn't seem to have much more than my email account—and the expectation that the folks on the receiving end were acting in good faith and making their best efforts.

MAY 2, 2009: 1,783 DAYS UNTIL TRIAL

Dr. Li started Cornetta, his new patient, with a prescription for ten Duragesic patches dosed at twenty-five micrograms/hour and sixty milligrams per day of Roxicodone. Cornetta's injuries—as well as his surgical scars and the hardware in his wrist—dated from a car accident ten years earlier. He listed no referral from another physician and brought no medical records.

Dr. Li didn't see Cornetta again until November, but the patient reported that, in the interim, he'd been using Duragesic patches dosed at one hundred micrograms/hour. Dr. Li increased his prescription to match the patient's request and doubled the dose of Roxicodone, prescribing 120 pills at thirty milligrams each.

In December 2009, Dr. Li continued the same prescriptions and added Xanax two-milligrams, ninety pills, to be taken three times a day. By January 2, 2010, Dr. Li changed the prescription, ordering Cornetta to change the patches every forty-eight hours rather than every seventy-two hours, earning Cornetta five extra patches each month.

One way to abuse fentanyl is to freeze the patches, making fentanyl "chiclets," as our medical expert, Dr. Gharibo, called them. Another way is to tear open the patches and suck out the gel, which is what Cornetta did. He was ahead of the data, a precursor to a deadly trend.

Experts since have identified three "waves" in the opioid crisis: overdose deaths from prescription opioids, resulting from increased prescribing in the 1990s; overdose deaths from heroin use after 2010, as opioid addicts shifted to a cheaper, more readily accessible drug; a third wave marked by increases, most noticeably starting in 2013, in overdose deaths from synthetic opioids, including legally manufactured and "illicit" fentanyl.[6]

In the medical, legal, and policy communities, contraband fentanyl is known as Illicitly Manufactured Fentanyl (IMF) to distinguish it from pharmaceutical fentanyl. On the street, it is sold illegally on its own, or mixed into heroin, "branded" as Apache, China Girl, China

White, Dance Fever, Friend, Goodfella, Jackpot, Murder 8, and TNT. Its presence in a bag of heroin can result in a fatal overdose; the possibility of death, which indicates high potency, can be a marketing strategy for heartless peddlers of poison. One kilogram—or just above two pounds—of fentanyl is worth sixty thousand dollars wholesale.[7] The same amount of fentanyl, converted into counterfeit prescription pill form, can bring in millions of dollars.[8]

It is sold, illegally, by drug dealers in the United States, who get it from Mexican cartel networks. There are also vendors from China who sell fentanyl, fentanyl precursors, or encapsulating machines online. Illicit fentanyl from China is purer—and therefore more potent and lethal—than Mexican fentanyl. There's a lot less of the Chinese fentanyl, but since it is pure, it can be diluted into greater resale quantities.[9] On October 2, 2018, Daniel Burke, Senior Operations Manager of the FDA's Cybercrime Investigations Unit, testified before the Senate Caucus on International Narcotics Control. "Online, at this moment," he warned, "there are tens of thousands of websites offering illegal pharmaceutical drugs to Americans sourced from clandestine supply chains." He added that his department "simply does not have the resources to investigate all the reports we receive regarding illegal online pharmacies."

We've come a long way from the days in 2012 when Joe Hall and I first saw prescriptions for fentanyl patches in Dr. Li's prescription data and read about them in Cornetta's hospital records. In fact, we've come a long way down a horrific path. In 2009, 2010, and 2011, synthetic opioids were involved in fewer than 15 percent of overdose deaths and synthetic opioids such as fentanyl were, in fact, not prevalent in the clandestine market for new psychoactive substances. In 2016, for the first time, there were more overdose deaths involving fentanyl and other synthetic opioids (not including methadone) than other illicit drugs.[10] That year, 19,413 people died from synthetic opioids nationwide, a 103 percent increase from 2015.[11] In New York City alone, 1,487 humans died of drug overdoses in 2017: more than half of those (842 deaths, or 57 percent) involved fentanyl.[12] Even in 2018, in New York City, when total drug overdose deaths dipped for the first time in seven years and opioid painkillers were involved in the lowest number of these overdose deaths since 2009, fentanyl remained the "most common substance involved" in fatal overdoses for the second year in a row.[13]

Of course, for Michael Cornetta's family and Sybil Stearns, none of those trends actually mattered, because Michael Cornetta wasn't any less gone for having been ahead of the curve. In fact, for the families of all those who died of an abuse of old-school pharmaceutical fentanyl in those earlier years, or who died of prescription opioids during the so-called second wave, or who have died at any point along this seemingly endless series of deadly waves, it must not feel any less hurtful or unjust or intolerable because their loved ones weren't felled by the trending killer drug at the time. All the love and loss was absorbed into statistics and long-term analyses, which are useful, of course, but the families were left behind in the wreckage after the waves receded: bereft, broken, confused, angry, wondering why no one seemed to be able or willing to do anything to stop it.

And they are left there forever, not even immune to the impact of the next wave.

In 2016, Michael Cornetta's brother lost his own cherished son to an overdose.

There are explanations, but there is no explanation. All we know is this: every data point marks love and grief.

Dr. Stan Li taking stroll outside the courthouse during the lunch break on
the last day of trial, hours before the jury rendered their verdict
(Credit: Anthony Lanzilote / The New York Times / Redux)

Medical Pain Management
Stan X Li, M.D

SELF PAY FEE SCHEDULE UPDATE

████████████████████ self pay fee for low complexity case is still kept on
100$ per visit.
Criteria of low complexity include:
. Fully compliant with Narcotic Agreement.
. One Doctor, one pharmacy.
. No early visit.
. Less than three prescriptions written in one visit.
. Less than 120 pills on one prescription.

Self pay fee for high complexity case will be increased to 150$ per visit.
High complexity cases include but not limit to:
. Any non-compliant behavior with Narcotic Agreement.
. Found to have more than one Doctor- one pharmacy. These patients must to stop
receiving any narcotic prescription from other prescribers, and the fee will be
increased to 150$ per visit thereafter.
. Get more than three prescriptions in one visit.
. More than 120 pills on one prescription.
. Early visit. The visit ahead of schedule will be charged 150$.
. The dosage of opioid is higher than 180 mg/day.
. Ask for replacement of lost or stolen medication or prescription.
. History of substance abuse, using illicit drugs, suicidal idea.

Price list posted in Dr. Li's clinic

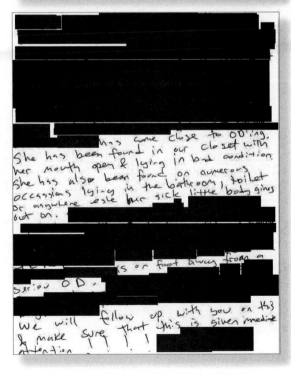

ATTENTION DR. STAN X.

This letter is in regards to our daughter & your patient ███████ ███████, as she is in very bad shape both mentally & physically as well. ███████ is a drug addict who has had a pill and hard substance problem for over 5 years already. ███████

███████

███████ if you haven't noticed is not healthy at all and she does not eat normally, sleep normally or breath & think normally. So its obvious that if you are a doctor of pain theraphy, then you must be able to see the pain our daughter is dealing with. Please you must stop prescribing her these deadly doses of drugs ranging from Methadone to you name it.

███████

███████

███████ has come close to OD'ing. She has been found in our closet with her mouth open & lying in bad condition. She has also been found on numerous occassions lying in the bathroom, toilet or anywhere else her sick little body gives out on.

███████

███████ is or foot away from a serious O.D.

We will ███████ follow up with you on this & make sure that this is given immediate attention.

A desperate parent's plea to Dr. Li (2007)

Below: Nick Rappold as a proud young member of the P.S. 107 Hot Shots. The school principal and Hot Shots coach both attended Nicholas' wake ten years later. *(Photos of Nicholas Rappold from his mother's personal collection, with her inscriptions on the backs.)*

NichOLAs AbouT
11 years
OLd

HE WAS SO
PRoud he
mAde THE
"107 HoT ShoTs"
His broTER burried
him with shiRT.

Nicky AT his
HOly CRoss
PROM.
2007

Nick Rappold posing for a photo before his
2007 high school prom

Michael Cornetta, remembered at Li's trial as "a beautiful man," at age thirty-two
(Photo courtesy the Cornetta family)

Above: The horrific Haven Drugs murders in Medford, New York, on June 19, 2011, marked a grim turning point in the opioid crisis and in the case. *(Credit AP Photo / David Rubin)*

Armed with search warrants, investigators seized more than 1,000 patient files and several additional boxes' worth of materials from Dr. Li's office and home. The evidence was kept under lock and key, accessible only in the presence of an investigator. *(Credit: Charlotte Bismuth)*

This is a case about a doctor who put money before lives.

Not just any lives – lives with which he was entrusted.

The defendant, Stan Li, is a board certified anesthesiologist and pain medicine physician who had a full-time job in a well-respected New Jersey hospital, near his home in New Jersey. You'll hear that he made several hundred thousand dollars a year working at the hospital as an anesthesiologist, five days a week.

But that's not why we are here. We're here because of what Dr. Stan Li did on the weekends.

Above: The case was, first and foremost, about real human losses. Charlotte kept a photo of Nicholas Rappold. *(Credit: Charlotte Bismuth)*

ADA Peter Kougasian waiting outside the courtroom during the trial *(Credit: Charlotte Bismuth)*

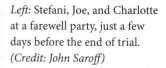

Above: Kougasian performing magic tricks for Charlotte's children in his office, December 2013 *(Credit: Charlotte Bismuth)*

Left: Stefani, Joe, and Charlotte at a farewell party, just a few days before the end of trial. *(Credit: John Saroff)*

Nina and Charlie proudly displaying a certificate during a visit to Charlotte's office. They never left without taping new drawings on the walls around her computer. *(Credit: Fred Hartwell)*

CHAPTER 9

Hope in a Bottle

We have to hammer on abusers in every way possible. They are the culprits and the problem. They are reckless criminals.

—EMAIL FROM DR. RICHARD SACKLER,
FORMER CHAIRMAN AND PRESIDENT OF PURDUE PHARMA,
CURRENT BILLIONAIRE, FEBRUARY 1, 2001[1]

Pharmacy tech was riding me about oxycontin [sic] being a bad drug. Corrected her by saying, good drug, bad people abusing it.

—PURDUE PHARMA SALES REP CALL NOTE, FEBRUARY 20, 2008[2]

APRIL 18, 2009: 1,797 DAYS UNTIL TRIAL

She talked; he wrote.

Tracy had a pink scar running across her cheek. Her hair was bottle-blond. She spoke quickly, nodding and gesturing to bring a story to life.

Dr. Li wore his white medical coat. He sat across from her, at the laminated wood desk in the small exam room. He looked down, reading the label on the prescription bottle that Tracy had given him, and filled out prescription forms.

She told him about the car accident—her blackout at the wheel, waking up in the hospital, getting up to go to the bathroom and falling down, the broken leg, her tongue ripped in two, the stitches in her mouth. The pain in her back, in her leg, in her ankle.

She told Dr. Li her life story—she wasn't sure why but she did, perhaps because there was a part of her that was still five years old, sitting at the table with her daddy, looking at her daddy and his gun, reliving that moment over and over again. Wishing she could stop time just before it happened—and stop *him*—so that the rest of her life could be easier. But that's not how it works.

So she told Dr. Li about her daddy shooting himself right there in front of her, just the two of them sitting at the table together.

From there, she went on to the next thing, as she tended to do, spilling out her entire story to make sure he understood the hurt: the sexual abuse, the rape, the car accident. Maybe it all sounded like a lot to him, but there was so much more. As she spoke it all unfurled in her mind, the times she'd ended up in the hospital and so many medications, psychiatric medications as she called them, to distinguish them from the other medications she'd been taking for her asthma, her heart, her blood pressure, her depression, her physical pain, and then there were illegal drugs: the crack cocaine, the heroin, whatever she could get her hands on, that answered a deeper call for something that wasn't relief; it was more than that, stronger than that—

"What do you need?" asked Dr. Li.

There were so many things she needed. What was he referring to? His pen hovered over the prescription form. He held the prescription bottle in his other hand. Oh—he just wanted to know what she wanted.

"Oxycodone," she said.

"I can give you two prescriptions," he said.

"How much would that be?"

"One hundred fifty dollars."

Okay. She had it. She had $150. So she'd take two prescriptions, if that's what he was offering.

He wrote the other prescription for Xanax, the sticks, as she called them. And that was it. Had he heard her? Had he seen her? She handed him the money. He put it right into the pocket of his white lab coat.

Numb. That's what she'd always wanted to be. That's what she needed to be. Numb. Now she could do that. When she took the oxycodone and Xanax together, she felt numb. She went home to the small two-bedroom she shared with her mother. It was in a compound of mid-level brick buildings, arranged in a U shape around a sectioned parking lot. Their apartment was on the ground floor, down the hall to the right of the lobby, all the way at the end. It was warm and tight, decorated and curtained, layered with their belongings and the scents of cigarettes and air freshener. Her mother worked long hours to provide for them, leaving Tracy alone. Time enough to take her meds and hide the ones she didn't want her mother to see.

The problem was, Tracy had been taking too much oxycodone and going to see Dr. Li too often. It didn't matter how he wrote out the prescription; she just took two oxycodones every time she felt pain, which was several times a day. It added up to a lot—it added up to running out every three weeks, so she went back every three weeks. It was worth the extra fifty-dollar early-visit charge, coming every three weeks and getting a full month's supply, but sometimes he asked why she was coming early. She told him what she was doing and how much she was taking. She told him that she was addicted to the oxycodone and Xanax. She talked; he wrote. Depending on how long it took him to write out two prescriptions, that's how much time she had with him. Just enough time to write out two prescriptions. Finally, one week he had recommended another medication, Soma. "It will help you take less oxycodone," he said.

It sure did. She didn't have a chance to do anything else. It was the be-all and almost the end-all. She took the Soma and blacked out, and woke up only because she was being resuscitated, with her mother frantic. The EMTs all over her. The noise. The in-and-out of awake and void. The hospital, again. Tracy's doctors told Dr. Li all about it before she had a chance to tell him herself, but of course she told him. She talked; he wrote. He had nothing to say. He had his face on him, that face he had when she talked, that made her feel like he didn't care. But he wrote when she talked, so—

Now that she knew what the Soma could do, she wanted it again, even though her mother didn't want her near that stuff. This was different, because she wanted to die, so she told Dr. Li to write her a script for the Soma again. She said it just like that. Did he even hear her? He had no reaction. She took the Soma, made herself a bowl of ice cream, and sat on the couch near the window, and that's how her mother found her, with her face in the bowl of melted ice cream; it was now just another story to add to all the others. She blacked out with her face in a bowl of ice cream, but she didn't die; in fact, she woke up and refused to go to the hospital with the EMTs, and her mother called the police to make her go to the hospital, so she went because they made her, and her mother got all upset and called Dr. Li and told him not to give her Soma anymore, and Tracy just had to keep going with everything even though it was all so much work every day just to get through.

Maybe Adderall was the answer? One of her friends had taken it, and it had given her so much energy. Maybe, she told Dr. Li during one of her next visits, maybe she should try Adderall? Dr. Li didn't know what it was. He looked it up in a big book of medications but couldn't find it. He didn't know how to spell it, it turned out. He just took out the prescription pad.

"How do you spell it?" he asked.

"A-d-d-e-r-a-l-l," said Tracy.

She talked; he wrote.

The Adderall didn't work out, nothing ever did, really, but when something didn't work out, they could always just go back to the basics, oxycodone and Xanax, two prescriptions for $150. She talked, he wrote, she gave him the money, and he put it right into the pocket of his white lab coat.

APRIL 2012: APPROXIMATELY 700 DAYS UNTIL TRIAL

There are moments of blessed innocence just before you learn or see something that rocks your consciousness. Despite world news, September 11, local crimes, my job, my divorce, the overdose deaths we'd identified so far, the Tamasi letters, the Laffer murders, there were still sorrows and harms I had not been able to imagine in early 2012.

Joe, Jon, the investigators, and I continued taking shifts in their conference room, hunkering down over patient files, slowly making our way through the more than twelve hundred records as we progressively obtained permission from the Court to review all of them.

There was a time when I did not know about Tracy Howard. One minute I was unaware of her existence and the next—I was at a loss to explain her survival. There has not been a day since that I have not thought of her. Not one day.

When I close my eyes, I can see her photo again. It was clipped to the left side of the thick, worn manila folder. She had bleached-blond hair and big brown eyes. It was impossible to attribute an age to her face. She looked both defiant and in need of protection. The file contained the usual paperwork—a sparse initial evaluation form, followed by a list on plain, lined sheets with dollar amounts noted in the margins next to each visit date, and under every date a list of the prescriptions issued along with bare-bones notations.

Reading the file was like watching a looped video of a house burning down, with people screaming for help. Tracy's mental health issues and addiction were apparent in Dr. Li's notes, but there was no indication that he'd been alarmed or pressed into urgent action by any of it. He'd taken note of her condition with detachment, documenting without judging, except that he was supplying her with stupefying amounts of addictive substances. It was painful to read. Based on the notes, I made assumptions about her personality and her relationship with Dr. Li, imagining a willful young woman who dictated her cravings. The day I met Tracy, all my assumptions dissolved.

Joe Hall and I drove out to visit Tracy and her mother, Andrea, at home in early 2012, less than a year after Tracy's last overdose. They welcomed us with warmth and Tracy offered to show us the lockbox where they secured her medication, to protect herself from herself. We sat in the cozy living room and I saw the couch where Tracy had passed out. Tracy and her mother were like two tigresses in captivity, the mother trying to keep her daughter alive, the daughter both grateful and trying to escape. Their love did not seem easy, but it was real. I thought about my mother and my daughter and the chain of helpfulness, helplessness, and occasional hostility that ties women together from generation to generation.

A few months later, I welcomed them both into my office. I always kept the harsh fluorescent lights off in the summer, so the big room, full of filing cabinets, was illuminated by the indirect sun. Still, it was a shabby, unfamiliar setting. In the shadows, Tracy looked like a little girl. She sat at the table, looking up at me with wide eyes, asking whether she would have to testify in front of strangers. The prospect was terrifying—but she wanted to find the strength to do it. She called me Miss Charlotte, gave sweet smiles to Joe, and delivered devastating information about herself, her father, her overdoses, in a natural and even tone, because that was just her story. She didn't realize how much it took not to curse the world when you heard it.

I met her doctors and visited two psychiatric hospitals where she had been treated. In one of them, I wandered a long, empty hallway looking for the ladies' room. A staff member watched me with wary eyes from a doorway. Two male patients appeared at the end of the hallway and began walking in our direction. "I'd lock that door behind you," said the staff member, before turning to close herself in her office.

MAY 15, 2014: DAY 57 OF TRIAL

Tracy and her mother were scheduled to take the stand. Peter and I were nervous wrecks. How were they getting to court? When would they arrive? Would Tracy feel able to testify? Would we be able to get through all the questions we wanted to ask her? How would she fare under cross-examination? We had the goods ready on the evidence cart: Tracy's file, along with every prescription Dr. Li had ever written for her and records from countless ER admissions—but would the young woman even make it into the witness seat?

"I can do this, Miss Charlotte," Tracy assured me in the hallway outside the courtroom, before the doors opened. "I want to do this for those kids who died."

She took the stand holding a small stuffed animal, a hand-sized fabric dog made by Victoria's Secret with romantic messages printed on the canvas—"call me baby," "I ♥ French kissing," "in your dreams." It was as childish as it was risqué. The truth, as she told it, was raw. "[M]y mommy helps me the most," she told the jury. "I love my mom." She spoke of her despair with simple honesty, as though every person on earth walked around hoping for the end. She told the story of her father's suicide as though that was a definition of childhood—and for her, it was.

"Did you take the pills in excess of the level he prescribed to you?" Belair pressed on cross-examination.

Tracy answered without hesitation. "I was trying to kill myself, yes."

Tracy admitted the lies she had told Dr. Li and defied Belair's attempts to mischaracterize her testimony. When he tried, for instance, to confirm the fiction of Dr. Li's family meeting with Tracy's father and stepmother, she clutched her dog and fixed her eyes on him: "How can I have a stepmom," she asked, "if my daddy's dead?"

As I watched Tracy testify and squeeze her stuffed animal, I thought about the difference between our outsides and our insides. We never know what is in someone's mind or heart. We can only judge based on the evidence we can see and hear. And it's never enough—we can never understand everything or achieve simple, perfect human interactions. I thought about my daughter, crying in her room at night, and my inability to help her because I was clouded by tremendous love and guilt and the built-in biases of my own childhood. I knew I could do better—but how? I looked at Peter and wondered why it was so hard for us to maintain a simple, professional relationship when we both strived for good hearts and were fighting so hard on the same side. My ex-husband, he was far from perfect, but what was I missing about my own behavior? Would we ever find a way to hear each other? Was it enough to keep trying?

At the end of the day that day, I knew more about courage, thanks to Tracy. I also knew more about the ferocity of a mother whose child is threatened, thanks to Andrea Howard, who told the jury about a call she made to Dr. Li after one of Tracy's overdoses.

Andrea lifted her chin and stared at Dr. Li. "I tell [sic] him he was a scumbag. He was a motherfucker. He was a murderer. He was a killer."

"Thank you," Peter responded. "What did Dr. Li say?"

"Nothing. He was very calm."

JUNE 16, 2014: DAY 89 OF TRIAL

Dr. Li was, in fact, very calm as he responded to his attorney's questions about his "treatment" of Tracy Howard, from May 2009 until August 2011.

"Doctor," Belair asked, "up to and including January 2, 2011, had you at all times prescribed the medications that you did for this patient in the exercise of good faith in trying to help her with her pain problems?"

Dr. Li nodded. "Yes."

"Up until [. . .] January 2, 2011, had the patient been compliant with your directions in this regard?"

Dr. Li's tone was even. "The compliance, I don't see significant she is not complying."

He had just reviewed her chart with Belair, which documented three overdoses, including two suicide attempts, and countless early visits. In fact, according to Dr. Li's own records, Tracy had never been compliant with his instructions. Perhaps he failed to see a "significant" lack of compliance overall because he'd managed to dismiss every single warning and incident at the time and then again on the witness stand.

His first warning about Tracy Howard had come just after her first visit in May 2009. "Call from New York Queens Hospital," Dr. Li had noted in his chart. "The patient took too much Xanax. Needs detoxification from Benzo. Benzo means benzodiazepine. Xanax."

When Tracy Howard returned to Dr. Li's office ten days later, he asked her about the incident. "So I ask her [. . .]," Dr. Li testified, "'why you went to hospital' and what was happening. And she reply to me, she went to hospital because she has upper back pain."

Contrary to the information Dr. Li had received from a fellow physician, Tracy Howard denied that she'd taken too much Xanax. "She say she didn't take too much," Dr. Li explained. "She said she went to hospital because the upper back pain."

"Did you accept what she said?" Belair asked.

"Yes."

"How did she appear when she was in your office?"

Dr. Li spoke plainly, without concern. "She appeared mentally normal. She is not like sedating. It's nothing special. Nothing shows she have intoxication from benzodiazepine, like sleepiness, something like sedated."

Dr. Li didn't stop prescribing. "I prescribe oxycodone thirty milligram times ninety pill," he said, "take one pill TID, means three times a day. And Xanax two milligrams, sixty pill, twice a day. Now I have seen the patient twice. My impression is she need Xanax for control her anxiety or panic attack. This patient, the way she talked to me, the way she appeared to me, is the personality have high level of anxiety and easy to get panic attack. I believe she needs Xanax for control her anxiety. That's why I continue the same dose of Xanax. Two pills a day. Two milligram, two pills a day, is not a very high dose. It's not going to cause overdosing, this dosage."

Even though it already had, I thought.

In addition to Xanax and oxycodone, he prescribed Adderall, telling the jury that Tracy needed it to "concentrate," to "focus on study." Tracy came every three weeks and received a full month's supplies. Despite early visits, excuses, medication requests, hospital procedures, injuries, Dr. Li continued prescribing—and even though she was a Medicare beneficiary, he was making her pay cash for prescriptions. He even kept a running tally of the money she owed him in the margins of her patient chart.

"The next one," Dr. Li said, referring to another call from another doctor, "is March 20, 2010. North Shore Hospital call. Patient to hospital. Run out meds. Means run out of medication. And also positive for heroin."

As it turned out, Tracy Howard came to see him the same day. It had been less than three weeks since her last visit.

Dr. Li read from his notes in Tracy's patient file. " 'March 20, 2010. As her word, "I try to hurt myself. My mother die. I was so depressed." Patient was on psychiatrist floor for seven day on Seroquel fifty milligram.' "

Tracy's mother, of course, was not dead—Dr. Li had just seen her in court a few weeks earlier. Belair and Dr. Li did not take the time to clarify this point of confusion. Instead, Dr. Li explained that since Tracy claimed to be feeling "better," he prescribed again that day, and the next time, and the next for more than another year.

The next warning came on November 13, 2010. A note written in Anna Guo's handwriting indicated that the office had received a call: the patient took Soma and had a bad reaction. As it happened, Tracy came to see Dr. Li later the same day. "Pain's the same," she told Dr. Li. "I'm going to Florida," she added, so he gave her more prescriptions. No Soma that time, but within a few months he prescribed it again.

Yet another physician called Dr. Li on November 30, 2010, with a report about Tracy Howard's condition. "'The patient was in LIJH, Long Island Jewish Hospital, for overdose of opioid and Klonopin,'" Dr. Li read from his notes. "'Decrease heart rate. She was "d/c" hospital. Now "d/c" means discharged from the hospital now. She was put on small methadone and then there's a telephone number psychiatrist.'"

In fact, Tracy had attempted suicide again on November 19, 2010. Tracy told the doctors at Long Island Jewish that her life "sucks," that she had been "depressed forever." That's why she had decided to kill herself with an overdose of pills, that's what she'd told the doctors at LIJH, and that's what Dr. Li would have learned if he had asked any questions or consulted the records. He also would have learned that, by the time Tracy reached the hospital, on November 19, in a state of overdose, she had used every Klonopin and Xanax pill he prescribed six days earlier. In fact, she had even purchased extra Xanax "on the street"—she had bought between nine and ten "sticks" daily. DAILY. She had given her boyfriend half her oxycodone pills—sixty pills—but she had used the remaining sixty pills. In six days. Because her life sucked and she wanted to die.

Dr. Li kept prescribing and the calls kept coming. The next warning came from Tracy Howard's "stepfather" on January 29, 2011. "This is confusing to me," Dr. Li testified, explaining why he disregarded the message. "I know the patient tell me her mother died and she have a stepmother. But she never told me her father died and she have a stepfather. So I just confused who is the guy making the phone call and I cannot confirm that."

Of course, it wasn't Tracy 's mother who had died but her father— he'd shot himself in front of her when she was a little girl. How could anyone forget that?

"July 2011," Dr. Li continued, referring to his notes. "The Chinese note means receive doctor phone call from hospital, ask to talk to Dr. Li, but the patient's condition unclear. The other side, the cell phone number, but when doctor, means Dr. Li, call back the person who picked up the phone said wrong number. So somebody tried to leave me [sic] and leave phone number, but when I call back and then the person says wrong number. So I cannot communicate with the person because the number is wrong or something wrong."

When he saw Tracy again, she denied having been hospitalized, so he prescribed again.

Dr. Stan Li was Tracy Howard's doctor. She became his victim and it is a miracle she survived his "treatment." He just didn't see it that way.

"So from December 4, 2010, [. . .] through August 14, 2011," Belair asked Dr. Li, covering the time period for which the grand jury had charged Dr. Li with reckless endangerment, "did you continue to treat your patient in good faith and attempt to help her with her pain and for [. . .] that matter her reluctance to see a psychiatrist?"

"Yes," answered Dr. Li.

"Did she suffer any injury, side effect, or harm during that period of time?"

"No." [. . .]

"Was she at risk of, was she at serious risk of injury or death by anything you did?"

"No."

MAY 9, 2014: DAY 51 OF TRIAL

I stood at the lectern with my binders of Bates-numbered patient files before me, an image of the page we were discussing projected for the jury, my list of questions; Dr. Gharibo had his own copy of the same binder; at the defense table, Belair paged through yet another copy of both the binders and my questions, following along and taking notes.

Belair knew everything about our work with Dr. Gharibo, and the doctor's background. He had known for a long time. Dr. Gharibo was our expert witness, so we had an obligation to disclose any prior statements he'd made about the case in addition to any information we'd supplied him about the case, and on which he had based his opinion.

Also, Belair had a printed list of most of the questions I planned to ask Dr. Gharibo: since the direct examination necessarily would be long and detailed, as it covered all twenty patients in the indictment, I had prepared my questions ahead of time. Since questions often incorporate facts or naturally reflect prior conversations with a witness, they have to be disclosed in advance to the defense if they are written down. Once in a while, I improvised a question, but for the most part, Belair had a road map.

Belair had a corresponding obligation with any expert witness he was planning to call, but we had yet to find out whether he would call an expert witness, let alone their name.

During Dr. Gharibo's direct examination, we dissected Howard's patient file in chronological order, entry by entry, date by date, prescription by prescription. Dr. Gharibo expressed his expert opinion about Dr. Li's treatment of Tracy Howard: "My opinion was that Dr. Li's treatment was below the standards of care. It consisted of inadequate history and physical examination for the treatment duration. The extent of the treatment was not supported by the diagnosis. There was continued prescribing of controlled substances. Despite multiple controlled-substance-related hospitalizations and suicide attempts and illicit drug use and presence of absolute psychiatric contraindication, one of the highest psychiatric profiles was present in [this patient] consisting of bipolar disease, history of heroin overdose, anxiety, depression, and suicide risk, as well as cocaine use. There were control issues with respect to the patient's taking controlled substances. The medication consumption was poorly controlled and that was made even further dangerous by disproportionate dose escalation. They were dangerous and unexplained, as prescribed by Dr. Li."

Belair bided his time. Nineteen days later, on May 28, 2014, he was the one standing at the lectern with Dr. Gharibo in the hot seat. Belair did not have an obligation to advance in chronological fashion through the patient charts, follow my organizational structure, or cover any or all topics. His only limitation was that he couldn't go beyond the scope of the direct examination. He controlled the narrative and kept it narrow: he poked in and out of the Howard records, asking Dr. Gharibo targeted questions to make his points, and ignored the rest. The points were clear: she obtained controlled substances from other doctors and Dr. Li sometimes decreased her doses of medication.

It was hard to sit through any of Belair's cross-examination of Dr. Gharibo, but their exchanges about Tracy Howard gutted me. I hoped the jury had heard Dr. Gharibo. I hoped they had registered his outrage at the thought that a suicidal patient's family should be given responsibility for her medications. "It's completely inappropriate for a lot of reasons here," Dr. Gharibo had insisted. "[. . .] One of them is that [the] patient is trying to kill herself, has ideas about killing herself, and that is also another absolute contraindication, you don't give a suicidal patient the tools to kill themselves with, coupled with demonstration of loss of control, but it goes beyond that as well. The patient is also exhibiting access to the illegal drug market and other psychoactive medications such as cocaine and heroin, which she could also use to kill herself with. So, she is an absolute contraindication to continue prescribing [. . .]. Anything has a high probability of hurting her at the minimum, if not killing her."

It seemed like common sense. Like common humanity. And yet, it was in dispute.

CHAPTER 10

Civil War

He got into a restless habit of strolling about when the cause was on, or expected, talking to the little shopkeepers and telling 'em to keep out of Chancery, whatever they did. "For," says he, "it's being ground to bits in a slow mill; it's being roasted at a slow fire; it's being stung to death by single bees; it's being drowned by drops; it's going mad by grains."

—CHARLES DICKENS, *BLEAK HOUSE*

APRIL 10, 2014: DAY 22 OF TRIAL

Erin Kingsley Markevitch had a head cold. She had promised to testify that day, and her grandmother was testifying, too, so Erin showed up. She pushed through. She waited for our first witness, a physician assistant from Brookhaven Memorial Hospital, to finish. When Erin took the stand midmorning, she had a determined look on her face and a box of tissues—for the cold, of course.

Erin told the jury that her parents had separated when she was four. She remained close to her father, Kevin, even after he moved out, but they had "rocky times" during her childhood. Kevin was an electrician who made a living from "odd jobs." Erin lived with her mother, a registered nurse who worked the overnight shift in a hospital from 7:00 p.m. to 7:00 a.m.

Early on, Erin had learned how to take care of herself and create order in her world. She didn't say this, but she radiated a sense of responsibility. She also loved her parents with all her heart—that was obvious as well.

When Erin was fifteen years old, she came home one day to find her father smoking crack in their living room. Kevin took up a lot of space—he weighed approximately four hundred pounds at the time. Nevertheless, fifteen-year-old Erin got physical with him.

"I went to knock it out of his hands," she told the jury. It didn't work. "He continued to light the crack pipe."

Erin told the jury that she soon learned to recognize the signs of her father's drug abuse.

"How could you tell?" Peter asked.

"The way he looked," she answered. "His eyes would be glassy, wide. His pupils would be very big. He would talk a lot. He would walk around. He was very sweaty. He was very sweaty and you could tell by his speech. [. . .] Sometimes it would be very fast or other times it would be super slurred and you couldn't understand. He wouldn't make sense."

Later Erin's grandmother, Anne Kingsley, would reach further back into her son's past, his adolescence, telling the jury he'd used angel dust and powdered cocaine. He'd had problems with drugs his entire life, she explained, abusing drugs on a regular—though not a constant—basis before 2007, and he'd gone in and out of rehab several times. Despite all of that, Kevin was a "teddy bear," his mother said.

Erin spoke to her mother every day, but she couldn't take her father's continued drug use. "Sometimes when I spoke to him, if he was high I would get angry and I didn't want to talk to him anymore," she told the jury. "If he did certain things—one time he stole a car, my mom's car—I would get very angry and refuse to speak to him if he did not get help."

In 2007, Kevin and his wife underwent bariatric surgery to treat their obesity. From the evidence cart, we pulled a photo Erin had taken after the procedure and showed it to the jury for just one quick moment. Her parents stood with their arms around each other. Erin's mother held her chin way, way up with pride, her brown hair falling to her shoulders. Kevin wore a black Harley-Davidson T-shirt and his long hair tied back into a ponytail. He stared right into the camera and smiled. His eyes were Erin's eyes, but Erin had her mother's cheekbones.

After 2007, her father turned to pills, Erin said.

Here's what Erin did not know: On September 22, 2007, her father had seen Dr. Li for the first time, providing a referral form and an MRI report. Dr. Li prescribed fentanyl patches, one hundred micrograms per hour every three days, and Percocet 10/325, 120 pills, four pills a day. That's what Kevin had told Dr. Li he had been taking, so Dr. Li just continued what his customer requested.

On December 8, Dr. Li discontinued the Percocet and prescribed 180 oxycodone pills at a 20 mg strength, six per day, in addition to the fentanyl patches. However, when Kevin came back less than three weeks later for more pills, and then early again, and again, Dr. Li cycled through various combinations of Percocet, oxycodone, Duragesic fentanyl patches, Opana, Xanax, and OxyContin, in full month supplies.

By April 2008, Dr. Li knew that Kevin Kingsley was taking more than what was prescribed—not just because of the early visits, but because his patient told him so. In response, he increased the doses of OxyContin and Duragesic.

When Erin told the jury about this time in their lives, she sounded almost nostalgic for the days of crack cocaine.

"I remember whenever he was on crack and things," she said, "the next time I spoke to him after he did that we would talk and he would let me vent to him and be mad at him and try to ask questions as to why he would do this, why he took drugs, what was going on, but he would still always be around the family and everything. Then, as time went on, when he started abusing pills he didn't want to be around anybody. He would take the pills in front of me. He didn't care. He didn't care how he looked in front of me. He didn't care who was around. He stopped seeing family and just kept to himself."

On December 20, 2008, Dr. Li discharged Kevin Kingsley from the practice, sending him off with a mammoth supply of controlled substances: fifteen 100 mcg/hour fentanyl patches; 120 OxyContin 80 mg pills; 240 oxycodone 30 mg pills; 120 Xanax 1 mg pills.

At the end of December 2008, Kevin overdosed. Erin remembered visiting him at Jamaica Hospital: "He was laying on the bed. His eyes were closed. He was out of it."

In January 2009, Kevin went back to see Dr. Li, receiving more OxyContin.

At some point after January 2009, Kevin decided to get clean. "He appeared back to normal," Erin told the jury, describing her reunion with her father in April 2009, when she picked him up from Arms Acres, an inpatient addiction treatment center in Carmel, New York. "He was happy. His speech was back to normal. He was regular. He was talking to everybody and introducing me to people. He just seemed more like himself."

In June 2010, a newly sober Kevin went back to Dr. Li. He told the doctor he had been in a "detox program" and was "off opioids" but complained of panic attacks. Dr. Li prescribed Xanax, two milligrams, three times a day—a two-milligram-per-day increase from what he had prescribed Kevin before the rehab program. Less than three months later, in early September 2010, Dr. Li reintroduced oxycodone, ending Kevin's short-lived phase of sobriety.

Late in the morning on Thursday, October 28, 2010, Erin called her mother's cell phone because they had plans to go out together. "My father picked up the phone," she said, "and told me that my mother was sleeping." Erin did not speak to her mother that day—which meant *ever again*.

APRIL 10, 2014: DAY 22 OF TRIAL

"As part of this lawsuit you are bringing against Dr. Li and other doctors," Belair asked Erin Kingsley Markevitch on cross-examination, "are you claiming damages for the loss of parental supervision of your father?"

"I believe so," Erin answered.

Belair had a ready response. "But he never supported you, did he?"

"No. Well, emotionally he did."

"I am sorry?"

"Emotionally he supported me, but never financially."

"Okay. Well, you're making a claim for money damages. He never supported you financially, true?"

"Yes."

It was a fair line of questioning, however hard to bear. It was Belair's job to try to expose Erin Kingsley Markevitch's potential interests to the jury and he did not shy away from that task. He was also hedging his bets: even if the jury didn't get the point or didn't agree, at least the transcript would be clear, if not to his client's benefit in this trial, then maybe on appeal or maybe even just in the parallel civil actions brought against Dr. Li by the Kingsley and Rappold families.

Belair cared what was said in the courtroom, but he cared much more about the record, and so he sometimes may have appeared to the jury as a Don Quixote–like figure, slashing at imaginary foes with undue violence, when he was, in fact, playing a long, strategic, necessary, and professionally sanctioned game. Belair operated in the legal universe where many words were spoken but only the words inscribed in the "record" mattered. It was also a universe where you could refer to fellow attorneys as your "brother and sister" one day and impugn their integrity the next, where your duty to defend your client with zeal required the emotional destruction of a witness, simply because their testimony offered an opportunity to make a devastating point.

As he did with Erin, Belair knew to rephrase questions until he received the required answers. He roared when a witness veered off track: "Move to strike!" Often the judge agreed, meaning that even though the words were said and heard by all, even though they were recorded by the stenographer and would appear in the printed transcript, those words did not exist for legal purposes and could not be considered. It was a powerful style and skill of lawyering, where first Belair crafted a series of questions designed to elicit only one possible answer, then he hit the "delete" button to wipe away any responses challenging his partisan premises.

Peter and I also appeared in this parallel universe, but we inhabited it with a different spirit. Neither Peter nor I could help but wear our hearts on our sleeves: he made self-deprecating jokes during sidebar conferences; my childcare obligations came up often in our scheduling conferences, making Belair privy to my imperfect juggle; every morning, we handed over all our notes and question lists; we would have given Belair our brains, Bates-numbered and inventoried, if the law had required us to do so, because we wanted to do everything not just "by the book" but beyond the book and, most important, we recognized and respected the importance of his work as the defense attorney. Belair, by contrast, was a perpetual mystery and a Janus-faced opponent. Perhaps he applied the cutthroat social codes of the civil courts, perhaps he felt offended by our decision to pursue criminal charges against a physician, or perhaps he was just channeling a bias against prosecutors that now has gone viral.

Belair bowed to the fictions of the law, to the rules of procedure, to the sacrosanct record, but he considered us—and treated us as—adversaries and expressed in dated and inappropriate terms what has become an unfortunate cliché: that prosecutors are different, in a bad way. "All prosecutors are special," he joked in the early days of trial, "in a sense of special ed." He added, "Just kidding," but those useless words fell into an uncomfortable silence.

APRIL 10, 2014: DAY 22 OF TRIAL

When Erin tried calling her mother again, later in the day on October 28, 2010, no one answered—"it would ring and ring." Eventually, her calls went straight to voice mail. Early the next morning, on October 29, between 4:00 and 5:00 a.m., Erin tried calling again when she was on her way to work.

Kevin picked up the phone.

Erin's voice was tighter as she recounted the events to the jury. She spoke faster.

"He sounded terrible, and I asked him to put Mom on the phone and he said, 'No, no, she is sleeping, she is sleeping.' I said, 'I don't care; I want to speak with her.' He put the phone down and tried to wake her up. [. . .] He came back on the phone and said, 'She is not answering.' I started screaming at him saying, you know, 'What the hell are you doing? Get off the phone with me; call nine-one-one; do something.' I hung up the phone hoping he would call nine-one-one. I later called back. Now I'm on my way back trying to go back home wherever she was. I called back again, and my father picked up and said that the ambulance was there. I told him to put me on speakerphone so I could hear what was going on. I just heard the— I tried screaming so that the paramedics would answer me because no one was listening to me and I wanted to know what was going on because I had no idea what was going on. I don't know how long I was on the phone."

Eventually, Kevin answered and told Erin they were on their way to Jamaica Hospital. By the time Erin arrived, her mother was unconscious, hooked up to a ventilator. Kevin was not there. When he arrived, "he was terrible," Erin sputtered. "He looked terrible. He was dirty. He was high as can be. He couldn't speak. [. . .] He was tripping into things and walking all over the place, just didn't make any sense whatsoever."

Kevin extended his hand toward Erin—it was stained with blood. "He kept saying, you know, 'I hit my head, I hit my head; look, I was bleeding,' but he didn't know how. He didn't know what he did. He didn't know anything."

Kevin told Erin that he would go back to rehab. "I said, 'I don't care; do whatever the hell you want,'" said Erin. Alone, she went back into her mother's room, where the doctors announced that the patient was brain-dead. Erin knew her mother would not wish to remain on life support. She signed the Do Not Resuscitate order. Her mother died. Kevin was not there.

Ever the responsible party, even in the moment of her greatest loss, Erin went to her parents' home to collect paperwork and clothing for her mother's funeral. When she rang the doorbell, Kevin opened the door.

"Where is your mom?" he asked. "What is happening with her? When is she coming home?"

"Not anytime soon," Erin answered, walking into the apartment.

She saw the pipe. She saw the crack.

"You have five minutes to get out of here before I call the cops," she said. She walked outside, accompanied by her boyfriend. Kevin came out, handed her the keys, told her he was going to rehab, and walked away.

Erin got what she needed out of the house but did not want to abandon her parents' animals, a dog and a cat. She returned later that evening after having shopped for pet food and found that Kevin had broken into the apartment. He snapped at her, then begged for the truth.

"I don't want to tell you," Erin answered. "I don't think you can handle it."

"Just tell me, just tell me," Kevin repeated—so Erin did.

Kevin curled up into a ball and cried hysterically.

"He came to me to give me a hug," Erin said, toughing it out through her tears and congestion, "and I stopped him and I said, 'I can't do this; I can't break down. I have too much stuff to do.' I said, 'I don't blame you for anything,' I said, 'but I can't do this now.' As I walked out he followed me to the kitchen and he began banging on the walls and screaming how he'd never get high again, he will never do this again, he is sorry, you know, he swears on my mother, he swears on me, he swears on everything, and I said, 'That is fine,' I said, 'Good,' I said, 'I only have one parent now so I need you and I need you to get help and do what you gotta do,' and then I said I would be here tomorrow and I left."

That line echoed in my mind all day and still lives there: "I only have one parent now so I need you."

Erin returned to the apartment the next morning, on October 30. This time, her father asked for his wife's purse. Erin had the purse. Kevin asked for the bank cards. Erin told him that she hadn't been able to find them, so she had already reported them as lost or stolen.

I thought of everything this young woman did on the night her mother died: the funeral arrangements; the pet food; the clothing; the purse, looking through it to see if everything was in order; calls to the banks and credit card companies.

Kevin asked for a check. "I didn't find any checks," Erin told him.

Kevin asked Erin to take him to the doctor, because he needed antidepressants.

"What are you talking about?" Erin asked.

"I don't have anything," Kevin pleaded.

Erin told Kevin that she couldn't afford to take him—she didn't have any money.

"I have to go to the doctor," Kevin insisted. "I have to go to the doctor; I have to go to Dr. Li."

Erin called her grandmother, who agreed to drive her son to his doctor's office.

The jury heard about the visit to Dr. Li from Anne Kingsley, Kevin Kingsley's elderly mother, who testified after Erin. After more than forty-five years of marriage to her late husband and after her son's death, Anne was left with four children and eight grandchildren, including Erin. When I walked Anne and Erin to court on the morning of her testimony, Anne tripped over a curb and fell—then berated herself for having fallen and refused any help. She was bleeding from her elbow. I don't think she even allowed us to get a Band-Aid for her. You didn't argue with Anne Kingsley. We did not discuss it, but she was rattled by the trial, nervous about taking the stand, and embarrassed to have shown any frailty. "I take yoga lessons," she reminded me. When it was her turn to testify, she lowered herself into the wooden chair on the witness stand and then straightened her spine up and looked ahead with determination.

When Anne Kingsley took her son to his doctor's office in Flushing, Queens, on October 30, 2010, it was not her first time. She had done so a few times in the last few years before his death, because Kevin had told her that he was in pain. He said he needed money for his doctor's appointments. Knowing her son's history of substance abuse, Anne was careful: She never just gave him money. She couldn't trust him with money anymore. Instead, she took him to the doctor herself and gave him money just for that purpose.

Of course, she believed that since he was going to see a doctor, it was okay. She thought that was safe.

Anne remembered the office in Flushing because "you couldn't park there." She never went inside with him but gave him money to pay the doctor once they pulled up to the office, then waited for him in the car—"not long, fifteen minutes"—drove him to the pharmacy, gave him money to pay for his medication, waited for him in the car while he filled the prescription, then drove him home.

That's what she did on October 30, the day after Kevin's wife died.

"Kevin said he needed more medicine to get through this, and he had no way of getting there, so I drove him to the doctor," Anne told the jury. "I drove him there, and then we just waited. [. . .] He said, 'I'll be right back,' and he was right back."

"How did your son look on that day?" I asked.

"He looked awful, awful. It just wasn't Kevin at all. It wasn't Kevin."

"Can you explain how?"

"He looked like a derelict, somebody that had no home, no any-thing. He looked raggedy, disheveled, like he hadn't showered, which I don't think he did in days, and he was wearing the same clothes. That isn't even important. What was awful was his—he looked gray and he just—it was like the skin was hanging down from him."

Dr. Li had written prescriptions for seventy-one patients already by the time he saw Kevin on October 30. "My wife died, I hurt my head," Dr. Li noted in Kevin's patient file, in quotation marks, to indicate that those were the patient's own words. That was the entire entry in the medical record for that day.

When Dr. Li testified about Kevin, he claimed that Kevin had con-fessed to having caused his own head injury. "[H]e's so sad, he inten-tionally hit the wall."

Dr. Li took Kevin's money and discharged the grieving, injured man from his practice with a full month's set of prescriptions: ninety Xanax pills in a 2 mg dose and sixty Roxicodone pills in a 30 mg dose.

Dr. Li was supposed to be Kevin Kingsley's doctor, but Kevin King-sley became his victim instead.

MAY 28, 2014: DAY 70 OF TRIAL

It was just another day at work.

"That's silly, Ms. Fishman," the judge rebuked me at sidebar. "That's silly."

During another one of Belair's cross-examinations, he'd asked a series of questions that the witness couldn't possibly answer in the way they were presented. Belair then faulted the witness for being evasive. It was a toxic mix of imperfect communication, contrary interests, conscious actions, emotions, fatigue, and legal formalities. We'd taken the dispute out of hearing of the jury, up to the bench, and I had, once again, failed to convince the judge that the witness was responding in good faith. I'd also clearly once again failed to embody the minimum threshold of professionalism and adulthood that would have spared me the indignity of being called silly in front of two other attorneys and a stenographer, and on the magical "record," in perpetuity.

These moments triggered dangerous depths of self-hatred. Maybe they were treating me like a child because I was behaving like a child. And not just any child—an insufferable one. Was I just as annoying to others as I was to myself? Was there a way for me to exist and disappear at the same time? It wasn't all an insecure fantasy anymore: my reputation was at stake. It was being crafted every day in that courtroom and documented forever. It could affect everything from the perception of other judges to my relationships with defense attorneys to my career in the DA's Office—but most important, it could affect my ability to do what I cared about the most: right wrongs. If the judge didn't trust me, didn't take me seriously, viewed me as inefficient or unable to learn from my mistakes or just plain "silly," my cases would suffer. "Your reputation is everything," they told us on the first day of ADA rookie training and every single day that followed—but was everyone's reputation being measured and sculpted according to the same standards? Perceptions of women in our office and the courts seemed to operate more like a seesaw than a spectrum: you were either a "Dragon Lady" with ice-cold water in your veins or a troublemaking child. "Calm down," one of my bureau chief's successors would say to every female ADA who walked into his office with an emergent problem. It wasn't cool to call women bitches in the open anymore, but who needed that word when there were so many others?

The judge did impart valuable lessons. Or maybe it was one lesson, illustrated in many different situations: Trials are not a truth-seeking proceeding. Trials do not exist to reconstruct the past or explain an issue. Trials are not intended to be comprehensive. Trials are not places where people are meant to understand one another or allow explanations of events. Trials, instead, are special proceedings designed to answer a limited set of questions, according to a set of specific and often arcane rules. Peter and Belair were master players, though they were driven by different spirits. On cross-examination, Belair channeled witnesses with skill toward the desired answers, vetoed responses that didn't align with his aim, and drew a benefit from the impression that the witnesses were resistant. While Peter never allowed witnesses to explain or wrest control from his hands, either, he relied more on confronting witnesses with the facts or exposing their motives through simple, selective questions. Meanwhile, I raged at every point of inaccuracy or misunderstanding, and every evidentiary gap that seemed to be getting in the way of clear, truthful, comprehensive, enlightening testimony—but I was missing the point of litigation.

APRIL 10, 2014: DAY 22 OF TRIAL

When Kevin returned to his mother's car on October 30, the day after his wife's death, he was holding the prescription forms that he had just obtained from Dr. Li. Anne drove him to a pharmacy on Metropolitan Avenue and accompanied him inside so that she could pay for his medication with a credit card.

I wondered if the jury noted that she had not just given him her credit card.

When they got back in the car, Kevin said, "I have to take this now," and drank down the pills with AriZona Iced Tea, his favorite. Anne drove him home.

The wake was scheduled to take place on Monday, November 1. Erin testified that, at four or five in the morning on that day, she received a call from her father. He accused her of having stolen his pills, either her or a friend of her mother's, to whom he referred as "that bitch."

"I screamed at him," Erin testified, "and hung up the phone."

When Erin arrived at the wake, Kevin was already there—he had arrived with Anne.

"[H]e was a mess. He was wearing dirty jeans, just a T-shirt and a jacket; his hair was a mess; he couldn't talk; he couldn't even stand up; his eyes were, like, halfway closed, couldn't even see his eyes, falling all over, couldn't speak." Kevin was falling asleep during the service, but after Erin spoke, he stood up.

"I'm sorry," Anne Kingsley said to the judge, because she was crying. "I could still see him there. It's the worst he ever looked. It wasn't Kevin. It wasn't Kevin standing there. He was just talking to us and it didn't sound like Kevin, and he was standing in front of everybody at that wake and saying how much he loved [her]."

"He was rocking back and forth," Erin testified. "[H]e was, like, talking to himself basically, just going over about my mom and him and how much he loved her and everything and how she never gave up on him. But he wasn't, like, looking at anyone; it was just like he was talking to himself."

"[That] picture is just never going to leave my head," Anne said. And then she apologized to Judge Sonberg, the jury, everyone—again. I told the judge that we had no more questions for her.

The judge told Anne that he would give her a few minutes to compose herself before cross-examination.

"I need a tissue," she said. The court officer handed her a tissue. She thanked him and added, "I thought I had enough."

In his cross-examination of Anne Kingsley, Belair asked her to confirm that Kevin had appeared always to be in pain in the last years of his life. She said no, so he read to her from the grand jury transcript of her 2012 testimony, in which she said that Kevin had complained of pain.

"If I have read that accurately," he asked, "was that your testimony at the grand jury?"

"Yes, that's my testimony, but that's not what you asked me," Anne retorted.

"Ma'am," Judge Sonberg admonished her—

She was right, but Judge Sonberg did not allow anyone to talk back to Belair—not even an elderly lady testifying about her dead son.

—"I'm sorry," Anne said. She turned to Belair. "Go ahead."

"Miss Kingsley," the judge continued, "arguing with Belair—"

"I won't argue," she promised, innocently. She sat up straight, ready to go.

"Well," the judge said, "well, you just started to. Let me just tell you that will only prolong this, okay."

Belair pressed on. During the years 2007 to 2010, did she see her son in pain? Yes, she had. Did she believe that he was in pain?

"Sometimes I did and sometimes I didn't," said Anne, looking straight at Belair. He didn't have many more questions for her.

Erin's cross-examination was much tougher. She had ended her testimony talking about her mother's funeral. Her father had showed up wearing the same clothes as he had worn to the wake. He could barely stand up. "[A]s we were laying her to rest," Erin told the jury, "we were able to throw roses at the casket and he was falling, you know, we were afraid he was going to fall in, basically."

"Is your father alive today?" Peter asked.

This was the only question we were allowed to ask about Kevin Kingsley's death: we could not allow the jury to speculate about its circumstances or cause, because Dr. Li was not charged with Kevin Kingsley's death. He was charged with Reckless Endangerment in the First Degree, the same charge the grand jury had voted in connection with Dawn Tamasi and Tracy Howard.

"No," Erin answered.

In fact, Kevin Kingsley died of an overdose on December 28, 2010. Less than two months after his wife's death.

And then it was Belair's turn.

He started with the civil lawsuit Erin Kingsley Markevitch had filed, claiming wrongful death and seeking damages from Dr. Li and other physicians. Belair spent several minutes extracting a concession that Erin could not recall having seen Dr. Li's name on any pill bottles prior to her mother's death. She also conceded that she had never known—until that moment, having heard it from Belair—that Dr. Li had once discharged Kevin Kingsley from his practice before taking him on again as a patient a few months later. Belair tried to push Erin to admit that her father had never not used drugs, but after a long and confused exchange she explained that "there were periods of months that he wouldn't use drugs, but there was never a long set period of time that he wasn't using."

Belair turned to the question of damages. Erin's civil lawsuit against Dr. Li was fair game for cross-examination: it revealed that she had an interest beyond civic duty and could give the jury a reason to discount her testimony. He asked Erin to confirm that she had been raised by her mother since the age of five. "My whole life," she corrected him. He didn't understand her response. "My whole life," she repeated.

Having scored his point for the civil case, Belair turned back to the criminal matter. Didn't her father tell her that he was taking medication for pain? That he was in pain? Yes. Yes.

And then, as he neared the end of his cross, he took a scattershot approach. Kevin Kingsley died just two months after his wife, Belair established. Was he still smoking crack at the time? Yes, answered Erin. Belair just let that hang. When he hurt his head and you saw blood, was he smoking crack at *that* time? Yes. The suggestion was clear: it was crack that hurt Kevin, crack that killed Kevin.

"That is all I have," said Belair to the judge.

He was just doing his job, I reminded myself. Trust the jury. Trust the facts.

SEPTEMBER 11, 2013: 190 DAYS UNTIL TRIAL

The motions were long and full of jargon. They were topped with Orders to Show Cause, followed by affidavits and appendices. It would have been just as well to scribble out the words "HELL NO" in big, thick marker on a piece of paper, but that's just not the way the law—especially not *civil* law—works. The clerk on the lower level of the Kings County Civil Court flipped through the sheaf of documents as I awaited his verdict: Had I forgotten some magic word? He finally stamped the documents. I hustled back to the subway and office to finish another motion, destined for Queens County. We didn't have time for any of this, but there was no way—*no way*—that we would allow Belair to make an end run around the criminal case.

The Kingsley and Rappold families had filed claim alleging the wrongful deaths of their loved ones, seeking compensation. Belair represented Dr. Li on those cases as well. After having shut down plea negotiations in early 2013 because Dr. Li was unwilling to contemplate any jail time, Belair kicked his defense of the civil cases into high gear: he scheduled the depositions of Erin Kingsley Markevitch and Margaret Rappold.

In a deposition, he would get a preview of Erin Kingsley Markevitch's and Margaret Rappold's trial testimony, and he'd have it on the record, under oath. It was an opportunity for him to cross-examine them with fewer limitations on time or substance, and it created an opportunity for discrepancies in their testimony—however unintentional—that he could later use to discredit them on the stand, during our trial. It was a smart move. We had to fight this, I argued. We couldn't let him bully our witnesses.

There was just one big problem: I hated civil procedure. Loathed. *Dreaded.* There was nothing I hated more in the universe of law—except maybe lawyers.

I threw myself back into civil litigation mode and called anybody I could think of from my law school class or former law firm who might be able to remind me of the arcane rules of Orders to Show Cause and Motions to Intervene. We developed a plan: request permission to intervene, inform the judges of the pending criminal case, and ask them to pause discovery in the civil cases. Our plan required a precise combination of motions, affidavits, and proposed orders, multiple trips out to civil courtrooms in Brooklyn and Queens to file our papers in person and appear on the case, as well as harrowing near-deletion experiences on the dicey web-based court filing systems.

It was war. Peter and I spent long hours sitting in ornate wooden courtrooms in Brooklyn and Queens, listening to lawyers harangue each other about contract disputes. Whatever friction existed between defense attorneys and prosecutors of the criminal bar, we were collegial by comparison to the civil lawyers. "You are a piece of shit," I heard one gray-suited man in his fifties, carrying a bunch of papers, say to another gray-suited man in his fifties, carrying his own pile of papers, in the hallway between two courtrooms. I looked around—was there going to be trouble? Did I need to alert security? The court officers and other lawyers waiting for the elevators didn't even twitch: it was business as usual.

OCTOBER 24, 2013: 147 DAYS UNTIL TRIAL

The Manhattan DA's Office offered me my dream job: Deputy Director of Training. I had applied months earlier, when we believed Dr. Li might plead guilty, but since then I'd lost hope of getting the job *or* of a plea agreement.

The offer was a thrill. I was honored: what could be better than to have a voice and role in raising new prosecutors, instilling values and influencing their entire careers and updating the training to reflect current thinking about criminal justice, implicit bias, and incarceration? I had to give an immediate answer, though, and make a commitment regardless of what happened with the Li case—which might mean leaving before trial.

I wanted the job. It seemed like the answer to everything. But there was no way I would jump ship.

"[Special Narcotics] has provided unfailing support to the case and the prosecution team over the past three years," I wrote to the Director of Training. "I wish to honor my commitments to the case and [Special Narcotics] now that we are slated for trial, and so I must decline the offer with regret."

We were doing this. We were really doing this. I was terrified. But tension or no tension, I was sticking with my case and my team. This was way easier than anything any of our victims—or their families—ever had done.

Maybe I could make it even easier. I made an appointment with my dermatologist. I pointed to the frown lines between my eyebrows: "This has to go," I said. My doctor pinched that skin, piercing it with a thin needle again and again to inject me with a commercialized form of snake venom. I felt numbness and tingling. For a few hours the reddish bumps made me look like a mosquito attack survivor, but then they disappeared, leaving a smooth surface.

My workload was the same. My stress was the same. *My behavior was the same.* I was a few hundred dollars poorer, but it was worth it just to hear people say, "Wow, you're so calm." Or better yet, sometimes they said nothing at all and we just got shit done.

I was ready for trial.

CHAPTER 11

The Gatekeepers

Between January 2012 and March 2017, [Purdue, Janssen, Mylan, Depomed, and Insys] contributed nearly $9 million to leading patient advocacy organizations and professional societies operating in the opioids policy area. For some groups, contributions from these manufacturers—alone—constituted significant portions of their total annual contributions and grants.

FUELING AN EPIDEMIC, U.S. SENATE HOMELAND
SECURITY & GOVERNMENTAL AFFAIRS COMMITTEE
MINORITY STAFF REPORT, FEBRUARY 2018[1]

FEBRUARY 23, 2012: 756 DAYS UNTIL TRIAL

Joe T. and I met Dr. Christopher Gharibo for the first time in his office at the NYU Hospital for Joint Diseases. The doctor wore a crisp white coat over business attire. He sat and listened as we proceeded through our scripted introduction: we described the patient files (photo and insurance claims clipped to the left, medical notes on the right); we explained that the Bates numbers at the bottom of each page had been added by our office, in order to keep track of every sheet of paper; we asked whether he was in the habit of taking notes and instructed him to retain anything and everything related to this assignment.

In preparation for the meeting, Joe T. had reminded me of our record-keeping obligations in the event we retained Dr. Gharibo as our medical expert: we had to keep track of everything we gave him, everything we said to him, and everything he produced, so that we could share that information with the defense. They had a right to know the facts, assumptions, and materials that may have influenced the expert's opinion.

All of this assumed, however, that Dr. Gharibo would agree to work on this case—and he looked skeptical. He was a pain management specialist who prescribed opioid painkillers to his own patients. He loved his work and trusted his colleagues. He previously had served as an expert witness, but he wasn't the kind of doctor who would say what suited the lawyers. It was clear that the report would contain his unvarnished opinion—and we would just have to live with that.

We didn't hear from him for six weeks, during which every investigative step was tempered with uncertainty. We were committed to following Dr. Gharibo's lead, so if he found that there was a legitimate medical basis for Dr. Li's prescriptions, we would end the criminal investigation and turn over the case to disciplinary authorities.

MAY 21, 2014: DAY 63 OF TRIAL

Belair's tone was nothing short of aggressive as he cross-examined Dr. Gharibo, who had come a long way since his initial skepticism. Belair had listened to Dr. Gharibo condemn Dr. Li's conduct in stark and unforgiving terms: now he sought to exploit Dr. Gharibo's outrage. He prodded and taunted Dr. Gharibo, hoping to provoke an unseemly explosion in front of the jury but willing to settle for an admission of bias. If the jury believed that Dr. Gharibo was intent on finding fault with all of Dr. Li's decisions, perhaps they would begin to discount some of his criticism.

"Isn't this the portrait of a caring physician?" Belair asked Dr. Gharibo, pointing to Dr. Li's treatment of Joseph Haeg. "You are not saying that Dr. Li wasn't trying to help his patients, were you?"

Dr. Gharibo was holding something back—everyone could tell. "I don't get the sense he was trying to help their pain," he answered, tensely. What was he holding back? Why was Belair pushing him on this?

"What was he trying to do, then, if he wasn't trying to help his patients?"

"He was prescribing controlled-substance monotherapy without taking advantage of other pain medicine approaches."

Belair raised his voice. "What is his interest in doing that if not to help his patients? Why is he doing it? What's his motivation?"

The answer rebounded quickly, in a tight, stern voice. "This is not pain management."

"I didn't ask you that!" Belair hollered. "Why is he doing it if not to help his patient? Give us a reason?"

That's where the judge's voice cut in, high and sharp and angry: "Counsels, *smirks off your faces!*"

Startled, Peter and I looked at each other. If our faces hadn't been contorted before, they were now. What on earth? We had been rapt, yes, captivated, yes, stunned, *yes*—but smirking? Was I even capable of smirking anymore, with my frozen frown lines?

While Peter and I composed ourselves after the judge's outburst, Belair pressed on, relentless.

"If he is not trying to help his patients, what's his motivation? What is he trying to accomplish? He is trying to help his patient, isn't he?"

Dr. Gharibo shook his head. "I don't agree with that. This is not helpful."

"Tell the jury what his interest is? What is he trying to accomplish if not to help his patients?"

Dr. Gharibo tried saying it a different way, without saying what he was trying to avoid saying. "He's prescribing controlled substances haphazardly without diagnosis and without regard to psycho-circumstances."

"Why is he doing it if not to help?" Belair bellowed. "Why is he doing it?"

The answer flowed out, quick and honest and brutal: "It's very mechanical. He's doing it potentially to make a living. He's doing it to feed an addiction network as part of his business model."

There would have been a stunned hush were it not for the fact that Belair kept going, kept pushing, kept talking; Dr. Gharibo kept answering, countering, explaining; Belair challenged him, admonished him, confronted him with past testimony in other cases, moved to strike Dr. Gharibo's answers.

Over and over again, Dr. Gharibo repeated a line that may have seemed anticlimactic to the jury but carried much significance to him: "This was not pain management."

MAY 8, 2014: DAY 50 OF TRIAL

Pain is subjective—it's a trope and the truth. You can't see pain. You can't test for the feeling of pain or verify the patient's experience of pain.

Pain has a purpose in the body. It is a reminder that we need to protect ourselves. "[W]hen we hurt ourselves," Dr. Gharibo explained during his direct examination, "we sensitize the neurological tissue to perceiving pain and that is helpful for our survival because otherwise, we would continuously injure that same area. So, that's acute pain." Acute pain, the jury learned, is often inflammatory. Yet if the source of acute pain, such as injury, has been fixed and yet the pain persists, "it doesn't serve any purpose and it is now maladaptive." While acute pain can persist even past three months, chronic pain, as Dr. Gharibo outlined, is typically defined as maladaptive pain persisting after six months.

In response to my questions, Dr. Gharibo gave the jury a rough history of pain medicine: It emerged as a subspecialty of anesthesiology, he explained, when anesthesiologists discovered that they could use nerve block techniques to relieve chronic pain and restore functionality to patients. Pain medicine developed into an interdisciplinary field, attracting and accepting physicians with fellowships in psychiatry, physical medicine or rehabilitation, anesthesiology or neurology. Its practice was "multimodal," Dr. Gharibo explained. "Multimodal means something that works through different mechanisms, different modalities of treatment. And what I am referring to there is, for example, physical therapy can be a modality, medications are another type of modality, or injections are another type of modality, biofeedback, acupuncture are a different type of modality, and surgery is a type of modality." The purpose of these treatments was to "give the patients their life back."

Dr. Gharibo was not a medical historian, however, and his job was not to give the jury a detailed and nuanced account of the specialty's history. Nor would it have been appropriate or permissible for me to ask—and for him to talk—about the marketing campaigns launched in the 1990s by pharmaceutical companies, which were designed to overcome physicians' reluctance to prescribe opioids to non-cancer pain patients. The jury was not there to render a verdict on a raging medical controversy but on certain date-and-patient-specific actions of an individual physician. We had even filtered out, through our juror questionnaire and voir dire, any potential jurors who might have carried knowledge or opinions about opioids, or pharmaceutical companies or even doctors, into deliberations. The trial, nevertheless, raised and reenacted, on a micro level, every theme of the ongoing debate about opioids.

Are opioid painkillers addictive? Are they addictive even for patients experiencing real pain? Are they addictive even for persons of "good character," from "good families"? Can you trust a patient's report of pain? Is non-cancer pain still "legitimate" pain, worthy of treatment? Can opioid tolerance look like addiction? Can patients addicted to opioids still feel "legitimate" pain? Do patients addicted to opioids deserve to have their pain treated? How do you treat the pain of those patients? Do doctors have a duty to avoid creating a risk of addiction? Do doctors have a duty to respond to the signs of addiction? What is the proper way to respond to a patient who abuses painkillers? Should a doctor ever initiate or resume opioid therapy for a patient who has abused illegal drugs?

Should a doctor ever initiate or resume opioid therapy for a patient who has gone through substance abuse treatment? Does a doctor's responsibility for the prescriptions they issue extend past the doors of their office, or past the date of discharge?

Dr. Gharibo set forth an affirmative mission and vision for the specialty of pain medicine. He ascribed to pain management specialists a responsibility—in fact, a "duty"—to "do a diagnostic work-up" of pain. First because "sometimes a pain diagnosis ends up being cancerous or infectious," but also because the focus of their specialty—pain—is a subjective experience that does not always directly point the way to its own relief.

"The job of the pain specialist," Dr. Gharibo explained, "is to take [the diagnosis] beyond just 'pain.' Pain is not just pain. There are different types of pain. Pain of a headache versus pain of an inflamed appendix in appendicitis versus pain of a wrist fracture [. . .] versus pain of sciatica versus cancer pain. So, our job is to find the pain source or sources. [. . .] [The] pain specialty is a multi-faceted specialty which kind of brings in these orthopedic, musculoskeletal, neurological, pharmacological, and psychological components together."

There were diagnostic tools and tests and resources to help with that work: there were movements the doctor could observe during the examination; functional assessments; medical imaging; referrals to other specialists.

This was the draw and promise and passion of pain management for Dr. Gharibo: an interdisciplinary practice of medicine, relying on rigorous diagnostic processes but investigative—and even creative—pursuit of physiological problems. With this testimony, he answered one of our first and recurring questions about Dr. Li's practice, having seen that it consisted of the same combinations and quantities of controlled substances for a narrow range of "diagnoses" that seemed to go no further than the patient's own original, simplistic complaint of pain. That question was a simple one: *Is this pain medicine?*

It was not, Dr. Gharibo affirmed. "A pain specialist would do combination therapy interventions, non-opioid, opioids, and physiotherapy measures, and other measures. That combination is what a pain specialist does." That was, he called it, the "science of pain medicine."

To be fair, we were not in court to engage in an intellectual debate about the origins and purpose of pain medicine. We had not called seventy-two witnesses and conducted a four-year-long investigation for the purpose of distinguishing pain medicine from other medical specialties. We were there because we were accusing Dr. Li of criminal conduct: specifically, 211 instances of criminal conduct, including two homicides.

Dr. Li was there because he had a constitutional right to be tried for those crimes before a jury of his peers. However, as the criminal defendant, he had no burden of proof. He had no obligation to mount a defense. Nevertheless, Dr. Li and his attorney decided that the jury should hear another side of the story.

They countered Dr. Gharibo's vision of pain medicine with their own. More accurately, they countered Dr. Gharibo's vision with the pharmaceutical company playbook. Mr. Belair, Dr. Li, Dr. Gharibo, and the defense expert—whose name we didn't learn until the day he testified—gave energetic voice to positions and disagreements that had split the medical community for decades. We'd done everything to keep the opioid epidemic out of the courtroom: the defense snuck it back in.

MAY 10, 2007: 2,506 DAYS UNTIL TRIAL

Six hundred *million* dollars: that's how much the Purdue Frederick Company, parent of Purdue Pharma, agreed to pay as part of a guilty plea in a federal criminal case.[2] As part of the plea agreement, the defendants acknowledged certain facts related to the misbranding and fraudulent marketing of OxyContin, a brand-name formulation of oxycodone, specifically that, "beginning on or about December 12, 1995, and continuing until on or about June 30, 2001, certain PURDUE supervisors and employees, with the intent to defraud or mislead, marketed and promoted OxyContin as less addictive, less subject to abuse and diversion, and less likely to cause tolerance and withdrawal than other pain medications [. . .]."[3] The company did so, among other things, by telling sales representatives that "they could tell health care providers that OxyContin potentially creates less chance for addiction than immediate-release opioids." They also spent millions of dollars funding so-called educational programs, distributing publications, creating and bolstering lobbying groups and think tanks, and influencing state medical boards.[4]

Yet 2007 wasn't the end of it—not in terms of the marketing practices across the industry, not in terms of the profits, and certainly not in terms of opioid-related overdose deaths.

In 2007, 18,516 human beings in the United States died of opioid overdoses (including natural, synthetic, and semi-synthetic opioids, methadone, and heroin). The bodies piled up as the years passed:

2008: 19,582
2009: 20,422 more
2010: another 21,089
2011: plus 22,784
2012: an additional 23,166
2013: 25,052 more people who'd been alive the preceding year
2014: 28,647 different human beings

2015: plus 33,091

Another 42,249 in 2016.[5]

How many people hearing these numbers remember a loved one, friend, or acquaintance who is included in the tally? How many people experienced a loss in not just one but *several* of the listed years? Why don't these numbers feel like they're hitting home until they actually hit home?

A new, separate lawsuit filed by the New York Attorney General's (NYAG) Office in 2019 charged that Purdue had persisted in its deceptive marketing even after the 2007 plea, and that Purdue, along with its competitors, including Janssen Pharmaceutica, a subsidiary of Johnson & Johnson, Mallinckrodt Pharmaceuticals, Endo International, Teva Pharmaceuticals, and Allergan, had relied on false claims to promote opioid products, which included Roxicodone (Mallinckrodt) and Opana (Endo), and had ignored, along with their largest distributors, the risks and warnings of diversion.[6]

It had been, the lawsuit charged, a multifaceted, well-funded, extensive, and influential campaign to overcome "opiophobia" and encourage the use of opioid painkillers as a first-line therapy—and Purdue Pharma wasn't the only company to wield dinners, speaking fees, sponsorships, and other inducements in an effort to boost sales.[7]

"Together," the NYAG's lawsuit charged, "these drug manufacturers (the 'Manufacturer Defendants') collaborated to falsely deny the serious risks of opioid addiction generally, and high-dose opioid prescriptions specifically. At the same time, they created and promoted the concept of 'pseudoaddiction'—a made-up term designed to recast familiar symptoms of addiction as signs that patients needed more opioid drugs. [. . .] Each Manufacturer Defendant spent millions of dollars over the following decade to push these fraudulent messages."[8]

Dr. Li's defense fell in line with the Big Pharma playbook uncovered by these lawsuits, adopting the notion that, so long as a prescription was written by a doctor, in response to a complaint of pain, it was legitimate. The defense also required the jury to agree that patients—regardless of their history—were responsible adults in whom doctors placed their trust. Patients exercised a conscious choice to abuse the medications and doctors were not responsible for those actions or their consequences. So long as the doses were standard and assuming they were taken as prescribed, they presented a minimal risk to the patient. Chronic pain patients should not be punished for the sins of a few bad apples (patients or physicians) by having their pain medication over-regulated and criminalized.

These were not all crazy claims, but they were a dog whistle to a subset of physicians and their medical "societies" who, under the influence of pharmaceutical company marketing and funding, maintained in defiance of mounting facts that opioids were a safe first-line therapy with a low potential for abuse or overdose for non-cancer pain patients.

Most important, by drawing the jury into a substantive medical debate on the merits and risks of opioid therapy, Dr. Li sought to muddy the waters of criminal intent. He was trying to make it more difficult for the jury to determine that he was not acting in good faith.

The two strands of the defense—the traditional criminal defense relying on the creation of reasonable doubt in the jury's mind and the "medical" defense—were advanced in equal measure, throughout the trial, in Belair's cross-examinations of our witnesses as well as in the defense case. On the medical front, Dr. Li and Belair added their own flair to the Big Pharma playbook, as required in order to counter some of the specific charges, but they never deviated from it.

JUNE 23, 2014: DAY 96 OF TRIAL

"You learned that chronic opioid use could lead to addiction; is that correct?" Peter asked Dr. Li on cross-examination.

"No," answered Dr. Li, without equivocation. "That's incorrect."

"You did not learn that?"

"No."

"You learned that chronic narcotics use could lead to overdose; is that correct?"

"No."

And yet, as the jury had already learned from one of our witnesses, Dr. Melinda Campopiano, medical officer at the Substance Abuse Mental Health Services Administration (SAMHSA), Dr. Li had sought and obtained training in buprenorphine treatment for patients with opioid use disorders.

In fact, the defense even questioned whether patients with "real" pain could fall into addiction. This issue became central to the trial.

Dr. Gharibo acknowledged the existence of a spectrum of views within the pain management community on opioid therapy, arising from differences of opinion about the medications' potential for abuse. It was common knowledge within the pain management community, in Dr. Gharibo's expert opinion, that there was a difference between dependence—the body's increasing reliance on opioid medications—and addiction, which he defined as "essentially using the medication for enjoyment, for the excitatory effect, which is a feel-good effect, [. . .] in a compulsive fashion." A patient, according to Dr. Gharibo, could be dependent without being addicted. However, it was understood, according to Dr. Gharibo, that opioids could have a recreational, "excitatory," "feel-good" effect on patients, *even patients with legitimate pain conditions*, and that the dosage, duration, and timing of a patient's opioid medications could either minimize or aggravate a sensation of peaks and troughs, where a dependent patient could become addicted and travel from highs to cravings to withdrawal without experiencing the goal of any pain management therapy: a steady, painless state.

As Dr. Gharibo described it, the spectrum of views therefore extended from the absolute refusal to prescribe opioids to chronic pain patients to "those that believe that opioids could be prescribed in chronic nonmalignant pain and they could be individualized for the patient in a functional fashion." Dr. Gharibo placed himself on that more permissive end of the spectrum, by explaining that he prescribed opioids to a select subset of chronic pain patients, with customized combinations of medications, supervised dosages, and a holistic evaluation of the patient's history and living situation.

Significantly, Dr. Gharibo excluded from the spectrum the views that Dr. Li and his defense expert represented, specifically that (1) there was no risk of addiction in a therapeutic setting, (2) there was no risk of overdose at therapeutic prescription levels, and (3) doctors were not responsible for the patients' lack of control over the medication.

The defense, however, was not having it. Dr. Li's team staked out a clear claim to a place on the spectrum of pain management—and not just on the extreme end, but in the middle.

JUNE 30, 2014: DAY 103 OF TRIAL

Dr. Alexander Weingarten, the defense expert, a pain management specialist from Long Island, New York, gave the clearest voice to the Big Pharma playbook. He created attractive binary scenarios for the jury—scenarios that had been propounded with success within the broader pain management community by bigger, more powerful actors.

According to Dr. Weingarten, there was the world of "legitimate" patients with "legitimate" pain and the world of "addicts." Dependence occurred in the former; addiction only in the latter. The difference was attributable to the patient's intent. "Physical dependence and tolerance," he explained, "are natural processes that all patients that are on chronic opioid [sic] will develop over time or many of these will develop over time. Tolerance: being used to the medicine where it doesn't produce the same effect as it did before and thereby they have a higher requirement to get the same level of pain relief. And physical dependence is defined as someone who is being treated for a legitimate pain issue but over time is dependent on the medication because the medicine is just stopped abruptly. They will have withdrawal symptoms. That's in contrast to [an] addict who's taking the medicine for no legitimate purposes. There is no reason in terms of medical certainty of why the addict needs his medicine. He is taking it for purposes that have nothing to do with the legitimate medical purpose. So that if he gets what we call addicted or dependent on the medicine, it's because of a nonmedical reason that he's on it and that's defined as addiction as opposed to medical dependence where there is a legitimate purpose that the patient needs the medicine for."

The only form of addiction that Dr. Weingarten acknowledged for "legitimate" pain patients was "pseudoaddiction," which, he testified, "can be related to physical dependence." "Basically, patients that act like they are addicts, they are running out of their medicine, they need a higher dose of medicine and they go into a withdrawal when they don't have the medicine. But pseudoaddiction is defined as patients who are not being given enough medication who do have legitimate medical pain issues. That's the reason why they need their medicine, but they are acting overtly like an addict; but they are not [an] addict because they are getting the medicine for legitimate medical need. But because of their being under-dosed, they manifest some of the same symptoms that an addict who doesn't get medicine for legitimate medical need would be manifested [sic]."

He was staying true to the script. As the NYAG's lawsuit alleged, opioid manufacturers disseminated such false information: one handbook asserted that"[p]hysical dependence is not the same as addiction" and promoted the concept of pseudoaddiction to convince the public that opioids are not addictive; another taught that behaviors such as "requesting drugs by name," "demanding or manipulative behavior," seeing more than one doctor to obtain opioids, and hoarding, which are signs of genuine addiction, were all really signs of "pseudoaddiction." And pseudoaddiction, as it turned out, was a condition of contested legitimacy and scientific grounding: it was based on a single case study of a single patient.

Our trial took place before the lawsuit, but views and postures described in the lawsuit were promulgated while Dr. Li was running his private pain management practice. Dr. Weingarten was an individual physician with respectable credentials who shared these beliefs and reflected them in his professional activities.

The mental gymnastics involved in evaluating Dr. Weingarten's motives, authenticity, and credibility were similar to the mental gymnastics required to make sense of his testimony.

Nevertheless, there sat Dr. Weingarten in the witness chair, the defense's designated expert, taking issue with Dr. Gharibo's characterizations of Dr. Li's prescriptions and practice. A battle of the experts, one physician's word against another, reflecting differences in approaches, beliefs, and values that were dividing the medical profession and the nation.

The second major front of the defense was that, in any instance, there was no inherent risk of overdose with the strengths and quantities prescribed by Dr. Li. These were "standard" doses, sometimes even lesser doses than other prescribers had ordered. Furthermore, it was appropriate to evaluate their legitimacy in a vacuum, setting aside the patients' history, credibility, environment, and conduct. About Joseph Haeg, Dr. Weingarten assured the jury that "[t]hese were doses that were well within acceptable parameters of prescribing, based on his original doses that he had come into the practice with. So that these were doses that were well recognized as being safe. Again, if taken according to the directions on the bottle, that it was prescribed as, would pose no undue risk of the patient [sic]."

Assuming that Haeg's report of his previous prescriptions were correct, assuming that the medications were taken in accordance with the directions on the bottle, assuming that the patient would only take what was prescribed . . .

In a typical question during his direct examination of Dr. Weingarten, Belair asked about prescriptions written for another patient:

"And did these prescriptions present any risk to the life or health of the patient?"

"No, not in the doses that were being used."

Not in the doses that were being used, because, as Dr. Weingarten explained, "[. . .] they certainly were within doses that did not expose the patient to any risk of injury or death, because these doses were well accepted by both the patient and both—and in the pain management community." These doses were not risky because the patient "accepted" them—did that mean they were not risky because the patient survived them? They were not risky because the doses were accepted "in the pain management community"—but *which* pain management community? Was it fair or even relevant to talk about "the doses being used" by the doctor when Dr. Li knew that the patient was using more than prescribed?

Dr. Weingarten was relying on—and advancing—a simple framework for understanding Dr. Li's prescriptions. As a threshold matter, according to Dr. Weingarten, if a legitimate doctor prescribed the medication in response to a medical complaint within the accepted range of medical doses, the prescription was *by definition* legitimate. The legitimacy of a physician's prescription, in Dr. Weingarten's view, demanded a medical relationship and a complaint of pain. "It was being prescribed for low back pain," he said of the prescriptions written by Dr. Li for Haeg, "which is what the patient's complaint was, and that in pain management is a proper purpose that legitimizes the use of Schedule Two type medications." The justification was a simple, self-nourishing loop: "And, again, the prescriptions were being prescribed in the context of treating pain," Dr. Weingarten added, "which is why these medicines are used, and so there was a legitimate purpose on that date when the prescriptions were given." If there was a stated medical purpose and that purpose was a recognized purpose, then the purpose was legitimate. If the circumstances did not point in that direction, well—actually, you could just ignore the circumstances.

"I'm sorry," Peter said to Dr. Weingarten on cross-examination, discussing Kevin Kingsley's last prescription. Peter had asked the doctor to assume the truth of Kevin's family's testimony about his appearance and behavior on October 30, 2010. "Even if, even if the patient has difficulty standing up," Peter asked, "even if his eyes are halfway closed, even if he is falling over, even if he looked gray, looked like a derelict, speech is slurred, and his words make no sense, that's an appropriate prescription?"

Belair spoke up. "Objection. There is no testimony that he appeared to Dr. Li that way."

"Well," said the judge, allowing the question, "it's a hypothetical with the assumption that that's how he appeared to his family members so that's permissible basis."

"Again," said Dr. Weingarten, "if he did appear that way disoriented, disheveled, then certainly one would have to be careful giving this patient medication. But again, the note appears to be saying that the patient spoke to the doctor. He had a pain complaint. The doctor responded. He even quotes him on his pain on his complaint. 'My wife died.' This does not appear to be the talk or the speech of someone that's totally disoriented."

In Dr. Weingarten's universe, it didn't matter how you looked, as long as you were able to show up and participate in the interaction. It didn't matter how well you articulated, so long as you could push out the word "pain." It didn't matter what happened or what the judge was instructing you to assume as truth, so long as Dr. Li's notes contained the necessary fictions and the patient wasn't dead in front of the doctor. To be honest, even in that corner case, I'm not sure what Dr. Weingarten's response would have been.

And this was the third front of the defense strategy, the origin of the most significant rift between the two experts: laying the responsibility at the feet of the patients rather than the physician.

Even if Dr. Li or the jury believed that patients with "real" pain could not become addicted to opioids, this belief was unsustainable if patients whom Dr. Li had believed to be "legitimate" proved to be using and abusing the drugs for illegitimate purposes. This belief was unsustainable if the patients' abuse and misuse of the drugs was obvious and predictable. As a result, Dr. Li's defense rested on another pillar: He was the innocent victim of sneaky, scheming patients. He had not known his patients were addicts masquerading as legitimate pain patients, and he had not known they were abusing their prescriptions.

In his direct testimony, Dr. Li proclaimed his ignorance of his patients' histories of addiction. They didn't check it off on the intake form, he said. They denied it during the initial visit, he said. That was just what the parents were saying, he said.

Dr. Weingarten's analysis of the patient files perpetuated the same bias: any facts that did not fit with the presumption of safety and legitimacy were ignored. It was a bias that purported to extend the benefit of the doubt to the patients, that purported to emanate from the physicians' trust in the patients. In fact, it was a bias that belittled, devalued, and dehumanized them.

"Now, Dr. Weingarten," Peter asked on cross-examination about Tracy Howard, "I would like you to assume for the purposes of the following question the following facts to be true: Miss [Howard] has testified that typically her visits to Dr. Li took approximately as long as it took to write the prescription. Would any legitimate doctor, engaged in the legitimate practice of pain medicine, treat this patient with visits that lasted scarcely longer than it took to write the prescription?"

"Well," Dr. Weingarten answered, "I tend to disagree with her. There were visits that he counseled her."

Peter cried out in astonishment: "Doctor—Doctor—Doctor?"

"That's not the question, Doctor," the judge admonished him.

Peter tried again after the judge reminded Dr. Weingarten of how hypothetical questions worked. "Would any legitimate doctor," Peter asked, "engaged in the legitimate practice of medicine, treat this patient with visits lasting scarcely longer than it would take to write the prescriptions?"

"Well, based on her testimony," Dr. Weingarten answered, "and based on her behavior throughout the course of the years, if that's, in fact, what she testified to, then I would certainly disagree that the doctor should spend more time with a lady, with a patient like this [. . .]."

Overdoses, addiction, mistakes—they didn't fit the paradigm. They had to be discounted or ignored altogether. Cut out. Discharged.

Or—reframed.

"Dr. Li could have certainly made a mistake about the diagnosis of gout," Dr. Weingarten conceded on cross-examination, talking about the notes in Haeg's patient chart for the last visit. "It's just a subjective thing that he wrote in the chart as a possibility. Whether he's wrong on the diagnosis, he's certainly treated him with the right medicine to help whatever was causing his pain."

"Whatever Dr. Li gave him was good medicine for whatever was his condition," Peter challenged him. "Is that essentially what you are saying, Doctor?"

"If you look at the totality of the visits, from visit to visit, the patient had problems, Dr. Li tried to help him with his problems. The prescriptions were prescribed based on the patient's problems, in the legitimate practice of medicine. So the answer is yes."

The physician was always right. If the physician was wrong, it was because the patient was bad. There was a certain logic to the approach, a flow: the doctor occupied his ivory tower, with white coat and prescription pad, standard medications in standard doses; there were "legitimate" patients who followed the rules and "addicts" who violated them; there was no risk because the doctor did not perceive a risk because the context precluded risk.

Of course, the "context" was not defined by reality, but by certain meaningful symbols, rituals, and code words: the clinic, the white coat, the prescription pad, the word "pain." The context was defined by certain necessary fictions: the "trust" between patients and doctors; the distinction between "patients" and "addicts."

In such a context, there could be no question, for Dr. Weingarten, that Dr. Li's prescriptions were legitimate and had legitimate medical purpose. That was the only possible conclusion.

In our microcosmic courtroom drama, Dr. Li played the role of the pharmaceutical company: an actor who is presumed to be benevolent because they operate in an industry devoted to human health; an actor whose authority and legitimacy is conferred by certain socially recognized markers, like corporate legal status or a medical degree; an actor who confuses goals for missions; who places their own profit interest ahead of the public interest; who refuses to acknowledge the suffering of others or, worse yet, may be indifferent to it; who avoids inconvenient facts instead of investigating them; who dissembles and dodges instead of taking responsibility.

Dr. Weingarten, meanwhile, offered the imprimatur and blessing of medicine to Dr. Li's practice. He was a practiced and ardent spokesperson for his vision of pain medicine. In fact, Dr. Weingarten had been the president of the New York State Pain Society, which propounded these views among the wider medical community. Dr. Weingarten also drew compensation directly from his work on pharmaceutical promotional campaigns. In 2014, for instance, the year he testified at Dr. Li's trial, Dr. Weingarten received fees and benefits from twenty-three companies, valued at $132,275.[9] Most of the benefits and fees came from Insys Therapeutics, one of the New York State Pain Society's corporate partners, [10]* on whose behalf Dr. Weingarten had participated in promotional efforts for the company's branded fentanyl sublingual spray, Subsys; however, Dr. Weingarten also spoke at or participated in events that same year related to the promotion of other drugs, including Oxy-Contin, Opana, and Suboxone.

Even to the extent that Peter may have obtained permission to question Dr. Weingarten about his sources of income, on cross-examination, he did not want to do so: the facts, Peter believed, were enough; Dr. Weingarten's system of circular logic, he believed, would condemn itself. Of course, we also knew that there was nothing un-

---

* Federal prosecutors in Massachusetts indicted former Insys executives and managers just a few years after the trial for having developed and implemented a scheme to bribe doctors in order to increase sales of Subsys—a scheme initiated in June 2012 and continuing until December 2015, including the time period of our trial and Dr. Weingarten's payments.

usual or disqualifying about a physician receiving such payments: our own expert medical witness also had drawn and continued to draw income from pharmaceutical companies.

These financial relationships reflected a complicated and ambivalent reality: the interconnectedness of medical practice and pharmaceutical sales; the softening boundary between science and marketing; the financial expectations, needs, and resources of physicians.

JUNE 11, 2012: 647 DAYS UNTIL TRIAL

Over the course of the investigation, Bridget had always asked about the challenges we faced—and provided remedies when she could. We needed help with data analysis? She hired analysts. Questions about homicide investigations? She brought in an expert. Gaps in the law? Bridget picked up her pen and notepad: she couldn't promise anything, but she believed the law could and should evolve to respond to new threats. If we were facing a situation that the legislature had not yet considered, she wanted to know what would help. We shared our frustrations and ideas. As we worked on assembling evidence, she considered and researched the legislative landscape, and participated in efforts to build in additional safeguards.

In June 2012, collective efforts finally bore fruit: the New York State Legislature passed the "I-STOP" bill.

This new law required the use of electronic, not paper, prescriptions and mandated physicians to check a patient's controlled-substance history before prescribing Schedule II, III, or IV substances. The law also elevated hydrocodone from Schedule III to Schedule II. We could understand why physicians might have mixed reactions to the law, perceiving an invasion of their discretion and an additional demand on their time, but saving lives took priority.

MAY 8, 2014: DAY 50 OF TRIAL

Where Dr. Li and Dr. Weingarten sought to limit the physician's responsibility, Dr. Gharibo sought it out and set it out, front and center. Both the decision to prescribe and the choice of medication belonged to the doctor; both were the doctor's responsibility. A doctor could refuse to prescribe—or continue prescribing—opioids to a patient, even over a patient's request to continue.

In fact, Dr. Gharibo emphasized the physician's responsibility for the choice of therapies and evaluations of the patient's environment over the patient's "trustworthy" or "untrustworthy" character. If a history of substance abuse was significant to Dr. Gharibo, it was because it indicated an increased risk for loss of control: opioid analgesics already were potent enough to cause uncontrolled behavior in patients who had never suffered from addiction. Their psychoactive qualities—the "excitatory" feeling on the upside, with the withdrawal as the levels of medication in the blood dropped—could make a patient with a history of substance abuse more inclined to reach for more. Loss of control over one's own consumption of the medication was a risk, as well as loss of control over the medication itself. "[F]irst and foremost," Dr. Gharibo testified, "the medication needs to be secure. It can't just be left out. It's like money, so to speak. You can't just leave it all over the place. People will take it. So you have to get a sense from the patient that they're in a secure environment."

It was the physician's responsibility to know how well a patient would secure their medication, "[b]ecause patients can abuse it and die. I think clearly it is a major issue in the United States over the last five to ten years or so. Other individuals get ahold of it. They either abuse it, misuse it themselves, or just sell it."

I challenged Dr. Gharibo with my next question, echoing a theme from Dr. Li's testimony: "But that's their choice, right? Why is that your concern as the prescriber?"

"It is absolutely my concern. It is important that I keep in mind the environment of the patient that the patient is in. You don't want to pre-scribe into an environment that feeds other people's addiction, other people's misuse, and puts everything around the patient at risk of mor-bidity as well as death. And it is illegal as well to knowingly prescribe to somebody who's diverting."

Even routine appointments, according to Dr. Gharibo, were oppor-tunities to gather information and adjust course. "If you make a deci-sion initially to prescribe opioids for a patient," I asked Dr. Gharibo, "do you have to reevaluate that decision?"

"Yes."

"Under what circumstances would you reevaluate it?"

"Each follow-up visit is really a reevaluation," answered Dr. Ghar-ibo, "that they are, whether they're compliant with the medication, whether if they're functionally benefiting from the medication, and there is a clinical benefit that gives them, ultimately translates into them getting their life back. And it is a screening process that checks for good efficacy, good benefit, and also checks into any irregularities that may occur as a result of the opioid as well."

What was the appropriate medical response, I asked, if a doctor finds that a patient has been noncompliant?

"If it happens, let's say, sporadically here and there," Dr. Gharibo answered, "and the patient has been with you and is compliant with other elements of the pain medication plan, then it's something that you educate the patient on and you, you accept some degree of latitude, but there comes a point if it becomes regular, if it's just something where the dosing is being driven up due to lack of compliance where you are picking up, you are not picking up improvement of function and instead you're picking up loss of control, compulsive, impulsive behavior without physical benefits to the patient and lifestyle benefits to the patient, so you pick that up as early as you can so that you can intervene and maximize safety for your patients.

"Our responsibility," he told the jury, "is like flying: safety first."

Safety required screening; safety required watchfulness; safety required verification; safety required appropriate responses to red flags. Safety required knowledge and care.

Dr. Li and Dr. Weingarten ignored inconvenient facts; Dr. Gharibo learned from them. For instance: Yes, patients sometimes lied. Patients, however, didn't lie to get more injections. Patients didn't lie to get more Advil. Patients didn't lie to get more physical therapy. Rather, they lied sometimes in order to obtain more opioids or more controlled substances. Dr. Gharibo knew the warning signs.

Whatever Dr. Li hadn't learned during his fellowship, Dr. Gharibo implied, he should have learned from experience. Dr. Li's clinical practice should have opened his eyes. In Dr. Gharibo's opinion, the warnings and red flags in Dr. Li's practice were monumental and overwhelming. They should have caused Dr. Li to reevaluate everything he thought he knew. Dr. Gharibo, as a result, took issue with Dr. Li's actions as well as his inaction.

Dawn Tamasi? "There is a highly disproportionate, outrageously excessive controlled-substance plan here that is virtually dosed to terminate somebody," Dr. Gharibo testified. "[T]his is also being given at the same time where there are huge warning signs to the physician that there is something profoundly wrong here with this patient and their controlled-substance addiction and misuse and abuse. And [m]any of these warning signs that [sic] are present in the record and yet [the] very disproportionate and excessive controlled-substance prescription plan is adhered to with almost nothing to mitigate it."

After receiving the letters from the family, which constituted "grave warning signs," Dr. Gharibo testified, a pain management specialist *could have no reasonable expectation* that the patient would take her medication as prescribed. The reasonable medical response would be "converting the patient to non-opioid substances that are not controlled, or at least at the minimum changing the controlled-substance regimen to a simpler regimen that is more of a steady state, cutting down on the number of pills and on the number of units that the patient is getting, talking to the patient about a rehabilitation program, starting a taper, starting non-opioids, and seeing them more frequently, and getting a mental health specialist involved."

What about Kevin Kingsley? In December 2007, Dr. Li received a letter from the New York State Department of Health, alerting him that Kevin had obtained controlled-substance prescriptions from multiple prescribers. "Well, this raises a very significant red flag," opined Dr. Gharibo, "in that I would consider certainly changing the regimen, not prescribing what I had been prescribing, and simplify the controlled substances, or maybe even consider cutting it out altogether." The warning signs in Dr. Li's practice, Dr. Gharibo testified, were unusual in their frequency and gravity. In his own practice, Dr. Gharibo testified, he conducted urine tests and checked prescription databases and detected "irregularity" only "five to twenty-five percent of the time."

"There may have been one case," he said, where he was notified that one of his patients had been treated in an emergency room for an overdose. Dr. Gharibo's definition of "overdose" also was broad, encompassing incidents that did not place a patient's life at risk and unfolding over a range. "The common feedback that I get from patients that indicate[s] an overdose is somebody having difficulty waking up in the morning or having difficulty maintaining their balance and getting around, and sometimes even falling, for example, as a probable side effect of the opiates that I am prescribing. There's a range of overdoses. That's on the lower end of the overdose range. The other end of the overdose range is respiratory depression and death and everything in between."

He had never received calls or letters or visits from family members asking him to stop prescribing controlled substances to a patient. Even as the Medical Director of Pain Medicine at NYU Hospital for Joint Diseases, a position that required him to review other doctors' cases, that was an "uncommon" occurrence, coming up "once a year to every couple of years." What would be the visible symptoms of a state of overdose? "Somebody being unsteady. Somebody being drowsy. Having very small pupils. Difficulty to arouse somebody. Sleeping too long. Another visible angle is somebody is gradually losing energy. Progressively they do less and less. There's a very insidious progressive development. It could be gradual progression, inactivity. So, somebody being very somnolent or drowsy or very difficult to arouse."

For his group of ten physicians, over a time period of approximately ten to fifteen years, Dr. Gharibo could think of only a "couple" of instances where patients received ER treatment for opioid overdoses. He was not aware of any instances of fatal overdoses; nevertheless, it was a risk that was of great concern to him.

Our responsibility is like flying. Safety first. In flying, however, the primary purpose is not safety but transportation. Similarly, the physician has a mission and purpose in treating a patient. While safety is a threshold issue, *the physician is failing in their essential mission and purpose* if they do not investigate the source of the patients' pain and develop a plan to address it, taking advantage of every possible channel for influence on the body.

And this was the clincher, the bottom line, the underlying radical difference between the defense's view of pain medicine and Dr. Gharibo's vision of the specialty: Dr. Gharibo did not believe it was his job to just prescribe medication, let alone a particular class of medication. Dr. Gharibo did not make more money if he prescribed more medication. The medication—all medication—was a tool. One of many.

He was not a warm and fuzzy witness. He was a fast-talking, sometimes combative witness, who charged a lot of money for his work. We paid Dr. Gharibo for his testimony. We brought this out on direct examination, but of course the defense was right to make the most of this significant sum of money: we paid Dr. Gharibo four hundred dollars per hour for the review of patient files and preparation of reports (fifty dollars more per hour than the defense paid Dr. Weingarten), and a daily flat fee of four thousand dollars for testimony (compared to thirty-five hundred dollars per day for Dr. Weingarten), for a total amounting to almost forty thousand dollars.

In addition to his salary and his consultancy fee, Dr. Gharibo also received payments and benefits from his work on behalf of pharmaceutical companies. In 2014 Dr. Gharibo had received fees, food, lodging, and other benefits valued at $107,966 from eight pharmaceutical companies, including over fifty thousand dollars' worth in connection with the promotion of Zohydro ER, a hydrocodone product.[11]

Yet Dr. Gharibo also treated Medicare patients and honored their benefits. He didn't just record his patients' complaints but investigated them. And if there was one thing that scared Dr. Gharibo, it was hurting his patients.

Perhaps, in Belair's view, Dr. Gharibo did no more than peddle another dangerous fiction—an idealized fancy New York City hospital brand of medicine that discriminated against doctors and patients of lesser means. Belair would have been right to the extent that Dr. Gharibo would stop at nothing in his efforts to reach the right diagnosis and the right treatment. Rather than just papering over—and perhaps aggravating—a mysterious, lingering, and maladaptive pain, Dr. Gharibo was ready to dig into it to give his patients back their lives.

For me, that was the portrait of a caring physician.

CHAPTER 12

Fireworks

SHE DID WHAT AT WORK?
23 SWEET & SEXY MOVES!
BEAUTY UNDER $10
THE CRAZY LIE I TOLD TO GET A BOYFRIEND
BEST SPRING EVER!
XOXO,
COSMO

—COSMOPOLITAN, MAY 2013 COVER

JANUARY 1, 2013: 443 DAYS UNTIL TRIAL

On a bright California morning on the first day of a new year, I sat at a long wooden table in a dining hall in Big Sur, California. Sunlight streamed in through windows streaked with salt spray. The beautiful deep blue Pacific Ocean ran all the way across our horizon and, once in a while, people whooped and cheered as whales breached the surface.

I recognized two women from my meditation group. I couldn't remember their names, but I remembered that they hadn't said anything bizarre during our sessions—so far. In fact, I think I had caught one of them rolling her eyes at the guy who'd praised his own "sexual flow" during our round-robin group introductions. I sat down and smiled awkwardly. They smiled back.

Our meditation instructor wore flowing white robes, crunched on persimmons like apples, and taught us the difference between a thought and a sensation. There was a narrator in my head, apparently, trying to make sense of my life, but it was telling a false story based on evidence so flimsy and biased that I never would credit it outside my own head. Meditation was not medicine, but it was a new and useful tool, allowing me to discern between fantasies of life and a tangible, current reality.

My new friends were warm, funny, a bit cynical, and also a bit broken, also finding new ways forward every day. We'd all come into the room with judgments and preconceptions about ourselves and one another. Staying in the room day after day, we found ourselves mistaken, surprised, understood, encouraged.

On one of the last days of the retreat and one of the first days of 2013, I sat cross-legged in front of a lanky blue-eyed Irishman, who popped in and out of the sessions according to his whim. The exercise was unbearable: to look into your partner's eyes without speaking for twenty long minutes, thinking first of what they may have looked like as a child, what they may have experienced in joys and disappointments, wishing them well, and allowing your mind to roam into their future. We were allowed to share one observation with our partner at the end of the meditation. I can't remember what I observed, because my partner said something so absurd that it left me a bit dazed and laughing.

"I saw a baby." He pointed to my belly. "You were carrying a baby." I didn't want anything to do with men ever again and I had two wonderful children already. I was all set; I was a "finished person," just not a very good one! Also, lest we forget, I was in my *late thirties*.

In the moment, it was easy to laugh him off. In the moment, I reasoned that he was trying to make me feel better, using the image of a baby as shorthand for something I clearly needed: a future. He didn't realize that he'd done so much for me already: my meditation partner, this unknown man, had just spent a long twenty minutes looking at me, eye to eye, without distractions, without words, without any exchange of any items of value, with just time and attention, *considering* my life. When does that ever happen?

MAY 15, 2014: DAY 57 OF TRIAL

Adrian Cruise didn't want to be in court. I'm sure the jury could tell. Still, he showed up and pushed through. He was wearing a crisp striped shirt with a smart tie and he was all business, describing a relationship with Dr. Li like you would imagine he would describe a series of transactions at work.

"It was very brief," Cruise explained. "I walked into the office and it was, it was rather quiet at this time. There was maybe a few patients there and I only, you know, had to wait a few minutes and then I was able to see the doctor. So, I was called into one of the rooms in his practice and he asked me why I was there and I was very forward in saying that I'm getting medicine, I'm getting Norco and Vicodin from some of my friends, and I was hoping you could help me get them (in my mind) legitimately. And he had no problem with that."

"What happened?" Peter asked.

"So, he asked if there was a specific medication. I said I was looking for Norco, and I believe I asked how much the visit would be. It was, again, it was a very brief visit. We talked very briefly about, again, it was more just really, why are you here. I asked about, if he could provide me with Norco."

There was no physical examination, Cruise insisted. Dr. Li did not check Cruise's blood pressure, pulse, heart, or lungs. Cruise paid either one or two hundred dollars (he could not remember how much) and obtained the prescription he wanted. So he went back. Again and again.

He went back every three weeks, even though he knew he was supposed to wait longer. It wasn't a problem with Dr. Li at first. In 2010, it became a problem. Cruise noticed that the practice had grown "dramatically" and Dr. Li was starting to become "more detailed," to "question why" Cruise wanted the medication.

"I mentioned to Dr. Li that I was running out of medicine," Cruise said. "[. . .] I was running out of the medicine and taking more than he was prescribing and I was having withdrawal and so, he mentioned that there is another medicine that can help with withdrawal and so, that became, that was one of the worst decisions I made, to take both, because it allowed me to start using a lot more and functioning because I had a way to withdraw with this other medicine and be able to function and work."

Cruise was talking about Suboxone. I couldn't believe that, even after all these years, he presented that decision as a failure of his judgment, rather than a criticism of the other guy in the room, *the doctor.* Over time, Cruise explained, he relied on Suboxone not because he wanted to stop using oxycodone, but because it allowed him to use more. A lot more.

"Dr. Li would say to me," Cruise explained, "that he was writing me prescriptions that, one was for pain and one was for withdrawal. He was writing [. . .] me prescriptions for OxyContin and he was writing me prescriptions for Suboxone or Subutex, and he would say to me specifically, if anyone was to ever look at this it wouldn't make sense why I am writing both prescriptions for you, and he would specifically say, you know, [. . .] he would ask me for a reason that he could put down of why I was either in pain or why I needed such medicine and it was at that time that I started to talk about my carpal tunnel and other ailments."

The carpal tunnel that, as Cruise had just testified, caused him little pain.

"And how would you manage that?" Peter asked from the lectern during the direct examination. "When you received a prescription, both the Suboxone and for an opioid, how would you manage the two of them?"

"I would either take the opiates during the week and while I was at work and either on the weekend try to—or I would on the weekend use the Suboxone, the Subutex to help me come off without as much withdrawal, or I would take all of the medicine as long as it lasted me, you know, multiple days in a row until I ran out of the medicine and then again used the Suboxone or Subutex to help with the—at that point it became very severe withdrawals."

Cruise later described the feelings of withdrawal as "nauseous, tired, chills, body pains, body aches."

This was, of course, the predictable risk and result of Dr. Li's prescriptions. Buprenorphine knocks the opioids out of the body's receptors but cannot match their full stimulation. It's a "mismatch," as Dr. Campopiano had described it, during her testimony about Dr. Li's training and licensing in buprenorphine treatment. Buprenorphine's partial stimulation of the receptors can launch the patient into withdrawal, "[. . .] so you are taught carefully how to make sure you are not going to do that to someone," Dr. Campopiano had explained. The partial stimulation also creates a higher risk of accidental overdose if the patient "go[es] back to taking a regular opioid [. . .]."

"Now, if you recall," Peter asked during his direct examination of Adrian Cruise, "what opiate was he prescribing to you along with the Subutex or Suboxone?"

"So, various. There was a time where he would write me for oxycodone, thirty milligrams, sixty milligrams; OxyContin, eighty milligrams . . . I believe it was thirty milligrams Roxicodone, but various opiates in various strengths. There were times I would ask for different strengths and different quantities because I knew that if, and actually that if I was to go to a pharmacy with the exact same prescription early they wouldn't fill it."

"So, what did you do?"

"So, I would ask Dr. Li, so instead of two sixty-milligram OxyContins I would ask for three forty-milligram or four thirty-milligram to get the same strength and then I would also ask him ultimately to increase it so I could get, you know, more strengths."

The dosages changed over time, usually increasing. The fees changed over time, usually increasing.

"As I can recall," Cruise testified, "I paid two hundred dollars and there were many times I would go early or ask for different medication. He would sometimes have a slight objection and I would offer additional money and he would accept that and ultimately write me prescriptions for that."

"What is as best you can recall the most you ever paid Dr. Li for a single visit?"

"I believe the most was five hundred."

Five hundred *dollars.* I thought back to my first Internet search for Dr. Li and how I had wondered whether anyone could be so cynical as to create an addiction in a patient and then profit from its cure. As it happened, that was not even the most cynical scenario I could have imagined—Dr. Li not only had created the addiction, but instead of offering the Suboxone as a treatment, he had allowed the patient to misuse Suboxone in order to extend and enable the opiate addiction. With Dr. Li's help, Cruise was taking advantage of the fact that Suboxone reduced his tolerance of oxycodone. He was using the Suboxone to get the most bang for his buck. Dr. Li, meanwhile, had applied his training in buprenorphine treatment and his federal license to prescribe buprenorphine to make matters worse for the patient and more profitable for himself.

The cross-examination was long and arduous. Belair hit hard on Cruise's credibility, painting him as a liar to the jury and baiting him by dragging out the questions. Cruise was an attentive but combative witness, at one point responding to Belair's question about a purported pain in his neck by saying that yes, in fact, he had a pain in his neck at that very moment. The judge was not amused. Belair then insisted that Cruise had complained of various ailments during his first visit with Dr. Li, pointing to notations on the initial physical examination form that might have given Dr. Li cover for the prescriptions. Cruise refused to acknowledge it. He may not have been thrilled to be

"Other than the Subutex or Suboxone and the oxyc
Contin and Norco, did Dr. Li prescribe any other medic

"Yes. He also prescribed me Ambien and Xanax."

It was a wonder this guy was alive. My seat at the pi
faced the witness stand. I couldn't believe he looked a
did, all shiny and alive and bumping with energy. He w
sential American dynamo and he'd been as driven in h
he was in his work. An addiction workaholic, doing mor
than anyone else, than even anyone might have thought
capable of handling. Ambien and Norco and oxycodone a
He'd ridden this roller coaster of addiction, abuse, cravi
drawal for years, structuring his prescriptions in direc
with Dr. Li like he might have structured financial produ
ents, taking the hits of success and failure directly, feelin
own body, taking the hits and making the deals.

The day ended before his testimony. The judge instru
come back the next morning. Cruise had plane tickets. H
He told the judge to strike his testimony, that he wouldn't
all if he had known. The judge ordered him to return. Cru
out—but reappeared the next morning, to our surprise and

There came a time, he told the jury, when Dr. Li refu
tinue prescribing both oxycodone and Suboxone. "[H]e sta
someone were to look at this, it wouldn't make any sense as
prescribing you both medicines at the same time."

"So what happened then?" Peter asked.

"So ultimately he had me choose."

"Which choice did you make?"

"I chose the opiates, the oxycodone."

"At that point did Dr. Li stop prescribing Suboxone to you

"Yes."

"Did he continue to prescribe opiates to you?"

"Yes."

Dr. Li never referred Cruise to substance abuse treatment.

in court, especially for a second day of testimony, but once there, he was determined to stand his ground. He told the truth, as embarrassing as it was, but he was not going to allow Belair to push him an inch further. They fought for hours. I wondered what was going through Cruise's mind: he knew he hadn't said or done the things that Dr. Li had recorded in this patient chart, but he couldn't explain the notes in Dr. Li's file.

Peter could have objected to the records during Belair's cross-examination, and I hadn't understood why he hadn't done so. I nudged him, passed notes—*that's not the right chart!!* Peter ignored me. When the judge asked if Peter had any questions for the witness on redirect and Peter stood up, I wondered whether my trial partner failed to perceive the risk of keeping this young man on the stand any longer.

I hated suspense. I wanted clarity and truth. It is an understatement to say that I did not have a lot of trial experience.

Peter projected another set of records onto the screen, asking the witness to confirm that they were in his name: they were. Peter asked the witness to confirm that certain notations on the chart shown by Belair were missing from this version: they were. Those notes were the ones the witness had fought about with Belair. Cruise looked confused. Peter could not—and would not—explain, but he wasn't there to make a case to Cruise. Peter was making a case to the jury.

MAY 2012: APPROXIMATELY 688 DAYS UNTIL TRIAL

Every piece of paper told a story.

Once we'd finished reviewing more than twelve hundred patient files, Joe and I combed through the search warrant materials from Dr. Li's home retrieved after his arrest: box after box of receipts, bundles of mail, sheaths of document drafts, home office documents . . . examining, questioning, sorting, wondering.

On a productive day in the spring of 2012, standing in the rays of light at the long end of the conference table, search warrant materials laid out in front of me in a specific order dictated by where they had been seized and by whom, dust particles suspended in the air all around me, I held a yellow folder with several Chinese characters on the cover. The folder opened into two pockets containing sheets of paper that looked like the ones in the patient files—some parts of the initial examination form, some lined sheets that the doctor tended to use for subsequent visit notes. There were handwritten notes from a young female patient, communicating her special requests with casual familiarity.

"*Dear Dr. Li,*" she wrote, "*I hope had you a great fourth of July lots of fireworks and parties. Unfortunately, I couldn't come today [. . .]. I was wondering, if you could give [my boyfriend] the two prescriptions of the Oxycodone Percocet (10 over 325) and Xanax one milligram to give me for my back pains because I am running low. I also read in the newspaper about the Tylenol in Percocet and Vicodin being dangerous on the liver. I was wondering if you could write me a prescription of either Roxicodone or Dilaudid to decrease the amount of Tylenol. [. . .] Thank you so much [. . .].*"

There also was a letter from the Office of Professional Medical Conduct, with a list of patient names. The names on the letter corresponded in part to the names on the sheets of paper in the folder. The young woman's name appeared on the list. But why would there be patient notes and files in his New Jersey home? I looked at the pages and flipped them over to confirm the presence of ink grooves and stains on the back. These were originals. But . . . why . . . what could this be? Oooh . . . maybe . . . wait . . .

I asked Joe to pull the patient charts for the same individuals and we compared the entries for the same dates, examining every sheet in the yellow folder. The forms in the "official" files had been rewritten, "improved"—*altered*. What we'd found in the yellow folder appeared to be the discarded originals.

Standing in the fifth-floor conference room with Joe on that bright, dusty day, holding the yellow folder and the altered files in our hands, we knew we'd finally experienced our first real break in the case: this was proof that Dr. Li knew that his patient files were insufficient or incriminating. We suspected it would take a lot of work to get the folder and its contents into evidentiary shape—and it did—but we'd never before shied away from a task just because it might be hard, and we certainly wouldn't stop now.

We obtained judicial permission to send copies of all these pages to the OPMC, and then asked the OPMC to make a comparison to Dr. Li's submission. Peter took the lead on this matter and the yellow folder made it onto the evidence cart. As the jury eventually learned from one of the OPMC's attorneys, who testified at trial, Dr. Li's submission to the agency had included the altered pages and omitted the handwritten notes. Nevertheless, Dr. Li also had signed the OPMC's certification form, affirming that all the records he'd sent were "complete, true, and exact copies" of the files he'd prepared and kept in the regular course of business. By doing so, not only had he committed the crime of Offering a False Instrument for Filing, but he'd also revealed consciousness of guilt.

MARCH 2013: APPROXIMATELY 355 DAYS UNTIL TRIAL

We were pushing into spring. I felt happy. Over salads in my office, I told one of my closest friends as much, adding that I was *done* with dating. I had recently signed up for a dating website and promptly canceled my subscription ("It's my first try at online dating," I wrote to their customer service department, "and I'm afraid I'm having major second thoughts. I'd like to cancel my membership altogether. Thank you— please confirm").

Please confirm that I don't need to put myself out there. Why should I? There was no need! I was so much better on my own. I didn't have to consult anyone about plans or decisions—other than my ex-husband about the kids, of course, and that was more than enough for me. Besides, nothing ever worked out, I said, before enumerating the faults of "all" men. My friend laughed and pointed out that I should not hold the entire gender responsible for the consequences of my own choices. "I saw John Saroff a few days ago," she added. "He's an adult. You should date him."

John Saroff? He was a former law school classmate, three years my junior, with twinkling eyes and a fantastic sense of humor. He'd always seemed too fun and too smart for me. He was also the guy from our law school class who knew everyone and drafted chipper letters requesting alumni donations: "How's the husband and family?" he had written to me once in a peppy fund-raising email in 2009. "Well, we are in the early stages of a wrenching divorce," I almost wrote back, before deciding not to respond at all.

He must be interested in younger women, I told my friend. And he must be still too smart for me, I thought. I was skeptical, but more significantly, I was intimidated.

My friend pushed back. I had just joined Facebook, so I looked him up with her peering over my shoulder. He was handsome, with the same twinkling eyes. In his latest photo, he held up a copy of *Cosmopolitan* magazine and mentioned an article he'd published. *Cosmo*? The bible of orgasms and dye jobs? That didn't make any sense, but I friended him anyway. He friended me back on the spot, with a nice message. I wrote back. And then, with my friend listening, comforting and berating me, I spiraled into anxiety.

A few days later, in a drugstore, I spotted the same issue of *Cosmopolitan* on the racks: "FRESH FLIRTY FUN," "23 SWEET & SEXY MOVES," "STUFF YOU THINK HE WANTS IN BED . . . *BUT REALLY DOESN'T*." I picked it up and flipped through . . . and there was John. Inside the "survival guide" for the "Young and Divorced" was John's article titled "It's Hard for Guys, Too." John Saroff had been divorced? John Saroff had been *married*? I had no idea.

The article was short, dense, and honest. He reflected on the failure of his first marriage and expressed hopes for another. "I want to be in a marriage," he wrote, "where the so-called hard conversations—those about life, love, money, and sex—aren't actually that hard to have, where there are safe spaces just to listen and talk. I want a marriage where both people make compromises, but not about our relationship or our happiness."

Oh.

Yes.

I sent John a note, complimenting him on the article. He wrote back. We set a brunch date for a Saturday in mid-April. Three days before brunch, I ran into him on the street. He was wearing a blue checked shirt, a puffy vest, dark jeans, and a big smile. His hair was short, stylish, and gray around the edges. He was funny. He was a fox.

The next day, I wrote an email to the two friends who had been urging me on: "I am not going to fall into negativity or insecurity. First, because I always tell the two of you not to be negative or insecure, and I am going to trust you that you will tell me when I look like shit or am being ridiculous. Second, because, in truth, I've had a really nice little feeling deep inside about this ever since I read his article, and it blew up into a slightly larger, even nicer feeling when I ran into him yesterday. Finally, because I will not allow [my past experiences] to beat the optimism and hopeless romanticism out of me. This is special, and so serendipitous. I don't care what happens. I am going to enjoy it. And I love you!"

"Just to avoid misunderstandings," one of my friends responded, ever the careful attorney, "I would not actually say 'you look like shit.' If I say that something you're wearing 'is not my favorite,' that means I don't like it."

On April 13, 2013, I met John for brunch. Optimism, intelligence, self-confidence, humor, active listening: what a strange and interesting man! When I left to pick up Nina from her dad's house to take her to a birthday party, I still didn't know how I felt, what I thought, whether this had been a date or whether we would see each other again. John knew I had two children, but did he realize what it would mean to date someone with a six-year-old and a nine-year-old, a custody schedule, and everything else that came with school-age kids (stomach flu, pink eye, end-of-year shows)? Most important, why give up my fragile peace? What if he rejected me—or us? How would I ever forgive myself for exposing my kids to more pain?

My fears and insecurities soon got the best of me. I attended a friend's birthday party that night and wrote to my friends again at midnight: "I feel old and in another phase of life. I don't know that I am up for this." Work was giving me plenty of challenges: I had no interest in challenging myself further in my personal life.

APRIL 21, 2014: DAY 33 OF TRIAL

Nearly three years after he'd pulled the sign off Dr. Li's reception window, Joe Hall read it out loud to the jury. It was titled "Self Pay Fee Schedule Update."

"'[S]elf pay for low complexity is still kept on one hundred dollars per visit,'" Joe Hall read. "'Criteria of low complexity include:

- Fully compliant with Narcotic Agreement
- One doctor, one pharmacy
- No early visit
- Less than three prescriptions written in one visit
- Less than 120 pills on one prescription.'"

High-complexity cases, the fee schedule indicated, "'will be increased to $150 per visit.

"'High complexity cases include but not limit to:

- Any non-compliant behavior with Narcotic Agreement
- Found to have more than one Doctor—one pharmacy. These patients must to stop receiving any narcotic prescription from other prescribers, and the fee will be increased to 150$ [sic] per visit thereafter.
- Get more than three prescriptions in one visit.
- More than 120 pills on one prescription.

- Early visit. The visit ahead of schedule will be charged 150$ [*sic*].
- The dosage of opioid is higher than 180 mg/day.
- Ask for replacement of lost or stolen medication or prescription.
- History of substance abuse, using illicit drugs, suicidal idea.'"

The sign had been posted on the reception window, Joe explained, in plain view of the patients coming in and those already in the waiting room.

It was a private medical office, but it was open to the public and subject to government oversight. The sign was visible; its terms were clear. It was no shocker to the clinic's regulars, because the sign simply formalized practices that had been in place for years in that weekend basement clinic: cash for prescriptions, with a penalty for drug abuse or wanting to kill yourself. Among all the patients who had visited that office and purchased prescriptions from Dr. Li, sixteen had ultimately died of overdoses, some within a few days, some within a month or a few months, others within a year of their last encounter with Dr. Li. All the facts were available: the sign was posted in the office; the prescription records were in a New York State government agency database; the death records were held by local medical examiners' offices; the families and patients, to the extent they were still alive, all lived locally; the local pharmacies saw Dr. Li's prescriptions with frequency and questioned his prescriptions but dispensed them anyway. Why and how had it taken so much and so long to stop him?

MAY 15, 2014: DAY 57 OF TRIAL

Dr. Li hadn't just submitted claims to Medicare: he also billed private health insurance companies for injections and high-complexity patient visits. With the Chief Medical Officer of a prominent private health insurance company on the stand, who personally had conducted chart reviews, including Dr. Li's, I asked (without showing Dr. Li's fee schedule) whether it was customary to calculate complexity based on the number of prescriptions.

"[C]omplexity," the witness answered, "is complexity of decision-making. Complexity in decision-making takes into account [. . .] if there is a diagnosis, how many different possibilities are being thought about by the doctor, if there is treatment, how many different possibilities are being thought about to treat, complexity takes into account how much information the doctor has to review, chart notes from other doctors, other tests, and takes into account the possible consequences, how likely it is the patient will die or get very sick. That's what determines complexity, not the number of prescriptions written."

The numbers of pills, apparently, didn't qualify as "complexity," either.

As for the practice of jotting down the amounts of cash Dr. Li had received from the patient in the margin of his charts, the Chief Medical Officer confessed that this was uncommon: "Doctors don't write dollar amounts in their charts."

This doctor, however, had done so. And he had done so for years. He had kept a running tally totaling half a million dollars in income. Dr. Li had exploited what was both the greatest strength and weakness in our system: trust.

"Now," I asked the Chief Medical Officer, "how does [your company] check if the information on the claim form submitted by doctors is accurate?"

The Chief Medical Officer answered without hesitation: "We don't."

"Why not?"

"Because the way the system works is that the doctors bill us, and we pay the claim. [You] can't imagine the volume of claims we get, and we have to pay them. We don't have time to stop and look and stop claims and look at them and ask for information. It is only in very unusual circumstances where we would request information, or sometimes for high-cost surgery the surgeons submit the operative report with the claim. Though, in general, we don't look at it."

"So how does [your company] have any assurance that the claims are accurate?"

The witness didn't hesitate. "We're dealing with doctors. We expect them to submit accurate claims."

JANUARY 17, 2014: 1,222 DAYS SINCE NICHOLAS RAPPOLD'S DEATH

The surgeon invited me to walk into the operating room with Charlie. This simple procedure—inserting ear tubes and removing adenoids—needed to be done under general anesthesia. We'd been waiting a long time, because the surgeries proceeded according to the age of the patients, from youngest to oldest. Charlie was hungry, scared, and tired. He'd been up since 5:00 a.m. and fasting since the night before. When the nurses asked him to lie down on the table, he didn't want to. He started crying when they put the mask on his face. In a few seconds, he went from crying to shuddering, loose limbed, limp—I scanned the surgical team's masked faces, could see nothing, and could see no indication that they were concerned. One perceptive nurse noticed my confusion. "That's just the anesthesia," she reassured me, as she escorted me out.

Our pre-procedure wait wouldn't have lasted so long if Charlie had been younger, meaning if my ex-husband and I hadn't waited so long to notice the problem, to agree that there *was* a problem, to diagnose it, and to agree on a solution, I thought. Most recently, he and I had even fought over the privilege of hosting Charlie's recovery. Still shaken from my completely routine yet terrifying minute in the operating room, I tried to throw off the anger. I should just be relieved to have obtained my ex's consent for the surgery, to know Charlie was in good hands, to have won the right to nurse my boy after the operation.

When they called us into the recovery room, Charlie was still asleep. We sat on either side of him and placed our hands on him—separately but both with love—to feel his warmth and offer him comfort. When Charlie was allowed to leave, I brought him back to my apartment, covering his ears all the way home because, after three years of muffled sounds, he could now *hear* the city and it was too loud.

Charlie's father was kind enough to pick up the doctor's prescriptions. I tucked Charlie into his bed, fed him obscene amounts of ice cream, and worked on a revised draft of a pretrial motion while he slept. My sweet boy.

It never occurred to me not to trust the doctors. They were the ones I trusted the most.

CHAPTER 13

The Kougasian Rule

Purdue should consider expansion across the pain and addiction spectrum. Pain treatment and addiction are naturally linked. [...] It is an attractive market. Large unmet need for vulnerable, underserved and stigmatized patient population suffering from substance abuse, dependence and addiction.

—PURDUE PHARMA INTERNAL PRESENTATION ON
PROJECT TANGO, A PROPOSAL TO EXPAND INTO OPIOID
ADDICTION TREATMENT, SEPTEMBER 10, 2014[1]

JUNE 23, 2014: DAY 96 OF TRIAL

It was time. Peter stood up and walked over to the lectern with his notes to begin the cross-examination of Dr. Li.

We'd rested our case on June 6. We'd survived Belair's motion for a trial order of dismissal. Dr. Li—who had no burden of proof and who could have chosen to remain silent—had taken the stand for direct examination on the afternoon of June 6. He'd testified on his own behalf for eight full days of trial over a span of two weeks.

Belair had taken him through every patient named in the indictment, every prescription, and even prescriptions written by other doctors, asking Dr. Li to expand on his knowledge and theories of pain
management and opioid therapy. Belair had avoided discussing certain
incidents—such as Alli Walton's last prescription on November 27,
2010, or the false insurance claim forms—but he had elicited Dr. Li's
best rationalizations: Dr. Li trusted his patients; the medications were
to be taken as prescribed; the patients did not seem overdosed while in
Dr. Li's office.

Dr. Li had grown comfortable on the stand under Belair's protective guidance. The muted clicks of the stenographer's machine, Belair's
slow, deep voice, Dr. Li's long answers, the slow ticking of time—it was
hypnotic. Once in a while, Belair bumped back into the piles of papers
he had heaped behind him, on the wooden divider separating the well
from the audience benches, and the papers went flying to the ground
with a whoosh. Other than those incidents, which brought everyone
back to life for a few minutes, the testimony pulled the entire courtroom into a focused trance. Even I was subdued, listening and every
so often handing notes to Peter. Peter, meanwhile, took copious notes,
consulting papers he'd pulled from his folders, circling and highlight-
ing with urgency.

When Peter began the cross-examination on June 23, 2014, he moved
and spoke with nervous energy. The jurors' eyes opened wide. Nobody
wanted to miss a single word. Only the clerks and court officers, immune
to drama by virtue of their years of experience, sat with placid—even
bored—expressions or went about their business, handling the important, invisible tasks that kept the criminal justice system afloat.

Peter had served as an ADA since 1979: thirty-five years. During his
rookie training, Peter had attended the lecture of a senior trial counsel,
Tom Demakis. At the end of the lecture, ADA Demakis listed his five
rules for cross-examination. "It felt like a veil being lifted from my
eyes," said Peter.

Rule One: Always lead.

On cross-examination, it was not only permissible to ask questions that suggested their own answer, but it was the best and only course. It was the difference between asking your own witness a question like "What did you see?" and forcing a cross-examination witness to make an admission, as in "You saw it, didn't you?"

Peter began with simple questions about the early years of Dr. Li's practice. His questions recalled Dr. Li's testimony about the contrast between his Chinese patients and the "pill" patients. The questions called for yes or no answers. He was asking for confirmation, not information. The questions weren't dramatic. They didn't have punch lines. Peter's tone was easy—but he was building, always building. At first, the structure was invisible. And then, after thirty or so questions, it took form.

APRIL 25, 2013: 329 DAYS UNTIL TRIAL

At 7:30 p.m., I met John for dinner. The seam of my dress had unraveled earlier in the day, so I was holding it together with office tape.

At 10:33 p.m., my friends emailed me, asking for a status update.

At 12:36 a.m., I responded: "Heading home. It was a date."

In the interim, two things had happened. First, before we'd even ordered dinner, with the clarity and systematic approach befitting a Columbia Law School graduate, John asked me a threshold question: "Would you consider having another child?" He wanted children, he explained, and if it was not something that I would consider then perhaps it would be better for us to remain friends. I was stunned: I was thirty-eight years old; Nina was nine; Charlie was six; they were everything and enough for me. And this was our first date. And no one had ever spoken to me so clearly about what they wanted or asked so clearly what I wanted. I ran a gut check and decided that I did not feel a hard no, so I said, "I would consider it."

Next, we proceeded to order, talk about everything under the sun, eat, leave the restaurant, pause on a street corner, turn toward each other, and kiss. We spent the next few hours doing more of the same over drinks and a gigantic chocolate chip cookie in a bar until it was after midnight and time to go home.

Suddenly, I had a boyfriend. Impostor syndrome set in again, but Buddy LaSala and Jon Courtney, my confidants, weren't having it: Life was life at every and any age, they admonished me. And he treated me right, they said.

It was true. When I talked to him about work, his answer was simple and surprising, a welcome counterpoint to all the voices telling me to relax: "Your anticipatory anxiety makes you better at your job. Keep going. Work hard. I'm proud of you."

JUNE 23, 2014: DAY 96 OF TRIAL

Rule Two of cross-examination: Get the defendant to confirm important parts of the People's case.

"Dr. Li," Peter asked, "you also noticed that as your patient population changed from the 'pain population' to what you call the 'suffering population' you developed many, many more patients; is that correct?"

Yes, Dr. Li conceded.

A lot more, in fact, Peter insisted.

Yes, said Dr. Li.

Peter followed up with questions about payments and we saw the path lighting up ahead, from the number of patients, to the fees, to the bank deposits, to Dr. Li's claim that he wasn't in it for the money. When Dr. Li dodged, Peter said "Thank you" to the irrelevant response and retreaded the same ground, but this time with documents to prove his point and elicit the unavoidable admissions.

There was a flow to the cross-examination that wasn't just about the rhythm or the control but also about the sheer volume of questions: the first few lines of questioning were rivulets, but as the minutes and hours passed, the material proved expansive, the current gained force. We all became aware that a river was flowing through and would not abate for some time. At the end of Dr. Li's direct examination, Peter had told me just one thing: he now knew that Dr. Li was lying. Gone was the Peter of yore, who mused about the possible humanitarian motives, who questioned whether it was appropriate for our office to pursue criminal prosecution. The deeper he went with his cross-examination, the more apparent it became that Peter was infused with the facts and a strong sense of mission. His bearing was straight and solid and full of vitality despite the fact that he had lost twenty pounds and needed to cinch his belt tightly. His expression had grown serious and determined. His decades of experience as an attorney and homicide prosecutor translated into gravitas and an impression of impermeability. He dispatched objections and interruptions with minimal acknowledgments, with politeness, without emotion, and without losing his grip on the courtroom, the witness, or the truth. It was Peter's job, now, to demonstrate to the jury, through questions and answers that made up cross-examination, that Dr. Li was a liar, that Dr. Li had been aware of every risk, that Dr. Li had consciously disregarded every risk, that in certain instances Dr. Li had even acted with depraved indifference.

Did Dr. Li understand what he was up against? Did Dr. Li understand how much Peter and I had wondered about his motives and intentions and knowledge? Did Dr. Li understand for how long we had afforded him the benefit of the doubt and what it had taken to turn us around? Had Dr. Li realized, in the early years of his practice in Queens, that his actions mattered? That he had been setting a course for this moment, for this confrontation?

Peter had no patience for Dr. Li's attempts to delay or digress. "Now," he said, after a tense and unproductive exchange, "when you're prepared to answer my question, Dr. Li, please let me know."

The courtroom fell silent. Dr. Li clenched his jaw. "Yeah," he said.

"Are you prepared?" Peter checked again.

"Yes."

And they moved on.

Some questions revealed hours of preparation. I learned about a few "secret" projects that Peter had been working on, which he had been teasing over the last few days. One such project related to the patient lists. Dr. Li denied that they reflected the number of patients he had seen—the lists were just for registration, he insisted. They didn't mean anything and should not be taken literally.

Rule Three: Have the defendant deny established evidence in the case.

"So, Dr. Li," Peter asked, "there would be one way to tell for sure if you saw one hundred and one patients on January 8, 2011, and that will be to—if you can somehow check every one of your files and see if you made a dated entry for each of those patients; is that correct?"

Dr. Li agreed, unruffled.

Peter swung around and grabbed a large black binder from our table. "All right," he said, "I would like this binder marked People's Exhibit number Two Thirty-Seven for purposes of identification."

"Sustained!" snapped the judge.

"Objection!" bellowed Belair.

"Sustained!" repeated the judge. "Move on!"

Peter thanked the judge and moved on as though nothing had happened, no problem, tossing away a binder that must have represented hours of work. Nothing came into evidence without the judge's careful vetting, especially if it represented any compilation of evidence that carried a whiff of argumentation.

As Peter continued to drill Dr. Li, binders and folders full of papers covered the desk, just as they did in his office, rising into layers and shifting into waves as he grabbed, used, and replaced various piles. Wherever he was, Peter was true to himself, just bringing his whole being and style without hesitation. How did it feel to just be yourself all the time, I wondered, without worrying about the perception of others? I always had hated his mess, but I'd come to envy his freedom to be messy.*

---

* During the summer of 2019, I read a draft of this book aloud to Peter, who had been hospitalized and confined to bed for several months already. Peter's face buckled with pain when he heard this line. Seeing his expression, I thought about cutting the

OCTOBER 6, 2013: 165 DAYS UNTIL TRIAL

John and I had devised a foolproof plan: frozen yogurt, followed by *Cloudy with a Chance of Meatballs*. The children and I would meet John at 16 Handles, there would be a few minutes of chitchat over a snack, and then we would proceed to the movie theater. Kid-friendly venues, limited conversation time, newly released animated movie . . . what could go wrong?

We had waited six months to introduce John to the children. I did not want to use them as a dating accessory and I was terrified of forcing them onto another unnecessary emotional roller coaster. Of course, it was important to me to know their opinion of him and to be sure that they could all get along, but I did not want to put any pressure on the kids to make the adult decision of selecting my mate. By October 2013, John and I knew we were serious about each other. It was time.

Of course, I had a pit in my stomach as the children and I walked up Second Avenue. I was nervous; they were nervous; John was nervous. I was the person they had in common, so I felt responsible for everyone's good time and positive bonding. John was sitting on a bench outside the frozen yogurt parlor. He'd been a camp counselor for years, he'd assured me before the encounter: he knew how to talk to kids.

Nina and Charlie knew John was my boyfriend. On the advice of a child psychologist, I had mentioned that I was dating someone a few weeks earlier; a few days before the meeting, I followed up with a scripted preview and some disclaimers. "You don't have to like him," I said. "I like him, but that doesn't mean you have to. Maybe you will; maybe you won't. Whatever you feel, it's okay, and it may or may not change with time. I just want him to meet you now because you two are the most important people in my life."

I watched the three of them as they put together their frozen yogurt sundaes. Was John judging my parenting as I made rulings on the kids'

---

sentence from the book, but that was the truth at the time—and all of us who ever had teased him about his messy office now would give anything to allow him that freedom again.

requests for toppings? Did the kids think John looked too young for me? Was he too young for me?

We sat down. John made conversational overtures. Charlie, age seven, was quiet. He ate his treat and swept his big brown eyes from John's face to Nina's as they started talking. Nina spoke earnestly, her little glasses sliding down her nose, her spoon poking at the stuff floating in her frozen yogurt.

Okay, I thought. Okay. I tried to relax.

I didn't catch the words, but just as I was indulging in the mental fantasy that this was turning out to be easy, there was a sort of glitch, like a record scratching. I saw Nina's confused face and heard John's edgy tone. What were they talking about? Had he disagreed with her about something? What? Why? Why? My protective instincts reared up. I moved us along to Phase Two. Time for the movie.

At the movie theater, I sat between Nina and Charlie; John sat beside Charlie, the farthest inside the row. When the movie was over, John walked us all back to the apartment. I had just hosted Nina's tenth birthday party, a sleepover for ten friends complete with a rented karaoke machine. We still had a couple of hours left on our rental, so we fired it up and John proposed to sing a duet with Nina in honor of her birthday. "Moves like Jagger" must have been next in the girls' sleepover queue. The song came on, but he didn't know the words, and neither did I. When the chorus lyrics appeared on the screen, John looked at me in a state of amused panic: "Kiss me till you're drunk, and I'll show you all the moves like Jagger, I've got the moves like Jagger." If he stopped singing, it would draw attention to the awkwardness; if he kept singing, it would get even more awkward. . . .

My ten-year-old daughter pretended he wasn't there and just sang, bouncing around with the microphone, either oblivious or diplomatic. John made light of it, putting on a silly voice and changing the words. I just wanted it to be over—all of it. My comfort zone, if there ever had been one, was exploding.

JUNE 23, 2014: DAY 96 OF TRIAL

The first morning of cross-examination electrified Peter: he moved and spoke with a robust, lively energy.

Dr. Li seethed.

It was time for Rule Four: Break down conclusions.

Peter asked about specific patients, starting with Michael Cornetta: no frontal attacks, just a tireless enumeration, entry by entry, fact by fact. Boring. Non-controversial. Yet with each short answer Peter had formed a damning chain demonstrating all the occasions and ways that Cornetta had demonstrated a risk of abuse and overdose to Dr. Li.

Dr. Li conceded the early visits, the notification from Dr. Hovanesian, the alerts from the New York State Department of Health, the CSI reports indicating Cornetta's multi-sourcing, but refused to acknowledge the import or relevance of any of those facts to his "treatment" of Cornetta or the changes in Cornetta's appearance. The Department of Health had alerted him to Cornetta's history of suicidal ideation? Yes, Dr. Li admitted, but Cornetta had never said to Dr. Li that he wanted to die. A suicide attempt had involved opiates? Yes, but that was only in Cornetta's medical history and on the day Dr. Li saw him after that incident Cornetta was "fine," the doctor claimed. So, Dr. Li, Peter confirmed, you prescribed the same medication that you had prescribed before the attempted suicide, was that right? That was right. It didn't matter that Dr. Li didn't agree with him. Dr. Li had to concede the facts, stripped of the meaning he'd tried to attribute to them. It would be up to the jury to draw their own conclusions.

And then there it was, simple as could be, a straight shot question to which Peter knew he would not receive a truthful answer, but it didn't even matter anymore:

"Dr. Li, you did that because you had a reckless disregard for the life of that patient; isn't that true, sir?"

Dr. Li only cared about the money and not getting caught; that was the message. That was the overarching theme and purpose of the cross-examination. Peter didn't need to go on for eight days or cover every patient: he picked the most telling illustrations and mined them.

Rule Five: Isolate those parts of the defendant's story that are implausible and untruthful.

On the altered OPMC files, Dr. Li maintained that he was just "completing the chart," like in the hospital. Peter cornered him, ever so patiently, on the fact that the blood pressure readings were inserted months and years after the patient visits and listened to the answers to draw out more admissions, more absurdities.

"You made up that number," Peter asked, referring to a patient's blood pressure entry, "is that correct?"

"Yes."

"And so, when you certified that those records were complete and accurate and made at the time that they [were] recorded, you knew that statement was not true; is that correct, Dr. Li?"

"It's true," Dr. Li insisted, clinging to a fiction.

"That's true to you, Dr. Li?"

Dr. Li explained that since he recalled that the patient's blood pressure had been normal, pulse had been normal, and respiration had been normal at the time of the patient visit—assuming he had, in fact, measured vital signs—he had been justified in selecting numbers within the normal ranges to fill in those fields. Completing the chart, just like in the hospital.

"When you were in the hospital, Dr. Li," Peter challenged him, "you made up blood pressures, too?"

Dr. Li knew there would be questions about the altered files if he took the stand. He knew that we knew about Joseph Haeg's patient chart. When Peter moved into that territory, Dr. Li's body tensed. He had a choice before him: how to answer these questions.

"Now, Dr. Li," Peter asked, "the last time you saw the patient was December 26, 2009; is that correct?"

"Yes."

"And three days later, you received a phone call from a man named David [Reed]; is that correct?"

"Yes."

"He was from the medical examiner's office, wasn't he?"

"Yes."

"He told you that your patient, Mr. Haeg, had died; is that correct?"

"Yes," Dr. Li said. There was still time.

"And he asked you to fax to him your patient file; is that correct?"

"Yes."

"And you did fax your patient file to him; is that correct?"

"Yes."

Peter raised his voice. "But before you faxed your patient file, you made some alteration; is that correct?" Dr. Li could still come clean. There was still time—not to save Haeg, but maybe to start saving himself.

"I don't remember," said Dr. Li, set and stubborn.

"Dr. Li," Peter admonished him, "you don't remember taking your patient file out and altering it before you sent it to the medical examiner's office?"

The blush emerging from Dr. Li's neck, under his collar, spread to his face. He looked like he was holding his breath and throwing the words out when he no longer could hold them in. "Not altered," Dr. Li blurted out, "just completing the chart." He'd made his choice. It was his boldest, baldest lie. "We do [it] all the time in the hospital," he insisted.

Peter demonstrated the extent of the changes. Standing alone, some of the "improvements" to the chart might have been defensible, even understandable. Taken together, especially with the certification of authenticity, they revealed Dr. Li's awareness of the deficiencies of his practice. It was a practice where none of the routine paperwork mattered, where Dr. Li cut corners on his physical examinations, and where the threat of oversight prompted concealment.

OCTOBER 13, 2013: 158 DAYS UNTIL TRIAL

John and I stood in my kitchen. I pretended to be putting away dishes but soon ran out of fake things to do. I was scared and angry and disappointed and sad and ambivalent but wouldn't say it and couldn't escape this conversation we were about to have.

Over the past week, since John had first met the kids, I had retreated from our relationship. I spent more time alone in my apartment, looking around at the quiet, empty space, thinking about how it would feel to let someone else in, with all of their computer cables and baseball almanacs. It had been more than four years since my ex-husband had moved out, and my home was settled, peaceful. It was arranged in a way that suited me. I didn't have to ask anybody else's permission to make changes or make any concessions. I reflected on my freedom to make decisions for myself and the children without mediating them through yet another stakeholder. Despite our best intentions and his years as a camp counselor, John's first encounter with the kids had been tense for everyone. Was I blaming him unfairly? Was it my fault? Was I not meant to be in a relationship? Was I better off just keeping things simple for me and the children? I didn't have a decision—but what I wanted, in the meantime, was to be left alone.

There also was a familiar pattern: every incident presented a binary choice of staying or going. I usually went. I'd done it in high school and in college when I cared too much and feared pain. I'd also been left my fair share of times and spent my entire childhood moving around, changing schools and changing homes. Saying good-bye (or rather, leaving without saying good-bye) was what I did best—except that all those separations and departures still hurt and made me cling to any possibility of stability and peace. But where did peace lie? And then there was the confusing data point of my marriage: I couldn't have stayed, but leaving meant that I had lost time with my children and complicated their lives. How could I trust myself to make any decision if I was doubting some choices but not others, accepting certain consequences but not others? Wasn't it just simpler not to try anymore?

John had noticed the growing distance between us. He'd asked if he could come over on Sunday afternoon.

He watched me bustle around for a few minutes, then got right to it.

"Either one of us can decide to end this relationship, unilaterally, at any point," he said. "And that's the way it is. I think we're really good together. I think we can build a wonderful family for ourselves, Nina and Charlie, and another child if we want to have one. If that's not what you want, that's fine, but I wish you would talk to me and give us a chance to understand what is happening. If you don't want to do that, and it's over, that's your choice. There is one thing you need to know: if we break up, that's it, because I don't believe in getting back together."

Of course, I had known it was a possibility that he might break up with me, but to hear it spoken aloud in that moment brought something to the surface: fear. Introducing John to the children and moving toward a future together as a family meant that I trusted him with my children's hearts as well as my own. It opened me up to the possibility of hurt, disappointment, messiness, and pain. I didn't want any of that anymore, ever again. I wanted safety, stability, predictability, and love. I was able to push out some words to that effect.

I was shocked, also, by the fact that John had been direct, clear, honest: I couldn't remember the last time I'd been able to have such a straightforward conversation. We talked, standing in my kitchen, about his first meeting with the kids, my concerns about my autonomy, and his belief that a loving, responsible couple could forge a better life together for the kids, even given a bit of messiness . . . or a lot.

The conversation didn't settle the question. John had presented me with a stark choice, requiring thoughtful consideration: "if we break up, that's it, because I don't believe in getting back together." If the consequences were clear and final, there'd be no letting myself off the hook, no second-guessing. Do I want to lose him forever *now*? I asked myself. No. I did not. I asked myself the same question the next hour, and every hour, until I asked it only once a day, then once in a while, then only when we fought, until the question became part of a longer internal monologue about how to find our way through hard times together rather than busting my way out alone.

I let him spend more time with the children. We negotiated the terms of our involvement in each other's lives—not always quietly or easily, but equally and incrementally, always building. John was not a fix, but he worked hard to become my partner and challenged me to express my fears, my love, my hopes, and my anger.

We grew comfortable talking about money, health care, plans, the children, work, pet peeves—everything. Mostly—thought not always—with the same straightforward spirit that he'd hoped for in his *Cosmo* article and demonstrated in my kitchen. It was helpful to have an outside perspective. He observed my difficulties with the custody calendar, with my ex-husband, with Nina, and together we set priorities and boundaries for ourselves, our extended families, and our friends. We agreed that so long as we both respected each other's boundaries and values, leaving was not an option. Between staying and leaving there was another way: fighting, talking, waiting, forgiving, expressing anger, seeking help, and holding ourselves accountable.

JUNE 23, 2014: DAY 96 OF TRIAL

Peter confronted Dr. Li with the fee schedule documents that Joe had seized from their display on the receptionists' window in the basement clinic. The fee schedule was couched in the language of medical billing—"low complexity" and "high complexity"—but it monetized vulnerability as much as addictive behavior, imposing penalties on patients for early visits and suicidal thoughts.

Dr. Li knew his fee schedule was unique and admitted as much—but sought to rationalize it as a reflection of his medical decision-making. Peter indulged the justification, allowing Dr. Li to describe conversations he claimed to have had with patients about reducing doses or avoiding dependence. Peter interrupted only to confirm that Dr. Li's charts contained no record of those discussions. It became apparent to everyone in the courtroom that these conversations were another fiction, an impossibility. Peter did the same with Dr. Li's office hours, assuming the truth of Dr. Li's claims in the questions and revealing their uselessness.

"[T]o see a hundred patients in twelve hours," Peter asked, working off Dr. Li's claim that he had extended his working hours to accommodate the crowds, "you could not spend more than just a very few minutes with most of those patients. Is that correct?"

"That's correct, yes."

How could Dr. Li say no? He had provided the twelve-hour estimate himself.

"You had just about enough time for those patients to walk in the door, ask them how they were feeling, write them a prescription, take their money, stand up, and call the next number? Is that true, sir?"

How could Dr. Li say no?

"That's not true," Dr. Li insisted, but the jury knew.

Peter sometimes gave Dr. Li breaks from the patient histories and prescriptions to talk about insurance billings. Peter drew out Dr. Li to admit that he knew his insurance billings were false, that he felt he was entitled to more than what the insurance companies would pay. Though Peter could not bring Dr. Li to admit that he had lied about his patients' records or his motivation for writing prescriptions, he knew that Dr. Li could not fail to admit that he knew the insurance billings were false.

Once Dr. Li confessed to those repeated lies, made for the sake of earning more money, the jury was entitled to doubt his credibility on other matters.

"[Y]ou knew that the date was false; is that correct?"

"I know the day is false."

Belair objected.

It was not objectionable, except to the extent that it was not what Belair wanted Dr. Li to say.

The judge overruled the objection.

"You knew if you told the truth on this form that the insurance company request would give you less money; is that correct?"

"Yeah."

When the stenographers took down Dr. Li's responses as "yeah," he was not, in fact, being casual or speaking in an informal manner. He was angry, curt, and reluctant. He was saying as little of the word "yes" as he could utter and still be understood.

"So you put something false on this form to get more money; is that correct?"

"No," Dr. Li retorted. "It's to get all the money I should get. It's not— They paid very little."

The truth was so simple. There was only one driver, one motive, one explanation.

JUNE 9, 2014: 1,364 DAYS SINCE NICHOLAS RAPPOLD'S DEATH, DAY 82 OF TRIAL

With his client on the witness stand, Belair dug through our evidence cart and asked for Dr. Li's perspective on the key exhibits we were marshaling to prove guilt. He began with the fee schedule.

Belair asked Dr. Li to explain: "Doctor," he asked, "what was the reason that you created this list, why did you do it?

Dr. Li was ready: "The reason, the major reason, is to enforce the compliance of the patient. It's like ask them to comply to the narcotic agreement. The second reason is we bill the insurance according to the time we spend on the patient, but for the self-pay patient it's just impractical for me to tell the patient I bill the time different, I charge according to the time I spent on you."

Dr. Li added that if he charged self-pay patients according to time, he would discourage them from speaking to him. "This will have a side effect. The patient will not want to talk to me anymore and the major time I spend on the patient is talking. Like asking history, ask the effects, side effects, of the medication, and teach the patient compliance, all these things. Talking to the patient, educate the patient, spend a majority of the time on the patient. If the patient do not want to talk more the quality of the care will be decreased. That's not good for patient. That's the other reason we're setting up for this compliance issue and the medication issue is easily accept by the patient. They just cannot argue why I charge you more because you are in compliance. If you want to pay less, compliance to the narcotic agreement."

Dr. Li was asking the jury to believe him. In order to do so, they would have to believe that he spent time talking to the patients, that speaking to his patients mattered to Dr. Li, and that he was striving to provide "quality care." Was that consistent with the rest of the evidence?

Belair turned to another item on our evidence cart: the numbered tickets. "Doctor, the jury has also heard that at some point in time you established a number system that you would give out to patients who came to the office; is that correct?"

"Yes," confirmed Dr. Li.

"Had you ever seen that done before in any health-care facility?"

"When I practice in China, yes."

"How prevalent was it in China?"

"Basically all the large hospital, all the busy hospital, they use this system. The patient came, they have a window, registration window, and then the patient get a number."

Peter took notes to prepare for his cross-examination and summation. I took notes to advance that effort—and to ensure that my face would be turned down toward the table, that my hands would be engaged, that my expressions would remain neutral. In his summation, Peter could present our view of the evidence to the jury. Until then, we just needed to hope that they were still watching, still listening, and still thinking. They were adults, empowered with the authority to determine a man's guilt or innocence: we hoped they would put in the thought and effort required given these high stakes.

JUNE 27, 2014: DAY 100 OF TRIAL

The judge interrupted Peter's cross-examination for the midafternoon break at 3:15 and resumed at 3:30 with the case of Tracy Howard. This time, Dr. Li was honest—and it was terrifying.

Dr. Li knew that Xanax was contraindicated for patients with suicidal ideation, but he did not believe in this precaution. Dr. Li was aware of the potential serious side effects of Xanax and knew that some of his patients—such as Eddie Valora—had made such reports, but he discounted them. Dr. Li knew that his intake form contained a field devoted to the psychiatric history of his patients but did not hesitate to admit that when he saw a young patient come into his office who looked more or less healthy, he assumed they were fine in that regard.

As Peter proceeded with his questions about Dr. Li's intake form and intake interviews, it became apparent that Dr. Li was not as famil-iar with the form as Peter. The tone of the cross-examination sharp-ened. The pace quickened.

"When a patient walks into your office," Peter asked, "you can't tell by looking at them whether they have a past medical history of depres-sion; can you?"

"Yeah," Dr. Li answered, "we ask a general question. I, basically when we look for a patient, a young health patient, we know pretty much, yes."

Tracy Howard's overdoses were not necessarily overdoses, Dr. Li maintained. When Peter confronted him with one of the hospital warn-ing calls, early on in Dr. Li's treatment of Tracy Howard, Dr. Li resisted the characterization of "taking too much Xanax and needed to detoxify from Benzodiazepines" as an "overdose." In his view, those incidents, no matter what label was attached to them, were just another doctor's "suggestion," as he put it. When Tracy Howard saw Dr. Li after her over-doses, she didn't look overdosed, he said. With respect to the call from the hospital about Xanax, specifically, Tracy denied having overdosed.

"Okay," Peter asked. "At that point, did you conclude that the hospi-tal had lied to you?"

Dr. Li brushed off the question. "Well, not necessarily lied to me, every physician has their own opinion for how to treat a patient."

When Dr. Li learned that Tracy Howard had received hospital treatment, he did not review test results or ask for records, nor did he test her urine: he just believed her and kept prescribing.

The point of the urine tests, of course, was to check that the patient was taking the prescribed medications but also to check for other substances, including illegal drugs.

"I trust the patient," Dr. Li repeated. "It's the patient/physician, it's a relationship; it's based on trust. If I don't trust her anymore, why do I continue to see her?"

"Well, Doctor," Peter retorted, "every time you see her, you make more money; isn't that true, Doctor?"

Belair objected.

Sustained. Arguments had to wait until summation.

Peter maintained an unforgiving pace, but the effort was all-consuming. He needed to maintain constant pressure on Dr. Li, who was back to dodging answers. Peter had to confront Dr. Li with documents, ask for his attention, focus him. In addition to asking questions, Peter also had to maintain a state of active and critical listening, to formulate follow-up questions in the right form and order.

He pushed and pushed until he got to another patient, a cab driver who abused oxycodone. Peter built up what proved to be his final salvo: the records indicated repeated early visits and an inveterate doctor shopper.

"You did not, at that point, believe that he was abusing medication, Dr. Li?" Peter asked.

"No, he's over take," Dr. Li countered. "[. . .] From this time, I really don't see any side effect."

"Can you drive?" Dr. Li recounted asking the patient, who said, "Yeah." "[H]e's doing the driving," said Dr. Li, as though to prove the point that the patient was just fine, as though any of us were comforted to know that this taxi driver had been deemed fit for the road by Dr. Li, as though it were an encouraging sign that a patient who was abusing his prescriptions and craving opioids was choosing to make a living by driving a cab.

"They're fine because they're driving," would say no one, ever, about a drunk driver.

"So, Dr. Li," queried Peter, "as long as on the occasions when he comes to your office, he seems to you to be pretty good, and he's not complying, then your conclusion is that he's not abusing drugs; is that correct?"

"No," Dr. Li answered. "[. . .] He's able to function. He's a driver. He's continued to do the driving. It's not causing any problem."

It's not causing any problem.

The overdose is just another doctor's opinion.

You can pretty much tell by looking at a young person whether they suffer from depression.

As Dr. Li insisted that he only agreed to see the patient again because no one else would treat him, Peter brought out proof that Dr. Li had, in fact, *known* that the patient was seeing other doctors. When Dr. Li countered that the database he consulted had a one-month delay, Peter just asked for confirmation that Dr. Li had, in fact, continued to prescribe to the patient even though it was also an early visit; that Dr. Li had even increased the quantities of Percocet prescribed; that Dr. Li had applied a fifty-dollar surcharge for the extra visit. Dr. Li confirmed those facts, but pointed out that he'd skipped the Opana prescription that time.

Peter wasn't about to quibble about total dosage comparisons, or the reasons why Dr. Li may have chosen to juggle between different medications and quantities for an early visit. Peter was clear now: he knew where to go; he'd known all along. Why would Dr. Li allow a noncompliant patient to return? What could be Dr. Li's incentive to see the patient again, to indulge the patient again?

"Now, on this day," Peter pressed on, "he only gave you one hundred and fifty dollars; is that correct, Dr. Li?"

THE KOUGASIAN RULE • 275

"Correct."

"And you told him that he owed you fifty dollars; is that correct?"

"Yes, written here, yes."

"Now, Dr. Li—"

Understanding dawned on Dr. Li's face. He nodded. "Then I did see the patient again."

There was one more rule of cross-examination that Peter had developed over his thirty-five years in public service and applied during this trial. It was the Kougasian Rule: "Listen to the defendant," Peter always said, "because he may be confessing."

The patient owed Dr. Li money. For that reason alone, and despite every red flag and warning of abuse, addiction, and danger to the patient and public, Dr. Li wasn't going to forgo another visit.

Peter knew that the People's cross-examination of the defendant was over. A few moments later, he took a seat, exhausted. In this trial there were two more challenges ahead for him: the cross-examination of the defense expert and the closing argument. Still, there were many more challenges ahead of Peter that were, as yet, unannounced, unexpected, and unwelcome.

CHAPTER 14

Angel

There is no love without hate; and there is no hate without love. The opposite of love is not hate, but indifference; the opposite of feeling can only be the absence of feeling. Disinclination, which is coloured by feeling, often only serves the purpose of concealing and protecting oneself against an inclination. Love and hate must go hand in hand; and the people we love most we hate also, because hate is grounded in the nature of love.

—WILHELM STEKEL[1]

**JUNE 11, 2014: 1,367 DAYS SINCE NICHOLAS RAPPOLD'S DEATH,
DAY 84 OF TRIAL**

On direct examination, Belair asked Dr. Li to comment on Dr. Gharibo's testimony about the prescriptions issued to Nicholas Rappold. "Dr. Gharibo, with respect to August 8, also says that you should have tried Motrin or tramadol or Tylenol or physical therapy before giving the prescription that you did," said Belair. "Do you agree or disagree with Dr. Gharibo?"

"I disagree," Dr. Li said.

"Please tell the jury why," invited Belair.

"Because when treating acute pain, the major goal is to get a very good pain relief so the pain do not develop to chronic pain. And if I believe the other modality is not sufficient, is not enough, I don't even try, because this is acute pain. The goal is get the pain under control. I don't waste the time to try other therapy and then delay the treatment, delay control the acute pain. Then the acute pain may develop into chronic situation. Then this is even worse. The same principle, we apply this to the operating room area, to the emergency room. We get the good pain relief first, to handle that, kill pain."

Dr. Li and Belair looked back at Rappold's chart. During the first visit on July 11, 2009, Rappold had reported pain resulting from a fifteen-foot fall and paid $100 in cash for a 120-pill prescription of 30 mg Roxicodone. On August 8, 2010, Rappold had returned to report pain from a twenty-foot fall.

Was this the same fall, described differently, or two different falls? This was the question on our minds, but Belair didn't ask it—and it appeared that Dr. Li hadn't asked, either.

According to Dr. Li's patient chart for Nicholas Rappold, the patient could not sit down on August 8. He had a tender spot on his back.*

"The evaluation," said Dr. Li about Nicholas Rappold during his direct examination at trial, "is the patient has acute back injury and [it is] causing low back pain. The treatment [. . .] is [to] give short-term opioid analgesic to treat the pain."

"Were you expecting the patient to be with you for a considerable period of time or not?" Belair asked.

"Maybe not," said Dr. Li. "Acute pain will be defined three months, so if the pain subside he may not come back."

On August 8, 2010, Dr. Li prescribed one hundred twenty Roxico-

---

* We had to take most of the charts at face value, because there was no proof that Dr. Li went back and "completed" any other patient files—but I still wonder.

done 30 mg pills and sixty Xanax pills, 2 milligrams each, in exchange for $100 in cash. The instruction was to take four oxycodone pills and two Xanax pills every day. Dr. Li prescribed the Xanax for its effect as a muscle relaxant, he said, but also to control anxiety symptoms. Rappold, in Dr. Li's opinion, looked "very anxious."

On August 14, 2010, after just six days had passed, Rappold returned to Dr. Li's office and said he had lost his prescription.

Dr. Li recounted Rappold's complaint. "He said every day he cry, he has just so much pain."

As a rule, Dr. Li said, and in accordance with his "Narcotic Agreement," he did not replace lost prescriptions. So instead of Roxicodone and 2 mg Xanax pills, Dr. Li prescribed one hundred twenty Percocet pills, 10/325 milligrams, and ninety Xanax pills, 1 milligram each, in exchange for $100 in cash.

Rappold came for the last time on September 11, 2010. He complained that the Percocet and Xanax were useless. Dr. Li prescribed 120 Roxicodone 30 mg pills and 90 Xanax 2 mg pills in exchange for $100 in cash and noted that Rappold's fee would be increased to $150 because of the noncompliant behavior. The fee schedule that we'd introduced through the receptionists, which Dr. Li had instructed them to post near the entrance, was in force.

As this exchange between Dr. Li and his attorney proceeded, I pictured Rappold and Dr. Li in that small examination room together. I wanted to pick apart the moment and examine everything. For everything we had on the evidence cart, I still had so many questions. Did Dr. Li look at Rappold's face? What words did he say? What was his tone? How much time had passed—if any—before he wrote the prescription? What would it have taken for him to put down the pen, interrupt the routine, and look at his patient? Look at him in a new way—hear him in a new way? Weigh the choices? Weigh the consequences?

I'm still trying to find a moment or an instance where Dr. Li would react the way I want him to react. I'm still finding fault with him for not having done so. In this particular scene, however, my attention is distracted from Dr. Li. I don't care as much about what he is thinking or saying or doing now, so many years later, because there is someone else in the room who is drawing my attention.

For everything we had on the evidence cart, there was nothing that could replace him.

He was a jokester.

He liked to look good for the babes.

I am addicted to painkillers and I need help, he told his mother.

"He went through a terrible withdrawal," Margaret Rappold told the jury. "He said he was in a lot of pain.

"He told me that he missed me, and I said, 'I'm right here; how could you miss me?'"

He blew her a kiss.

There is so much we don't know and cannot change.

Mothers, brothers, doctors, friends, judges, lawyers, toxicologists, police officers, Medical Legal Investigators, medical examiners, patient charts, pill bottles, photographs—we can chase them all down and question them and call them to the stand and question them some more and cross-examine them; we can try to piece it all back together, to understand how it could have happened.

But it's just not enough. It will never be enough.

NICHOLAS RAPPOLD'S LAST DAY OF LIFE

It was their tradition. The L-ride, they called it. Streaming onto the Clearview Expressway from an on-ramp in Queens, cruising eastward on the highway until Manhasset, then looping around and driving back. They listened to music. They talked. They smoked weed. They took pills.

It was nighttime. The highway flowed with cars and lights and signs. The sky never really turns dark in New York City, but it gets darker as you go east, so the lights got brighter. Or was it the music? Or the weed? Or the pills? Or just the teenage-memory-neurons-lighting-up magic of the moment, the three friends from high school together again?

Nicholas, Kaci, Marlie. Nicholas drove—it was his Jeep, his night.

Nick and Kaci had dated in high school. When she texted earlier that evening, asking if Nick could pick her up from Manhattan, he said yes. She couldn't get any drugs at her northeastern university. The lifestyle was too slow, so she was coming home. Did he want to hang out and get high? Hang out, for sure. Hang out and get high with Kaci Yates? That was a yes. It was a Monday and he had to work on Tuesday, yet he said yes. He knew he had a problem. Still, he said yes.

He was no angel, Margaret Rappold used to say.

Nick already had sold 100 of the 120 Roxicodone pills to his friend Marlie Bensen for twelve dollars each. Her boyfriend had already dropped off the cash. But Nick still had the Xanax—he never sold that; that was all for him. Could he get more oxy? Maybe. Not from Dr. Li on a Monday night, though. Things had been off with his friend/supplier Noah lately, but maybe he could work something out.

"He blew me a kiss," Margaret Rappold had told the jury, "and he ran out. He said he had a date and that was it." Kaci was the date.

Nick picked up Kaci at 10:00 p.m. He looked happy. He looked normal. She slid into the passenger seat of his black Jeep and they were off, talking and driving and starting with the pills. She saw two orange prescription bottles in the center console. Maybe there was one more prescription bottle in the side door, maybe not. As soon as they set out, Nick gave Kaci a Roxy from one of the two prescription bottles in the center console. She looked at the pill in her hand: small and blue with the special stamp she recognized. She crushed it with her phone and snorted it through a dollar bill.

Nick swallowed his Roxy, then gave Kaci a Xanax from one of the orange bottles and took some himself.

How many Xanax pills did Kaci take over the course of the evening? Between two and five, she later said. How many Xanax pills did she see Nick take? Between four and ten, she said.

There was one thing Nick needed to do before they picked up Marlie. "There's a guy who owes me money," he told Kaci. Nick drove to the Dunkin' Donuts in Whitestone, where he met another young man. Kaci didn't know him, she said—she just knew *of* him.

Noah Hobbes and Nick knew each other from high school. They hadn't been in a great place for a while, but they hugged it out: two former classmates, two friends, two hockey players, two young men with active addictions, two pill dealers from a neighborhood where everyone scored pills, took pills, sold pills.

"It was an epidemic in my neighborhood," Noah later told the jury.

Whoever had pills sold to others. Nick was usually the one supplying Noah, but sometimes it worked the other way around. He'd always fronted Noah the pills and waited until Noah sold them all to get his money back, but lately he'd wanted his money faster, sooner, right away. And Noah hadn't been paying up. They walked away from the car, leaving Kaci behind. They walked up the block and talked it out—how much Noah owed (maybe $150 or $200), why he hadn't paid up yet (he was angry; he'd been holding out), what would happen next (they set up a payment plan), and how their business had affected their friendship. Noah could tell that Nick was intoxicated—Nick seemed forgetful; he moved and spoke slowly. They came to an agreement and walked back to the car.

While Nick took a phone call, Noah discovered he had a customer: the young lady sitting in Nick's passenger seat. She stepped out of the car and told Noah that she wanted Roxies. She handed him some bills, but it wasn't enough. Was she trying to free-ride on what he owed Nick? Noah wondered. He refused to sell at a discount. If he didn't get the full amount, he wouldn't be able to repay his other supplier. Kaci went back into her purse and dug out more money. Noah gave her four or five pills wrapped in cellophane.

None of that happened, according to Kaci. She didn't buy anything from him, she said. She bought them later, she said, from someone else. But Kaci also said that she and Nick had run out of oxycodone before they saw Noah and took more (along with more Xanax) as soon as they left Dunkin' Donuts.

Noah asked for a ride to a friend's house, five or six blocks away. Nick tried to take the wheel, but Noah wouldn't let him—Nick was clearly too high to drive, even for Noah. Kaci took the wheel, and they dropped Noah off.

Marlie was waiting for Nick and Kaci to pick her up at home. When Nick had first called Marlie earlier that evening to ask if she wanted to come out, she'd said no, because she was mad at him. Nick had promised to sell her the whole batch of Roxies, all 120 pills, but then he cut her share down to just 100. What was he going to do with the other 20 pills? she'd asked. He was supposed to be getting clean.

And there was something else: if he didn't sell her all 120 pills, she'd have fewer for herself. She'd have to resell at least 60 to pay him back, which would leave only 40 for her—and she was addicted, too. Marlie and Nick had been best friends forever, like siblings, but now they were more like business partners: each one looking out for themselves, fueling their own habits.

"Come on," Nick finally convinced her. "I'm picking up [Kaci], we can smoke weed and get high and go for a ride. The three of us together, like before."

"All right," Marlie had agreed, even though she was mad. "All right," she'd said, and he'd promised to pick her up later. Marlie decided not to bring any pills with her, so that she could keep her stash for herself.

When Nick and Kaci finally arrived, they climbed out of the car to hug Marlie. Then Nick got behind the wheel, Kaci sat in the front next to him, and Marlie got in the back seat. It was fun to be together again, but she was also watching, thinking, evaluating, and worrying.

NOVEMBER 19, 2011: 431 DAYS SINCE NICHOLAS RAPPOLD'S DEATH, 852 DAYS UNTIL TRIAL

While Joe Hall was searching Dr. Li's office in Flushing, another team of agents and investigators combed through his blue two-story poolside New Jersey home. From Dr. Li's kitchen, the team brought back a stack of handwritten lists: pages upon pages of patient names, listed in the order they were seen by Dr. Li. There was one list for every weekend "Open" day, going back several years.

We set the lists aside. We hadn't seen the patient files yet. We didn't know most of the names. Dr. Li knew—and had known for years—that Dawn Tamasi was a heroin addict, that Tracy Howard had tried to kill herself, that Joseph Haeg was dead, that Kevin Kingsley had tried to get clean—but we didn't know any of that, yet.

Months later, once we had obtained permission from the Court to read all the patient files, we went back to the lists—back to the time when so many more people were still alive and Dr. Li still had time to save them.

The lists were hard to put down and wrenching to understand. Some of our victims had been there on the same days, alive. They were *all alive* back then.

The list for July 11, 2009, named Dawn Tamasi as number 4; Joseph Haeg, number 35; Adrian Cruise, number 44; Nicholas Rappold, the sixty-first and last patient. How much attention, we wondered, does a doctor give his sixty-first and last patient of the day?

The list for December 26, 2009, revealed Joseph Haeg to have been the twenty-fifth patient out of sixty-one. Three days later, he was dead.

There were seventy-eight patients on the list for February 27, 2010; ninety-six on March 6, 2010; seventy-seven on March 13, 2010; one hundred on June 26, 2010.

On October 30, 2010, Kevin Kingsley was the seventy-second patient out of eighty-six. It was his last visit to Dr. Li. Two months later, he was dead.

On August 14, 2010, Nicholas Rappold was the eighty-first and last patient to be seen that day. Nicholas came back one last time, in September, and then he, too, was gone.

Dr. Li was supposed to be Nicholas Rappold's doctor, but Nicholas Rappold was just another customer to Dr. Li. Nicholas Rappold should have grown up to become a man: instead, he became a crime victim.

NICHOLAS RAPPOLD'S LAST HOURS OF LIFE

Nick was upbeat as he drove; he talked a lot. They smoked pot. Nick took a few more Xanax. They on-ramped onto the Clearview Express-way and cruised for a couple of hours, steady and fun—at first.

Marlie felt a pit in her stomach a couple of times when the car seemed to loosen itself from Nick's grip. He seemed quieter. Kaci saw that Nick's head was nodding at times. The car veered out of the lane.

"Nick, are you all right?" Marlie asked.

"Yeah," he said, "I'm fine."

"Pull over," Marlie said. "Pull over; you can't drive anymore. Kaci, are you okay to drive?"

"I'll drive," Kaci said.

They pulled over. Kaci and Nick switched seats.

"Let's go home," Marlie said. "Drop me off?" she asked.

They stopped at a 7-Eleven on the way. Kaci got out of the car to buy Nick a drink. Nick confided in Marlie that he was hoping to sleep over at Kaci's. "Don't," Marlie pleaded. "You can stay with me," she said. "[Kaci] has a boyfriend. I don't want you to get hurt."

"Stop being my mother," Nick said. "Start being my friend."

Kaci came back with water and a caffeinated drink for Nick. She got back behind the wheel and drove to Marlie's house.

Marlie gave Nick a kiss and said good night. "Let's all go to IHOP in the morning," he suggested. She squeezed him tight, gave Kaci a hug, and went into the house.

It was past 1:00 a.m., maybe 1:30, maybe even 2:00. "I'm coming home," Kaci finally told her mom, who'd been calling her all night. Kaci just wasn't coming home fast enough.

Kaci parked around the corner, on 165th Street, near 35th Avenue. "Come with me," she said to Nick. "You can sleep at my house," she said. He agreed. There were still some pills left in the bottle of Xanax in the center console. Kaci held on to Nick as they walked around the block, holding him up. He was stumbling.

Kaci's mother, Lydia Yates, met them at the door. She saw her daughter—relief, anger, frustration, relief. She could tell that Kaci was intoxicated. Not this again, thought Lydia. Not again. But at least she's home. At least she's safe.

Lydia saw Nicholas and—no. Just—no. His eyes were red. He was slurring his speech. He could barely stand up. He was very polite, but she could tell he was very, very drunk. She'd known him for a long time, but this wasn't happening under her roof. Kaci still had a boyfriend! Lydia drew Kaci in. "Can't Nicholas stay?" Kaci asked. "He's tired," Kaci said. "I don't want him driving home."

"Absolutely not," said Lydia. "He can go home," she said. "He doesn't live that far away. Under no circumstances can he stay here," she said. "Say good-bye," she told Kaci.

"Wait five minutes," Kaci whispered to Nicholas. "I'll call you. I'll let you in."

Lydia sent Kaci up to bed and said good-bye to Nicholas. He was very polite, again, said good-bye, and left.

Lydia set the house alarm.

Kaci went upstairs and waited a few minutes for her mother to go to bed. She called Nick's cell phone—no answer. She texted him. Nothing. She called—and called—and called. She texted.

At 4:00 a.m. on The Day, Nick's mother woke up. "I shot up and I just had a feeling something was wrong," she said, "and I ran downstairs and put on my sneakers and ran outside in my pajamas and started to drive round the neighborhood looking for him and I didn't find him, and I got back home about ten after five." At five o'clock in the morning, Lydia got up to get ready for work. At 10:30, a friend of Nick's called her to ask if she knew where he was. No, she said, she did not. She saw him last around 2:00 a.m., she said. Thirty minutes later, Kaci called. Nick was missing, she said. He hadn't shown up for work. Could Lydia come home during her lunch break so that they could drive around the neighborhood and look for him? At 11:30, Lydia left work. She drove home, picked up Kaci, and turned the corner—"his car is still there," Kaci said, pointing. It was exactly where they'd parked the night before.

"Stop, Mom, stop," Kaci begged.

Kaci ran up to the car. Lydia followed her, but she couldn't see inside because of the tinted windows. Kaci opened the driver's-side door and screamed—then collapsed. Lydia ran up and saw Nick, slumped over the center console. She put her hand on his back and she knew he was dead.

A Con Ed worker heard the scream and called 911. A crowd assembled. Some were there to do a job. Others came just because they loved Nick.

EMTs confirmed that "the young gentleman was not salvageable." Police officers secured the car and called in the homicide squad. Nobody touched anything until the Medical Legal Investigator from the medical examiner's office arrived on the scene. The police officers struggled to keep the growing crowd under control.

Kaci was frantic. Marlie arrived with her mother and her sister. Other friends of Nick's arrived. It was mayhem.

Margaret Rappold arrived. Her brother met her there. He took care of everything because she could not. The police handed him a white plastic bag containing Nick's wallet, phone, necklace, earring—and a prescription pill bottle with Dr. Li's name on it, dated September 11, 2010, just three days earlier. The bottle contained thirty-five Xanax pills out of the ninety that had been prescribed.

Margaret's brother identified the body and drove the Jeep home.

Bystanders and friends shouted questions, asking what happened. Angry mourners complained about Nick having been sent away from Kaci's home.

Lydia pulled Kaci away, went home, and locked all the doors.

What if you love some, and not others?

What if you save some, and not others?

It was an epidemic in the neighborhood.

CHAPTER 15

May It Please the Court

Well, I don't think oxycodone is indicated just because a patient has tenderness. I did not see any objective findings to state to give this patient a narcotic. It's standard to give patients a nonsteroidal, which is naproxen. And given his history he has been on Suboxone, which is a medication used for addiction. So I did not [. . .] see any objective evidence as part of my neurological examination to require a narcotic on this patient at that time.

—DR. TERRENCE CHAN, ON HIS EXAMINATION OF
NICHOLAS RAPPOLD, AUGUST 10, 2010

MARCH 14, 2014: 6 DAYS UNTIL TRIAL

John and I were swamped. He'd just started a new job and I was about to go on trial for at least two months, if not longer. On our custody nights with Nina and Charlie, we couldn't get out of our offices fast enough to get to the grocery store and be home in time for dinner and cook and oversee homework and hear about their days and take a breath to be human again and clean up and have enough time to work again after dinner. Even while we were all still together, I missed my family already and fell into a snappish, martyred mood. John suggested that we order takeout every night, but our budgets didn't allow it. I longed for my grandmother's bountiful cooking and unconditional love, but this was New York City in 2014, so we joked about hiring a private chef instead. Underneath the humor was a serious concern: we'd both been married and divorced before; we feared the corrosive effects of fatigue, stress, guilt, and resentment on our relationship.

We sat down to talk about it, but I didn't want to: I was nervous about sounding critical or complaining too much or having a fight. It always had been "easier" to just push through and deal with the consequences later. John set a professional tone to the conversation and we told each other the truth. We discussed our division of labor, listing and reallocating tasks. We talked about money, calculating how much we spent on food every week and agreeing on how to split it in a way that felt fair. We debated how much we could spend to outsource a few dinners a week for the duration of the trial, whether in the prepared foods section of our supermarket or with outside help. We talked about our health concerns and the family's tendency to eat pasta at every single meal. There was no shortage of cash-strapped aspiring chefs in New York City: Could we tap that demographic pool to help our family? Recalling the offers I'd often received for discounted cuts from apprentice hair stylists, I posted an ad on local cooking school websites: *Family seeks student to prepare bulk meals during a busy time for reasonable fee.*

On March 20, 2014, during the first lunch break of our first day of trial, I received an elegant missive by electronic mail. "Dear Charlotte, Herewith menu for trial delivery. Should we move forward together, I can always include crudité and dips for you to take to work, or croquettes or falafel etc. Please let me know your thoughts." The sample menu was stunning: chickpea and squid stew, wild fish in coconut curry, poached pears. And who doesn't love a croquette? It was also, as I notified John, "heartbreakingly expensive," and I could only imagine my kids' reactions to squid stew.

We finally met our match in Jay,* an exuberant young man who turned the kitchen inside out but always filled our refrigerator, with a smile. We could afford to be his guinea pigs once a week and he granted me the luxury of sitting down with my children when I ran home from court, for hugs and books and precious conversation, before they left again for their dad's. It was *almost* perfect.

"That's the way they're meant to be served," Jay said one night, suddenly a tad defensive when John cut a meatball in half to reveal the red, "rare" meat inside. The kids and I panned our heads from one man's face to the other, wondering what would happen. The kids were still learning about adult conflict. I thought I knew men—and this didn't look good. I also knew John. There were two sacred foods in his family: his father's Thanksgiving turkey and his mother's Super Bowl meatballs. Would someone get angry? Would this pleasant evening turn sour? Couldn't there be just one moment without tension, where everything wasn't a huge deal, for heaven's sake?

John caught my eye. He raised an eyebrow, stabbed the halved meatball with his fork, and ate it. Honorable members of the jury: this was evidence of love.

JUNE 6, 2014: DAY 79 OF TRIAL

Peter stood up. "Your Honor," he said, "the People rest."

Belair moved for a trial order of dismissal, asking the judge to rule that we had failed to present sufficient evidence of the charges. The judge assured Peter that he would give Peter and me a few minutes to confer before hearing our response.

"I know from experience," he said, "that neither one of you is going to get up without talking to the other first."

"That's teamwork, Your Honor," answered Peter, and the judge agreed. Ultimately, the judge denied Belair's motion: barring any unforeseen disasters, the case would go to the jury.

---

* Name changed to protect his privacy.

But this exchange stuck with me: honorable members of the jury, this was persuasive evidence of a partnership. We had credible testimony from a judge, based upon his firsthand observations: Peter and I were, finally, a team. Mutual respect had won out. Fatigue had dulled the edges of Peter's humor and, as a result, I was less defensive, less reactive. Most important, we had, by the end, always forced ourselves to behave as a team even when we did not feel like a team. It had become a habit and it made us better at our jobs.

MAY 12, 2014: DAY 54 OF TRIAL

For our first Valentine's Day together, my gift to John had been an invitation to spend more time with us and an extension of his love of eccentric socks: an eccentric bathrobe. It was blue and British, with polka dots. A delightful piece of clothing—something he could be proud to wear as he helped take our garbage bags down the hall to the chute. Or, as it happens, opening the door to my ex-husband . . .

Nina was ten years old, juggling the demands of fifth grade and struggling to remember all her books between her two homes. My ex-husband and I made regular trips to the school, where the security knew to set aside the forgotten goods for Nina and she knew to pick them up from him. On this Monday of the trial, however, the call had come too late: I was already in court. By text messaging under the table, I begged my ex-husband for help. We had been in tension about how to help Nina with these slips but agreed that this was no time for a teachable moment. He ran over to my apartment, got a key from the doorman, and went upstairs—and, luckily, thought to ring the doorbell before going in. John answered the door . . . in his new, dotty bathrobe.

They'd met before, but never this early in the morning, never without me, never with one man in a state of undress, and never as co-parents. As they hustled to gather and pack up the belongings of the ten-year-old girl whom we all cared about so much, my ex-husband paused.

"You look adorable," he said to John.

Honorable members of the jury: this was evidence of good faith.

JULY 8, 2014: DAY 111 OF TRIAL

From the beginning of Dr. Li's testimony on June 6, through Dr. Weingarten's testimony, ending on July 1, I helped Peter prepare for the cross-examinations, handled the projector, and passed him too many Post-it notes containing too many questions. No more heavy lifting for me: Peter was on the spot. Calling on the Tom Demakis rules of cross-examination and marshaling a careful selection of patient vignettes to illustrate Dr. Li's lies, consciousness of guilt, and criminal intent, Peter powered his way through.

The defense case ended with an unanswered question and a sustained objection: Belair had brought Dr. Li back to the stand for redirect, and on recross Peter attempted to demonstrate that Dr. Li had used the profits from the pain clinic to pay off his mortgage.

"Your Honor," said Belair, "I'm going to object as beyond the scope."

The judge sustained the objection.

"Okay," said Peter. "Your Honor," he added, "nothing further."

There was no redirect. There were no further defense witnesses. Belair introduced a medical record as his last exhibit.

"That concludes the evidentiary portion of the case," said the judge, concluding the evidentiary portion of the case.

Concluding any portion of this case was a shock to the system.

When the trial had been ahead of us, it seemed monolithic: it had appeared as a huge, heavy, consistent burden of effort, stress, and uncertainty that stretched from March 17 until some uncertain date. We were like drivers on a road who see a dark, foreboding cloud ahead, who then notice that it has begun raining and, when the rain stops, are stunned to find that the dark cloud is behind, that they already passed through it. We had been unable to imagine that our experience of what appeared to be a great, unique difficulty would come in a familiar, manageable form. As we had chewed up each day, we had felt like we were not diminishing the cloud, but rather just pushing it back one more day.

And now we had the end in sight. But what end?

Still, hope turned the lawyers into giddy compatriots. If barbed wire had bound our triad of prosecutors/judge/defense together, the stings were falling away. The mood lightened. We peppered a long discussion about jury instructions with good-humored exchanges.

The judge asked whether Belair intended to deliver a summation (he did) and we tried to map out the following day of trial.

"How long do you expect yours to be, Mr. Kougasian?" the judge asked Peter. "Do you have a rough guess?"

"It's about eleven ounces, I think," Peter said, thinking of the pile of paper on which his summation would be printed. "Well, again depends on how much I have to respond to Mr. Belair, I'd say between an hour, an hour and a half maybe."

"That short?" The judge was surprised.

"That short, maybe a little more," Peter answered. "It's hard to say."

The judge opened up a discussion about his proposed legal instructions to the jury, the "charge." "I noticed an awful lot of yellow stickies on your copies, Miss Fishman; I was afraid to ask," he joked. "So," he continued after we wrapped up a few other matters, "Miss Fishman, why don't you tell me what issues you had with my charge."

"Yes, Your Honor," I answered. "First, I should mention that most of the stickies are points of interest for me."

"Oh." The judge smiled. "Okay."

"They are not for you," I added.

"That's a relief," he said, and heard my comments with an equanimous, productive spirit.

On the morning of July 9, we discussed the schedule for summations. The judge expressed a hope that Peter would be "on target" with his estimation of a summation lasting between one and one and a half hours.

"I am never on target," interjected Peter. "I should tell the Court." I had no idea whether Peter was joking or engaging in more self-deprecation. At most, he had sent me and Nancy a few passages here and there, to check or edit.

The jury entered, and the judge began instructing them on the logistics and law relating to summations. "[W]hile you are deliberating," he warned them in advance, "we take all your electronics from you. I know for some of you that is like taking a pacifier from an infant. So be prepared.

"Honorable members of the jury, I confess a fondness and nostalgia for dry, good-natured courtroom humor."

JULY 9, 2014: DAY 112 OF TRIAL

Belair began his summation by arguing that we had brought the second indictment against Dr. Li because we had realized that the first indictment, concerning only Michael Cornetta, would not hold up. "It's very tough for people to admit that they've made a mistake," he said, "and, unfortunately, human nature sometimes just says, okay, well, what's the expression, double down, go for broke, go over the top."

My head was about to blow up. We didn't make a mistake—we followed a trail of death. We received unprompted calls from members of the public. We met Tracy Howard and Dawn Tamasi. As for "human nature," well, "human nature" was not the entity making the decisions. In fact, there was not one person making decisions—there never had been. There had been countless people involved in investigating, double-checking, questioning, verifying, vetting. If there was any one person making any decisions, it was Bridget—and "human nature" was not a force that moved her so easily. She may not have had ice water running in her veins, but after all, she was from Wisconsin.

I am making light of it now, but it was serious: Bridget's decisions to allow us to pursue this case, on the first and second indictments, were ones that she had worked over and heard debate on for months. But as I sat fuming, Belair continued, turning to the question of Dr. Li's good faith. "Maybe he's negligent," Belair suggested, before doubling down. "Again, I say that the proof does not show that, but if you should so conclude, that doesn't make out the case for which he is charged."

Belair went for broke: "You will see that virtually everything that he did was for the patient's benefit." Dr. Li wasn't a "pill pusher," he argued, asking the jury to remember that Dr. Li had warned his patients about abusing the pills. "That is not something that a pill pusher does." This became the theme: Dr. Li did not act as a pill pusher; he demonstrated good faith. The patients, meanwhile, were not just liars—"they were very good liars," argued Belair, evoking Tracy Howard and Dawn Tamasi.

"She was a tough cookie," Belair continued about Tracy Howard, talking about Dr. Li's refusal to drop her as a patient until she finally left his practice to see a psychiatrist. "It's a happy ending," he added.

I thought of Tracy on the witness stand, stuffed animal clasped in her arms.

"I'll tell you something that I told you in the opening statement as well," he pressed on, reprising one of his favorite defenses. "Nobody who took Dr. Li's medications the way he prescribed them ever had an overdose. Nobody who took the stand in this case ever said, anybody who was in his office ever appeared there to be intoxicated, stoned, wobbly, weaving on his feet, sweaty. I don't know about sweaty—let's withdraw that—slurring their words. Nothing like that. Nothing like that."

As for the extra charges, for early visits and suicidal ideation? They were just a deterrent, Belair said.

His most powerful argument was about the burden of proof. Look at Dr. Li, he asked the jury, having instructed Dr. Li to stand up. Do you see him as a citizen or a defendant? If you think of him as a defendant, Belair cautioned them, you already have begrudged him his rights. If you think of him as anything less than innocent, your verdict will not be a true verdict. There was no burden on Dr. Li. He had to be presumed innocent. The burden was on the prosecution to prove every element of every charge beyond a reasonable doubt. "[A]ny verdict you will render which is not beyond a reasonable doubt," Belair insisted, "is something less than a true verdict. It's a compromised verdict." He was right. It was powerful.

I agreed with him on only two other points: first, our jury had demonstrated extraordinary patience; second, we would all be scarred by the experience. "You'll probably be seeing these charts in your nightmares for years to come," Belair said, referring to Dr. Li's patient files.

Belair revisited Dr. Gharibo's testimony, attacking his credibility and reminding the jury that opioid painkillers, even according to Dr. Gharibo, were a legitimate form of treatment and that treating pain was a legitimate purpose. He set a contrast to the high bar of the law, where, in order to find Dr. Li guilty of Reckless Endangerment in the First Degree with respect to Tracy Howard, Dawn Tamasi, and Kevin Kingsley, the jury had to find that Dr. Li acted with depraved indifference.

"You have listened to Dr. Li testify," Belair boomed. "He took you through all the patients, all the reasons that he did things. Did he strike you as being depraved? Wicked? Evil? Is that the way he struck you? Or did he strike you as somebody who is dealing with, in many instances, very tough patients?"

I thought of the piece of paper taped to the wall above my computer in the office: "The opposite of love is not hate, but indifference."

Also, I thought about our burden of proof: The homicide and endangerment charges did not require proof of an intent to harm. They required a finding of recklessness.

"Now, you might think that Dr. Li is a little gullible," Belair argued. "Maybe he is; maybe he isn't. But even if you think he is gullible, even if you think that, that's not acting—that's not bad faith. He is acting in good faith. Gullibility is negligent if it's negligence. But if he is doing what he thinks is best for his patient and he gets conned by some very good con artists [. . .]"

Belair was on a roll: "The doctor who is trying to take care of his patients; who is trained to believe them; who believes them; who doesn't need this job for the money. He [gave] his wife a job so they can get remarried; come back to the United States and be reunited with their daughter. He didn't need it for the money. This was a family deal. Remember that? On Saturdays Dr. Li and Mrs. Dr. Li, Miss Guo, and their daughter would go to Flushing, and the daughter would go to the Chinese school. And when they finished, usually late, they would go for what kind of meal? A Chinese meal. What else? But this is not something—this is not something that he did because he was greedy as suggested by the prosecutor; and he didn't act as if he was greedy. Of course, in this case, what happens is the heroes become villains and the villains become the heroes."

The deaths were "sad," but not Dr. Li's fault, Belair argued. Building on his arguments about the patients' lack of reliability, the doctor's good faith, the absence of any perceptible risk, there was no way for Dr. Li to control how these patients abused the medications—and he could not be held responsible.

As for the "contractual matter" of the insurance fraud, Belair insisted that Dr. Li had been wronged. "Why wouldn't they want to send it, if they were serious about the thing and this wasn't just a Kangaroo Court effort, why wouldn't they send the thing to Dr. Li and say, 'You owe us three thousand dollars,' whatever it was, whatever it was, and then they could get paid?" It was the prosecutors' influence, Belair contended. "[W]hat they tried to do is to dress it up, flounce it out, and make it sound like a crime."

" 'Let's make this like a ghost,' " Belair imagined us saying, sharing his version of events with the jury. "Something to cloud the eyes of the jury. A trick. A trick that doesn't belong in the criminal court."

Belair condemned the prosecution in a vigorous finale. As the defense summation wound down, Peter became very still. Bracing. Breathing for the next heavy lift.

A verdict in favor of Dr. Li, Belair concluded, was "the only verdict that a fair reading of all the evidence in this case would permit." He thanked the jury, and before we broke for lunch the judge addressed the jury. "We will resume at two fifteen," he said. "And from what Mr. Kougasian has told me, I expect he will be able to complete his summation this afternoon."

Honorable members of the jury: this was optimism.

JULY 9, 2014: DAY 112 OF TRIAL

"During the course of this summation," Peter began, "I expect that I will be on many occasions disagreeing with Belair and sometimes, in fact, quite often I think the disagreement will be strong. But at the outset, I want to identify one area where we were in complete agreement. And that is in our gratitude for your service as jurors."

I ran my eyes over the jury box, stopping on each face to think, Thank you, making a particular effort to bear no expression whatsoever upon my exhausted, relieved, semi-frozen face. No matter what the outcome, I was grateful for their service. In practical terms, these folks had spent eighteen weeks stretched between family, personal responsibilities, professional obligations, and a complex, dense, tragic criminal case. I could only imagine the variety of issues, dilemmas, and challenges this had raised for each juror and alternate.

Their constancy was evidence of civic responsibility.

Peter paused after thanking the jury, then modulated the tone of his voice. He enumerated all of the suffering we'd heard about in the courtroom: "How could it happen that Margaret Rappold would awake in the middle of the night with an intuition that something was wrong with her son, go searching for him only to discover the next afternoon that, in fact, he had perished the night before, dead of a combination of oxycodone and Xanax? How could it be that Tracy Howard ended up in emergency rooms again sick on overdoses and suicide attempts only to get the same drugs, sometimes in even larger quantities, again and again? How could it happen that the [Tamasi] family would find their daughter [. . .] passed out in a closet or in a bathroom? And how could it happen that they would plead with the prescribing doctor, only to have drugs prescribed to her in such amount and such combinations that she lived, as she described it, 'like a zombie'?

"How could Kevin Kingsley, staggering and incoherent with a self-inflicted wound to the head, go to a basement clinic and emerge with a prescription for thirty milligrams of Roxicodone, two a day for thirty days, an opioid medication he had just detoxed from? [. . .] How could a nineteen-year-old named [Alli Walton] come to a doctor a recreational user of Percocet and end up so addicted to oxycodone that one afternoon she forced her way into the doctor's lunchroom to plead for one last prescription? How could twenty patients walk in a doctor's basement clinic, [hand] up the money, and walk out with prescriptions for powerful drugs with [. . .] no medical justification?

"How could this have happened? It happened because they all have the same doctor. The defendant, Dr. Stan Li, sitting in this courtroom today, who will soon face your judgment. It happened because Dr. Li put his desire for money ahead of his duty as a doctor to help his patients or at least not to harm them. It happened because he put money above, even above the simple duty that we all share, to obey the law."

This would become clear, Peter promised, as he examined the crimes of recklessness with which Dr. Li had been charged. "Understand," Peter emphasized, "Dr. Li is not charged with intending to hurt anyone. He is charged with recklessness: with ignoring the evidence right before his eyes."

"What is recklessness?" Peter asked the jury, repeatedly, then answered the question by reminding them of the testimony about Kevin Kingsley. "His own mother said that he looked gray, raggedy, disheveled. His daughter said at about that time he couldn't talk. Couldn't stand up. His eyes were halfway closed, and he was falling all over. What is recklessness? *That is recklessness*. Recklessness is looking into another person's half-closed eyes seeing the deterioration in body and mind, knowing by training and experience that drug abuse is the cause of the suffering [. . .]."

Peter turned to Tracy Howard.

"What does it take to prescribe Xanax and opioid to [her]? This, by the way, is [. . .] the patient who Belair in his closing remarks characterized as a tough cookie. This is the witness who testified before you clutching a stuffed animal. This is the tough cookie who tried to take her own life. And admitted as much to Dr. Li.

"What is recklessness? That is recklessness. Recklessness is to look into the face of a patient with a record of repeated overdoses, early visits, hospital reports, of use of heroin and cocaine, and suicide attempt, and say, 'I don't see a significant failure to comply.'

"[Tracy Howard] testified, how long were the visits? About as long as it took to write the prescription. What is recklessness? *That is recklessness.*"

At 3:30 p.m., the judge interrupted Peter to give the jury a bathroom break.

"Okay," the judge told us at sidebar, "Mr. Kougasian tells me that his hour to an hour and a half estimate is significantly off and that he anticipates that it would take him until five thirty or so to finish." We had permission to keep the court officers working for an extended day, he explained, meaning until 5:30, but if we weren't sure to finish by then, it would be best to stop at 4:45 and resume the next morning.

A humble Peter confessed his uncertainty: "I cannot realistically say I'm sure," he told the judge. "It's very hard for me to estimate. I haven't rehearsed this."

Belair seconded the motion to stop at 4:45 p.m. and resume in the morning. The judge expressed his hope that Peter would require only forty-five minutes or an hour in the morning to finish. "I want them to get the case before lunch," he emphasized. Peter agreed that time was of the essence.

"And the extra time," the judge continued, "gives you a chance to—"

"Pare it," offered Peter—

"To trim rather than to expand," the judge clarified.

Though he'd been humbled at sidebar, Peter came back strong at the lectern after the break, attacking Dr. Li's credibility. "He wasn't gullible when he signed the certification that said these are the original records made at the time of the occurrence and put it in an envelope and sent it," Peter argued. "That's not gullible. That's a person who doesn't tell the truth. That's a person who certifies falsely. That's a person who said things from the witness stand under oath to you that weren't true again and again."

Peter contrasted Dr. Li's purported certainty with the concerns, hesitations, and extensive examinations described by the other, legitimate doctors whom we had called as witnesses. "By my guess," Peter said to the jury about those doctors, "you will conclude that they were intelligent, caring, and compassionate, and none of them was willing to prescribe the same doses and combinations as Dr. Li. There is no moral dilemma here. Dr. Li was not practicing on a battlefield where he is forced to make immediate moral choices, knowing that whatever he decides will end up in tragedy. He could do the same kind of deliberate medicine that those doctors in the emergency room practice, but he didn't."

Peter addressed the dilemma we'd discuss at such length in Joe T.'s office: how to distinguish bad medicine from a crime.

"I want to make it really, really clear," he emphasized, "and I think it goes to something that Mr. Belair said. I want to say it's going to be now the second time that I agree with him. No doctor should be in a criminal court because he engaged in poor but acceptable practice. Doctors have to be protected to make mistakes. Doctors have to be protected to be mediocre. Dr. Li is not here because he has given poor but acceptable practice. Dr. Li is not a doctor without talent. [. . .] He's a well-trained doctor. He knows what he is doing. He knows what medications are about. He knows what these combinations do. [. . .] That's why before he sent the records to the OPMC, he knows he has to make changes. That's why before he faxes medical records to the medical examiner, he knows he's got to alter that document.

"One of the most remarkable aspects of the evidence you have heard," Peter submitted to the jury, "is the lengths to which Dr. Li will go to distort the record and hide the truth when he believes the truth is to his disadvantage, when Dr. Li is conscious that he has done something wrong."

Shortly thereafter, we quit for the day. Peter was up most of the night. I know not whether he trimmed it down. The next morning, he resumed his summation at 9:30 a.m.

"Now, look," Peter asked the jury, recalling Dr. Li's denials of greed. "Could Dr. Li simply not be aware how much money he's making at his practice in cash? That would be absurd. This is a doctor who wrote down in his medical records how much cash was paid, how much cash was owed. This was a doctor who literally took the money from the patient and put it in his pocket. This is a doctor whose focus at all times was on the money.

"It wasn't that he trusted his patients," Peter declared. "It's that he didn't care. [. . . The] tragedy did not come from trusting patients. It did not come from a doctor who was gullible; it came from a doctor who was reckless."

Referring back to the metaphor I had used in my opening, of licensed prescribers as gatekeepers for controlled substances, Peter drew his summation to a close.

"Those doctors," he said quietly, "are the keepers of a gate that is meant to limit these powerful drugs to legitimate uses and in the legitimate doses with genuine medical supervision. Those doctors are the keepers of a gate, not a tollbooth. The gate cannot open for anyone who happens by with enough money. You saw in this case the tragedies that can result when the gate becomes a tollbooth."

The witnesses and documents we had presented over eighteen weeks of trial, Peter concluded, were evidence of manslaughter, reckless endangerment, criminal sales of prescriptions, filing of false documents, scheme to defraud, and grand larceny. He asked the jury to return the only just verdict: guilty.

With that, Peter finished his two-day, four-hour summation. He had said everything there was to say, as well as he could have said it. Our work was done—it was time for the jury to do their duty.

We took a short break before the judge read his final jury instructions, reviewing the elements for each charge and the jurors' duties during deliberations.

The jury got the case before lunch and worked until 5:00 p.m. They did not sit on Friday but reconvened on Monday and resumed deliberations. I volunteered to remain in the courtroom and pull any exhibits they requested. The last thing I wanted to do was be in the office, talk to anyone, or answer any well-intentioned questions ("What's happening? What do you think will happen?") about the trial. I read a book and worked on my to-do list. Peter and Jon sometimes joined me in the courtroom. One afternoon as the three of us sat in the last row of the empty courtroom, Jon and I wore down Peter's resistance and he agreed to do one or two magic tricks. A few disappearing coins, some telepathic thinking with his ubiquitous deck of cards—for a few minutes, his energy and pep came back.

Day by day, the jurors asked for exhibits in a manner that suggested they were proceeding in order through the indictment, with the exception of the homicide charges, which they saved for last. We measured their progress according to their requests: a flip chart and easel, patient charts, translations, claim forms, legal questions about the Scheme to Defraud and Grand Larceny charges, the definition of "serious physical injury," and finally, the controlled substances recovered from Nicholas Rappold and Joseph Haeg and another reading of the legal instructions pertaining to the manslaughter charges. On Thursday, the jurors signaled that they might be able to reach a verdict before evening, then changed their minds.

We reconvened on Friday morning. The jury filed back into their room to continue deliberations. I sat in the courtroom with the officers, court staff, and Belair's associate. We broke for lunch. I went outside and noticed Dr. Li sitting at a sidewalk table in front of the park, right next to the courthouse, eating his lunch under sunlit trees and a blue sky.

Honorable members of the jury: Did he know it might be his last day of freedom?

CHAPTER 16

Sorry for the Loss

Dr. [Russell] Portenoy said it was "quite scary" to think how the growth in opioid prescribing driven by people like him had contributed to soaring rates of addiction and overdose deaths. "Clearly, if I had an inkling of what I know now then, I wouldn't have spoken in the way that I spoke. It was clearly the wrong thing to do," Dr. Portenoy said in the recording.

—THOMAS CATAN AND EVAN PEREZ, "A PAIN-DRUG
CHAMPION HAS SECOND THOUGHTS,"
WALL STREET JOURNAL, DECEMBER 17, 2012

JUNE 23, 2014: DAY 96 OF TRIAL

While we toiled away in court, New York State's Governor Andrew Cuomo signed multiple bills into law. The New York State Legislature had voted on a package designed to address the opioid epidemic.[1] Among them was an amendment to the Enterprise Corruption statute, making Criminal Sale of a Prescription for a Controlled Substance an eligible "criminal act." Another bill amended Section 220.65, which criminalized the sale of a prescription for a controlled substance, to include sales of controlled substances by practitioners or pharmacists in so-called pill mill cases. The sponsor for that particular bill, former New York State Senator Kemp Hannon of Nassau County, cited the Li case—and the Medford murders—in his remarks to the press: "In 2011," he said, "Dr. Li, who reportedly saw up to 120 patients a day, engaged in illegal prescribing practices resulting in the death of as many as 9 people, and prescribed more than 2,500 pain pills to the gunman who killed 4 people at a pharmacy in Medford, Suffolk County, was indicted under a penal law provision prohibiting the illegal sale of a controlled substance by a physician. Due to a loophole in the law, New York State lacks similar provisions to address practitioners and pharmacists that illegally and knowingly dispense."

With the governor's signature, these bills—along with other legislative initiatives to expand substance abuse treatment, access to naloxone, and increased staff for the Bureau of Narcotic Enforcement—became law.

Other changes arose from inter-agency collaborations. Before we went to trial, the NYPD updated its overdose death scene protocols to guarantee the preservation of evidence: pill bottles, prescriptions, cell phones. We hoped there would not be another case like this one—but we certainly wished to prevent future prosecutors from encountering the same obstacles.

JULY 18, 2014: DAY 121 OF TRIAL

At 2:23 p.m., the foreman signed and issued the following note: "We, the jury, have reached a verdict." Peter and I texted our colleagues. I thought about calling Margaret Rappold but decided I did not want her to be anxious for the next hour—I would call her once we knew.

The judge instructed the court officers to bring in the jury. I sat straight in my chair and tried to breathe. To my left, Peter took notes on a legal pad—or pretended to take notes in order to keep himself together. The door to the jury room remained closed. Any minute now they would come out and announce the verdict. I couldn't decide what to do with my hands. I could hear murmurs and rustles behind me. We had spent four months in this courtroom on the ninth floor of 111 Centre Street, waiting and working, questioning and fighting, studying and preparing—just us, Belair, his associate, Dr. Li, the judge, the jurors, and the court staff, with occasional visitors.

I don't know how much time passed. At some point, the courtroom just felt different. I decided to turn around.

Almost every seat was occupied.

Joe Hall was just behind me. We locked eyes and he brought his chin up in one of his trademark expressions of readiness. Whatever happened, we had done our best. Just a few feet away sat Nancy Ryan. She met my eyes and held hers steady. Whatever happened, we had done it with integrity.

Behind them, our team and colleagues filled the rows. I saw Jon Courtney, Buddy LaSala and his fellow investigators, Erin Kingsley Markevitch, Sue O'Connor, Jean Stone, Stefani Miotto, Joe Tesoriero, and other office supervisors. I saw fellow ADAs from our office, young and old, sitting in a solid row of support. I saw so many others who'd stood with us, who'd hustled into court to witness the verdict.

I thought about Bridget, who couldn't be there. She had been determined to take an early and strong stand to fight the opioid epidemic and had the courage to authorize and encourage the groundbreaking prosecution of a corrupt doctor.

I thought about John, who couldn't make it in time but was glued to his phone, waiting for news. He had seen me through this last and hardest year of the case.

I scanned every row, every face, counting my teammates and my blessings. I had started alone, then just with Joe Hall, then just with Joe and Stefani—but we were an army now. Every person in this courtroom—and so many more who could not be present—had contributed to this case. No matter what happened, every single one of these people knew what Dr. Li had done. More important, every single one of these people knew of his victims and would be forever changed by their stories.

I reached out to tap Peter's arm. "You should turn around," I told him. He did, and his face revealed the same strong emotions. At that moment, more than a dozen court officers, weapons in hand, entered the courtroom and lined its walls. For homicide verdicts, protocol demanded extra security.

A few rows behind Dr. Li, I noticed two women. One of them was Anna Guo.

Peter and I looked at each other. I knew what he was thinking: by the end of the day, we would know more. We turned back to face the judge and await the verdict. I uncapped my pen and let it hover over the verdict sheet, ready to follow along as they proceeded through each of the 211 counts.

JANUARY 4, 2016: 656 DAYS SINCE TRIAL

On January 4, 2016, Nina, Charlie, John, and I pressed through the crowd of a small downtown theater on a Monday night at 8:00 p.m. for a magic show. We sat through a juggling performance, and then Peter came on, wearing one of his frumpled trial suits. As he began speaking, I noticed that the slight speech impediment he had developed was still audible—it was like a thick lisp, like the aftermath of a dentist's numbing shot. He didn't know what it was, he'd said the last time we had seen each other; the doctors were still running tests. After a few minutes, it became less noticeable, as Peter picked up speed and started packing in the tricks.

He was quick, funny, and deft. He asked for a volunteer from the audience. The kids and I raised our hands, but he picked a young woman to our left, a skinny blonde with a bohemian cool outfit. She was a model, she told him, from Sweden. Her name was Tilda. He built her into the act, questioning her, teasing her, using her as a foil for his tricks and jokes, with stinging and hilarious humor. I was laughing at first—and then I caught my breath.

She was me.

I was her.

Peter's teasing and our tense dynamics had all been part of an act. I had struggled for so long to understand his attitude toward me—why hadn't I just seen his magic show earlier? I hadn't known that I had been cast in a role. Had I known, could I have refused to play the scene? Could I have handled his comments differently? I had responded with earnest talks about our "communication dynamics," bracing myself to walk into his office and work through our latest conflict; meanwhile Tilda—bohemian Tilda, the quirky Swedish model—stood there with her head cocked to the side, the jokes bouncing against her confidence and even, sometimes, rebounding back toward Peter with a sly response.

The next day, I sent him an email. "Remember how, every day of the trial, you would say, 'By the end of the day, we will know more,' and we never knew more? Well . . . I KNOW MORE!! I KNOW MORE!!" I had realized, I told Peter, that from May 2012 until July 2014 I had been Tilda. "[W]hile it wasn't always funny to live," it had been funny to watch. "I hope you're not worried about your speech," I added. "You sounded very fluid and very natural—and did I mention funny? I hope you're getting some answers from the docs, and not beating yourself up about it."

"Dear trial partner," Peter wrote back, "So gratifying that you now understand that you were tormented by the very, very best. What you got for free [. . .] during the Li trial, Tilda paid $48.00 for. That's a lot of kronas. Anyway, your remarks are very kind, and even more reassuring. Thank you so much for coming, and for your support. You can't imagine how much I practiced and rehearsed for this show. I am so glad that I sounded natural. Yours," he signed off, "Uncle Pete."

So much of life is invisible as it is unfolding. By the time you understand it, it's gone.

JULY 18, 2014: THE 121ST AND LAST DAY OF TRIAL

The two homicide counts topped the indictment. Any second now. The court clerk addressed the foreman. "Has the jury reached a unanimous decision?"

"Yes."

"How say you as to the first count of the indictment charging the defendant, Stan Li, with the crime of Manslaughter in the Second Degree? Do you find the defendant guilty or not guilty?"

"Guilty."

We did not flinch. Silence filled the courtroom during the clerk's pause. I allowed the tips of my fingers to move, placing a small blue check next to the first count of the indictment. *That was for you, Joe Haeg.*

"How say you as to the second count of the indictment charging the defendant with Manslaughter in the Second Degree? Do you find the defendant guilty or not guilty?"

Foreman: Guilty.

That was for you, Nicholas.

Reckless Endangerment in the First Degree for Dawn Tamasi: Guilty.

Kevin Kingsley: Guilty.

Tracy Howard: Guilty.

They found Dr. Li not guilty of Reckless Endangerment with respect to Adrian Cruise. I disagreed but respected their decision and could see their reasoning. I placed an "X" next to that charge on the verdict sheet.

Michael Cornetta: Guilty.

Reckless Endangerment in the Second Degree for Alli Walton: Guilty.

The clerk continued to read out the charges, and the foreman continued to answer.

The jury found Dr. Li not guilty of a selection of charges for Criminal Sale of a Prescription for a Controlled Substance, with respect to patients and dates where the evidence elicited through both direct examination and cross had, in fact, left some doubt as to the existence of a legitimate medical basis.

Maybe there could be truth, after all—born of confrontation, examination, deliberation, and consensus.

Thirteen times the foreman pronounced the words "Not guilty." Otherwise, the words "guilty," "guilty," "guilty" echoed in the courtroom.

The clerk read the verdict back to the jury and confirmed its accuracy. The judge thanked the jury for their service and told them they were now free—but not obligated—to discuss the case. He promised to come thank them again, personally, in the jury room once he had concluded his business with us, the attorneys.

Once the jury was excused, Peter asked that Dr. Li be remanded into the custody of the Department of Corrections. Belair opposed the request and asked that bail be continued, but the judge denied the request. Officers handcuffed Dr. Li and led him out of the courtroom. The judge set a date ninety days hence for Belair's post-conviction motions and ended the proceedings.

"I have to call Margaret," I told Peter, and ran out of the courtroom. I stood outside the doors as people milled about.

She picked up the phone on the first ring. She knew the verdict was in—one of the investigators had texted her. "Margaret," I said, "they found him guilty." I couldn't say anything else. She spoke, and I listened, turning to face the wall as I held the phone to my ear and wiped at my eyes with my suit jacket.

I went back into the courtroom and found Nancy, Joe, Jon, and Peter huddling around the wooden barrier separating the well from the public benches. We reviewed the verdict in hushed voices. There was a pause in our conversation when we noticed that Anna Guo had approached our group. She looked at us, bowed, and smiled. I nodded, confused. She turned and walked out of the courtroom with her companion.

When I walked outside with Joe, we agreed that it was bizarre not to carry the case with us anymore. It had inhabited us for four years. We could lay it to rest. The amount of time, work, and effort that had gone into the investigation and trial seemed unreal, impossible. Like someone else had done it.

Peter, Joe, and I divided up the list of witnesses and family members and spent the rest of the afternoon making calls, sharing the verdict, expressing our thanks. We provided some input on the press release. I went home as soon as possible. I hugged my children and John. I spent a few days cleaning up my office and then took a few weeks' worth of leave from work.

I was tired and missed my family.

When I came back, I negotiated a new position within the office: Director of Training for the Office of the Special Narcotics Prosecutor, the "local" equivalent of the job I'd pursued earlier. I needed a break from the gladiator arena and looked forward to mentoring new ADAs. It was a turn away from the antagonistic atmosphere of the courtroom, toward affirmative, constructive, positive work influencing a new generation of prosecutors. I felt guilty and weak for giving up on trial work for the moment, for being the woman who was opting out, but I'd had enough of the adversarial system.

DECEMBER 19, 2014: 155 DAYS SINCE TRIAL

I wore a version of my dress-and-blazer trial uniform for Dr. Li's sentencing hearing, but my expanded waistline revealed the passage of time and changed circumstances. As we waited inside the courtroom, Margaret Rappold placed her fingers on my six-month-pregnant belly and blessed its tiny occupant before taking her seat. She wasn't sure she had the strength to speak. Peter, Joe, and I hovered near the entrance to the well, watching as the courtroom filled once again with all those who had borne witness to the crimes and their prosecution. Erin Kingsley Markevitch braced for her important role: a victim impact statement. A few members of the jury took seats together in a row near the front—we acknowledged their presence with surprise and a respectful distance.

Court officers milled about, the clerk shuffled papers, the judge entered, and Belair unfolded his hands from their resting place on his chest: it was time for sentencing. We parted from Margaret Rappold and Joe and entered the well.

The door in the back of the courtroom opened and Dr. Li walked out, in handcuffs, between two court officers. If the verdict and incarceration had changed his mindset, we could not tell.

The clerk called the case: "This is calendar number two, *People of the State of New York versus Stan Li*, Indictment Number 4940/2012, defendant present, on for sentence."

At the clerk's prompting, and for the absolute last time on this or any case, I entered my appearance: "Assistant District Attorney Charlotte Fishman, for the People, Your Honor."

Judge Sonberg announced that he would order Dr. Li to return the money he'd stolen from Medicare and private insurers, then asked the clerk to arraign Dr. Li for sentence. The clerk read out the crimes of conviction and announced that, before sentence, the Court would allow the People and the defense to make statements. The judge turned to me: "You have a victim impact statement?"

Erin stood up, clutching a piece of paper, and walked to the lectern. She thanked the judge for letting her speak. "This man's crime," she began, "is so heartless—and preventable. He took an oath to preserve life. [. . .] His crimes were so far-reaching to so many families, it is unimaginable to think about. My parents' and my lives were destroyed by this man.

"And long before I knew of him," Erin continued, "I claim to all my family and friends that my life was destroyed—began being destroyed—in December of 2008, which is when my father first OD'd in his life. And it is also the time I found out he started seeing this man."

The courtroom was silent. Erin spoke with urgency, holding back her tears. She retold the story of her mother's death, but with the emotion and reasoning that she had not been able to express in the question-and-answer format of a witness examination. "My father was so distraught on pills and drugs that he didn't even realize my mother had not woken up," she reminded the judge, illustrating the risk Dr. Li created to others when he sent his patients out into the world like zombies. "He was not there for me when I had to sign the DNR for my mother," she said, describing how her father's addiction had deprived her of his help and support. "And the very next day," she continued, "all he wanted to do, instead of planning my mother's funeral with me, was go see this man, this doctor. I told my father that I needed him because he was the only parent that I had left. Going to see this man was more important to him.

"I have to live with the memories and the nightmares of my father that day," Erin cried. "My father died on December 28, 2010, of an overdose. My father. This man chose not to help my parents, but to hurt them. He showed total disregard for my father's life. I did not have my father to walk me down the aisle when I got married. And when I have children, they will never know their grandparents. To think that this man one day would—could walk his daughter down the aisle or hold his grandchildren makes me sick to my stomach. My grandmother who could not be here because of medical reasons—could not handle being here—will never hold her firstborn. She couldn't even handle talking to me on the phone this morning. And to think that so many families, not only my family, suffered and will continue to suffer the same way I am or similarly is horrible. And I just beg of you," she finished, with emphasis, "to make him—to make this man an example and to show doctors who show total disregard for human life will be punished for the fullest extent of the law. I thank you."

The judge asked me if there were any other victim impact statements. "May I have one moment, Your Honor?" I asked. He nodded. "Sure." I walked out of the well and went up to Margaret. Her eyes were red and wet, but she nodded. She wanted to support Erin and speak for her son.

"Your Honor, the People request Ms. Margaret Rappold be allowed to address the Court."

When Margaret Rappold reached the lectern, she looked up at the judge. "I wasn't prepared to speak," she started. "However, I would like to say a few things about the impact on my life since my son has died. My name is Margaret Rappold. My son Nicholas was one of the two young men that Mr. Li was found guilty for manslaughter. I don't call it manslaughter. I call it Nick-slaughter. The impact on my life—I did write a letter to you, Judge, telling you how I felt, and I just feel that my heart was broken. It was just that he put his hand right through my chest and ripped my heart out. There is a void there that will never ever be filled again. They say things aren't final until it is written in stone. And when I go to the cemetery and I see the name Nicholas on the stone, it tells [sic] me very little consolation to kiss it and to tell him I love him, and I miss him.

"All I could do now is think about that, as a Catholic, we were always told to forgive," Margaret Rappold began, in a surprising and devastating gesture of mercy. "And I do forgive Dr. Li for what he did. It was wrong. I feel it was because of greed. But I forgive him. But I will never, ever forget what he did to me and to my family and to everyone who was associated with my son. He was a young man and I'm sure not an angel. He did not deserve to die. And no mother should go through what I'm going through. I think about him every single minute of the day. His face flashes in my mind. I miss him terrible," she sobbed. "And I know Dr. Li is sentenced—he will see the light of day at some point. But my son will never see the light of day again and I'll never see my son."

She stopped. "That's all I have to say. Thank you."

The judge thanked her and instructed the court officers to move the lectern into the well for me. "As Your Honor sat through eighteen weeks of trial in this case involving the testimony of over seventy witnesses," I began, "and as Your Honor has received and reviewed the People's lengthy sentencing memorandums, I will address the Court on just a few matters relevant to sentencing." First, I acknowledged the letters submitted by Dr. Li's friends and family. The support he received was to his credit, I said, but did not change our recommendation and should not affect the Court's decision.

"Your Honor," I argued, "the thrust of many of the letters was that [the] defendant is a very well-educated man who worked hard to improve his own life and that of his family and who is extremely knowledgeable and competent in his field of practice. The People have never claimed otherwise. Indeed, over the course of this trial, the People sought to prove, and did prove, that the defendant benefited from the best medical education in the U.S., was highly accredited in the field of pain management, and had a great deal of medical experience. This is not a doctor, Your Honor, who did not know better. In fact, the letters are a further indication that the defendant set aside his education and training when it came to treating the patients named in the indictment."

I cited one of the letters, from a former Chinese patient of Dr. Li who had praised him for refusing to prescribe painkillers. "Your Honor, as the jury found," I pressed, "the defendant had a very different approach with the patients in the indictment." As for the other letters from some of Dr. Li's patients, I added, they should be taken with a grain of salt, because "their files demonstrate the type of insurance fraud for which the defendant was ultimately convicted, including false dates of service for injection procedures." It was unlikely, I emphasized, that these patients had known of the fraud committed in their names before they wrote these letters.

On behalf of our office, I asked for the judge to impose maximum consecutive terms on the two manslaughter convictions, of from five to fifteen years, amounting to an indeterminate term of from ten to thirty years.

This sentencing argument was the culmination of all our work: also, it could evoke the emotion of the case, the human cost, the totality of the circumstances, the social importance. It could express our anger.

These were not crimes of passion, I argued. Dr. Li was licensed and experienced. He was empowered by the state to write prescriptions for controlled substances. He was entrusted with the care of his patients but violated all of those obligations. Consecutive sentences on the manslaughter counts also would reflect the individual value of each of the lives lost, I pleaded, and the two young men "leave behind grieving families that were helpless against Dr. Li's decision to keep selling prescriptions.

"The proposed sentences also reflect what the People consider to be the most damning aspect of [the] defendant's conduct," I asserted. "Your Honor, with every single one of those patients, at every single visit, the defendant had an opportunity to behave as a doctor rather than as a seller of prescriptions. He did not take those opportunities even when confronted with startling information about his patients' overdoses, suicide attempts, injuries, or addictions."

I thanked the judge and Belair for their time and attention on the case and sat down.

Belair rose to make his appeal on behalf of Dr. Li. He began by informing the judge that Dr. Li's wife had, once again, divorced him. "As Your Honor will recall," he said, "she previously divorced him when she was unable to obtain employment as a doctor in the United States. He remarried her and promised he would create a job for her in the pain management program that he ran. His twelve-year-old daughter will now likely return to China with his wife because that is where the wife went last time she divorced him. His family life is over."

It was Mr. Belair's job, of course, to try to evoke sympathy for Dr. Li in his sentencing argument. He continued, therefore, by informing the judge that Dr. Li's medical license had been revoked (finally, we thought, and how shameful that it had taken so long and so many deaths) and that even if Dr. Li survived his prison sentence, "he will be looking for employment in the status of a felon convicted of manslaughter."

I felt little sympathy. He'd worked hard and it was a shame to lose it all, but he'd been given many opportunities to change his ways.

"In about a month, a little over a month," Belair added, "Dr. Li will be sixty-one years old. He suffers from cardiac atrial fibrillation, which, thank God, right now is asymptomatic. In many respects, his life is over."

My rage was building. Sixty-one years old? He already had lived almost three times as long as Nicholas Rappold. A heart issue with no symptoms? How about a healthy heart no longer beating? Dr. Li's life was not over. His life, as he imagined it, with piles of cash and no accountability and other people picking up the pieces for him—yes, that was over. But he could still breathe and feel and *change* and *live*.

Belair cited letters from fellow physicians, attesting to the difficulty of treating drug seekers and to their disbelief that Dr. Li intentionally would harm his patients.

Dr. Li's patients lied to him, Belair emphasized. They told the truth in court, but "Dr. Li did not see these patients present in the way that they presented here."

That's right, I thought—he saw them in worse shape. Post-suicide attempt. Post-overdose. Bleeding from the head. Mourning a dead wife. Confused. Haggard. He also saw them in his medical office, where it was his job to ask them questions, examine them, diagnose their conditions, review their medical records, send them out for diagnostic tests, and do no harm.

Belair concluded by asking for the shortest possible sentence—the minimum indeterminate term (a range of time rather than a definite period), which meant that Dr. Li might be eligible for release after five years.

SEPTEMBER 27, 2014: 72 DAYS SINCE TRIAL

On September 27, 2014, John and I spoke our vows of marriage in my parents' backyard, with just our families and children in attendance. Our glorious matchmaker, freshly ordained by the Internet, officiated. We took a picture with Nina and Charlie, the four of us holding one another and smiling in the golden rays of a setting sun, the trees around us still lush. My belly was rounded and tight under my dress, but no one other than me, John—and, I suppose, my meditation partner from the 2012 retreat—knew that there was a baby inside. When we sat for dinner, my mother choked on a shrimp. John's father, a cardiologist, saved her by performing the Heimlich maneuver, sending the shrimp flying on a high arc out of her throat—and right into my mother's outstretched hands. Even on the brink of disaster, she was thinking about containing the mess. It was a magical day.

Lucie was born in March 2015. She was my "bonus baby," bringing unexpected joy to the entire family. I loved my new job, but during my maternity leave I started writing bits and pieces of things during odd hours of the night and in between feedings. I relished the luxury of staying close to my big kids: I could walk them to school and pick them up and talk to them and hear about their days, making the most of the time we had together.

Would it be possible to rekindle my old, crazy dream of becoming a writer? John and I agreed that I could give myself a year, maybe two, to attempt a career change. I went back to work in October, unsure of myself, but within a few weeks, I knew I was done. I repaid the salary I had received during my leave and turned in my badge at the end of November. During one of my exit interviews, one of my colleagues said she'd been tempted to do the same, but so much of her identity was tied up in this work. So was mine, I said, and that's why I had to leave.

DECEMBER 19, 2014: 155 DAYS SINCE TRIAL

Now it was Dr. Li's turn to speak at his own sentencing proceeding. I was angry and curious. Given Mr. Belair's presentation, it was unlikely—but maybe not impossible—that Dr. Li would show remorse, but still, I held out hope.

"Most of this patient already taking high dose of opioid analgesic before coming to see me," Dr. Li began, referring to his "American" patients at the Flushing clinic. "Many of these patients have both problems of severe pain and the high level of opioid tolerance. I did not create this problem. The problem already existed."

He was trying to help them, he said. He encouraged them to cut the doses, and "never try to push any patient to taking more medication." He asked them to comply with the narcotic agreement, he said.

"I never intend to harm any of the patients," he said, making a transition to the case of Joseph Haeg. In the same monotone voice, he then proceeded to review the entire patient file, repeating the testimony on direct examination in which he had given justifications for every prescription. He finished his review of the Haeg case with a flat recitation of events: "At the third day after his last visit, Mr. Joseph Haeg was found dead in his bedroom. And the medication bottle [sic] left in the bottle is much, significant less than what was supposed to be. I mean, the opioid analgesic—so he took much more medication than the instruction. He died from an overdose of oxycodone and Xanax. Sorry for the loss. During the course of the treatment I had tried my best to help Mr. Joseph Haeg to reduce his pain. [. . .] I never intend to harm the patient."

Sorry for the loss. Did he mean it? I couldn't tell. It didn't sound like it. Especially not when he repeated those same words for every patient.

"I saw Mr. Rappold only three times," Dr. Li said. "I treat his acute low back pain caused by acute fall injury. Rappold also abused substances and he also sell drugs and buy drugs. He did not tell me about this. The last prescription I prescribed to him, the pain medication, it was oxycodone thirty milligrams, one hundred twenty pills, for one-month supply. Rappold filled the prescription and then he sold the pills. First, he sold one hundred pills. Then later he sold the rest of twenty pills."

That was a complete misstatement of the testimony and evidence at trial, but the worst was yet to come. Dr. Li continued reading from his prepared statement.

"On the day Rappold died," Dr. Li read, "he was kicked out from his home by his mother because he was abusing substances—"

I was beside myself. Margaret Rappold was in the courtroom. What was he thinking? There was no such evidence and this was beyond cruel.

Dr. Li kept going.

"—He had no place to stay. He stay in his car all night on the street and he died in his car. He died from overdose of oxycodone and Xanax. Sorry for the loss."

I glared at the surface of the table. I could not look at Dr. Li.

"The source of the oxycodone caused his death was not come from the prescription I wrote onto him. I saw Mr. Rappold only a few times for his acute pain. I had no plan to prescribe him medication to him for long term. I never intend to harm the patient."

"Kevin Kingsley," announced Dr. Li. His position had not changed. Uncuffed for the moment, he held his notes between his hands, the papers propped up on the table, both elbows down. Glasses on. Monotone voice.

A self-righteous recitation of prescriptions and justifications preceded Dr. Li's thoughtless dismissal of Kevin Kingsley: "His wife died. He has two episode of acute injury of his head and on his shoulder. For each acute injury, I prescribed small number of pain medication. That was oxycodone, thirty milligrams, sixty pills, for one-month supply, and the one time only for each injury. Two months after his last visit, Mr. Kevin Kingsley died. He died from substance abuse. Sorry for the loss."

Dr. Li stopped there with the patients. He did not talk about Dawn Tamasi or Tracy Howard. Instead, Dr. Li finished with a short speech in which he repeated several times that he had done his best. "I never intend to harm any of the patients," he said, and he was done.

It was the judge's turn. In three years, I had never heard his thoughts on the case. Finally, we would know more.

"When sentencing in a matter of this complexity," the judge began, "I frequently look to history to see if there is some insight I could gather. And I found this quotation from Lao Tzu, the great philosopher: 'There is

ou had
i could
of the
id that

urance
of dis-
nes had

ied [to]
ie prac-
ie hun-
ngs that

patients

u didn't
the pre-
ients or
ient for
iination
as write
s, or the
the pa-
er proof

.appold,

rence to
? Xanax
ing him
ild have
Xanax.

. There is no greater disaster than discontent.
ine than greed.' And I really do think that
ce in this case."

Li's "remarkable" background: surviving
ie Cultural Revolution, admission to medi-
the United States, the licensing process, the
lowship. It showed, the judge said, "an in-
, perseverance, determination. And because
ise and trying to figure out what to do, my
could find any benign explanation for what
ime I thought I saw this little glimmer that
olanation, thinking about it twice, it van-
n explanation for what happened here. The
s in its crassest terms—that you adopted,"
Dr. Li, "in establishing this pain manage-
nitially two days a week but eventually one
where you lived, remote from where you
Friday, was designed to create disaster."
I was hearing.
e judge continued, "whether you stumbled
oid pain relievers as a way to make money
you had planned or at some point decided
ou weren't getting enough traffic from the
ishing coming for epidurals and that you
omething to ramp up the business. Or it
word got out that you were an easy writer
g the addict community, apparently that
ece that makes me [believe] it's not benign
were confronted with the global surgery
if you do a procedure, you can't bill for
office visit in the same day. And as early
g false claims to insurers saying you had

seen a patient on a day when you hadn't seen a patient and tha[t]
performed an epidural the next day or two days later so that y[ou]
get paid twice. So, at some point, whether it was the econom[ics of]
practice or just a desire to make money, the pure greed, you f[elt]
writing prescriptions was the way to go."

We had pressed so hard to develop the Medicare and i[nsurance]
fraud investigation, because they were early and sure indicato[rs of]
honesty and self-dealing. To hear that the evidence of those cr[imes had]
been processed and digested by the judge—it was a huge relief.

"The reason I say the economics of the practice were desi[gned to]
lead to this," the judge was saying, "is that the clinic nature of [the prac-]
tice, the fact that in a given day you might see sixty, eighty, [or a hun-]
dred patients, then there was no way that you could do the th[ings]
we would expect a doctor to do when a new patient comes in."

The judge expressed his disbelief at Dr. Li's claims that the[y]
had fooled him.

"And it just seems to me that you didn't want to know. Y[ou didn't]
want to challenge. All you wanted to do was be able to write [a pre-]
scription and take the fee. Patients would send in other pa[tients,]
relatives to pick up their prescriptions when it was inconve[nient for]
them to come or when they were unable to. There was no exa[m]
performed. You provided no medical judgment. All you did w[as write]
a prescription and sign your name. You charged those patien[ts, the]
insurance companies, the same way you would have done ha[d the pa-]
tients been there present. And it seems to me, there is no bet[ter proof]
than that you were really selling prescriptions."

The judge began talking about specific patients: Nicholas [Zito,]
Kevin Kingsley, Tracy Howard, and Adrian Cruise.

"You're a pain management doctor," the judge said in ref[erence to]
Kevin Kingsley. "Why in the world are you prescribing Xana[x? It]
isn't a pain medication. He has other doctors. Someone's gi[ving him]
Lexapro. Someone's giving him Celebrex. The right answer sh[ould have]
been, 'Go to the doctors treating you. Tell them you need th[e

Not me.' He said he had a panic attack. Pain management doctors don't deal with panic attacks. That's not what you're trained to do. You're trained to deal with pain. He has another doctor. You didn't say, 'Go see someone else.' You said, 'I'll take your money,' and wrote a prescription [. . .]."

The judge revisited Dr. Li's treatment of Nicholas Rappold—the lack of diagnostic work, the failure to ask any questions. "You were acting as a medicine dispenser," he said to Dr. Li, "not a physician." And Adrian Cruise's credible testimony, the judge said, made clear that his visits to Dr. Li were "purely a financial transaction."

"And last," the judge added, in a heavy voice, "[Tracy Howard], who had to have been probably the most pathetic of the patients that testified. When she first came to you she had been under medical care for some time. You didn't ask to see any of her prior medical records. You didn't ask if she was using illegal drugs, which she said she had been." There had been so many warnings, the judge said to Dr. Li, from other doctors, family members, and Tracy Howard herself about misuse of the medications—and yet "you continued to prescribe [. . .]."

The judge was ready to impose the Court's sentence upon Dr. Li.

The judge began with the manslaughter counts, sentencing Dr. Li to two concurrent indeterminate terms of from five to fifteen years, meaning both sentences could range anywhere from five to fifteen years and would be served at the same time. Dr. Li also would serve three years, at the same time, for his prescription sales to Joseph Haeg and Nicholas Rappold.

To those sentences, the judge added another consecutive block, made up of the time Dr. Li would serve on the crimes of Reckless Endangerment in the First and Second Degrees, as well as the Criminal Sales of Prescriptions for a Controlled Substance with respect to the remaining patients.

The third and final set of sentences related to the insurance fraud and falsified records crimes, which the judge characterized as "the most arrogant of the bunch."

Altogether, the judge sentenced Dr. Li to between ten and twenty years in state prison.

With that, it was all over. "Officers, take charge," said the judge. The court officers surrounded Dr. Li, helped him to his feet, and walked him out of the courtroom, back to a holding cell. He is incarcerated at the Fishkill Correctional Facility in New York State, where he will become eligible for parole in March 2024.

JULY 8, 2017: 1,087 DAYS SINCE TRIAL

The foreman and his fellow juror in Seat Number 2 were married in July 2017, three years after they rendered a verdict in the case. We had known nothing of their romance during the trial.

A couple of years later, I received a birth announcement for their son. We have never spoken, but they have made me, Joe, Peter, and Margaret Rappold hopeful that there is always an invisible goodness that may arise from tragedy. It doesn't take away the pain or fill the gap, but it's an engagement with life and love—and another good argument for jury duty.

Epilogue

Bridget G. Brennan, New York City's Special Narcotics Prosecutor announced today the conviction of Dr. HECTOR CASTRO, an internal medicine practitioner, on 39 counts of Criminal Sale of a Prescription for a Controlled Substance. A Manhattan jury found CASTRO guilty on all counts following a three-week trial in Manhattan Supreme Court [. . .]. Evidence presented at trial demonstrated that CASTRO, founder and medical director of Itzamna Medical Center, located at 205 East 16th Street in the Gramercy section of Manhattan, illegally sold prescriptions for the potent painkiller oxycodone for $125 each. The doctor acted other than in good faith by providing prescriptions for non-medical purposes in exchange for cash.

—MAY 28, 2015, PRESS RELEASE FROM THE OFFICE OF THE
SPECIAL NARCOTICS PROSECUTOR

Bridget G. Brennan, New York City's Special Narcotics Prosecutor, announces the guilty plea of Dr. LAWRENCE CHOY [. . .]. Earlier today, CHOY pled guilty to 34 felony counts, including two counts of Manslaughter in the Second Degree, five counts of Reckless Endangerment in the Second Degree and 27 counts of Criminal Sale of a Prescription for a Controlled Substance. Sentencing is set for

September 10, 2019. CHOY is expected to receive a seven-year prison sentence under the terms of his plea.

—JUNE 18, 2019, PRESS RELEASE FROM THE OFFICE
OF THE SPECIAL NARCOTICS PROSECUTOR

As major pharmaceutical companies look to capitalize on the opportunity, the playbook unfolding in India seems familiar. Earnest advocates share heartbreaking stories of suffering patients; physicians and pharmaceutical companies champion pain relief for cancer patients and persuade regulators to grant greater access to powerful opioids; well-meaning pain doctors open clinics; shady pain clinics follow; and a spigot of prescription opioids opens [. . .].

—"HOW BIG PHARMA IS TARGETING INDIA'S OPIOID
MARKET," SARA VARNEY, *KAISER HEALTH NEWS*,
AUGUST 28, 2019

OCTOBER 17, 2019: 1,918 DAYS SINCE TRIAL

I reached a hand toward the monitor and tapped a button, lighting up the screen. My baby was still sleeping, curled up in her crib. It was 5:18 a.m. How could I feel so awake? Lying in the dark next to John, I tried to go back to sleep, but became aware of a vibrational feeling of alertness in my brain. It might be anticipation: I was traveling to Albany in a few hours to hear oral arguments in Dr. Li's last and highest state appeal from his conviction. There was another possibility: the buzzy feeling might be a side effect of my new antidepressant. I'd chosen pharmaceutical relief over crushing anxiety, but there was always a trade-off, including the irrational fear that I was "not myself" with the medication, and the reality that I couldn't live with myself *without* the medication. At least I'd had the privilege to make the choice consciously, under the supervision of a trusted physician.

In either case, there was no more sleep to be slept. I headed downtown to Penn Station. In the brightly lit station, hundreds of humans were already gathered to travel, serve coffee, clean, patrol, or stay warm. I waited in a long line of travelers and watched as a gaunt young man in torn, stained clothing gyrated to the music playing from his smartphone. He bumped into columns and tripped over his own feet, tangling himself up in the laces of his mismatched and oversized shoes. He couldn't have been more than twenty years old. He was so high, so low, and so lost. I boarded the train and headed north.

Peter and I had attended the case's first appellate argument together, in the fall of 2017. In New York State, all defendants are entitled to appeal their convictions to the Appellate Division, where a panel of judges receives and reads briefs from both sides, then hears oral arguments by the attorneys based on the trial record. Dr. Li's case had been heard in the First Department, in an ornate chamber just off Madison Square Park. I knew the courthouse well; it was where I'd argued my first cases on behalf of the Manhattan DA's Office, nearly a decade earlier. In 2017, I had a different vantage point: no longer "The People," but just one of the people, sitting on the side reserved for civilians.

Peter had been sitting right next to me. There'd been some signs of his progressing disease, diagnosed as ALS—he held a handkerchief to his mouth to conceal the tremors and loss of muscular control—but he'd *been there*, in a public place, in a suit. How miraculous that seems now. Back then, just a few years ago, he could walk on his own, sit on his own, breathe on his own, even write. Since we couldn't speak in the chamber, we passed the day's court calendar between us, exchanging bantering notes about the proceedings. I only realized after we left the building that, in fact, we couldn't really speak: we waved good-bye.

On appeal before the First Department in 2017, Belair had challenged the convictions on several grounds, ranging from insufficiency of evidence to inconsistency with legislative intent. He'd lost: the Appellate Division unanimously upheld the convictions on all counts.

"The jury's determination with respect to the credibility of the People's expert testimony on these counts is given great weight," the

Court had written in its decision, released on November 30, 2017, "and [the] defendant's general contentions regarding the improper nature of the prosecution and the proper nature of his usual prescription practices do not overcome the showing made by the People with respect to the medically unlawful prescriptions. Regarding the reckless endangerment in the first degree convictions, there was ample evidence to support a finding that [the] defendant's prescription and treatment practices with respect to these patients created an imminent danger of an overdose that could have been life threatening, which thereby evinced depraved indifference to human life."

Dr. Li did not have an automatic right to appeal to the state's highest court, given the Appellate Division's unanimous decision, but the Court of Appeals granted him permission to do so. We speculated and waited, first for the briefs, then for the Court to set an argument date.

In his appeal to the state's highest court, Belair challenged the homicide convictions. First, he argued that the People couldn't charge Dr. Li with the crime of Reckless Manslaughter as a matter of law, because Dr. Li did not administer the drugs that caused Joseph Haeg's and Nicholas Rappold's deaths. Second, he claimed that even if Dr. Li could be charged as a matter of law, there was insufficient evidence to support the homicide convictions.

By the time the Court published its calendar for the fall of 2019, scheduling the Li case for arguments on October 17, 2019, there was no hope that Peter might join me for the journey to Albany. As I woke up in my own apartment and bed in the morning, mixed my baby's bottle in my own kitchen using my hands and moving around on my own two feet, walked out of my building, waited in line inside Penn Station, watched fall foliage scroll past my train window, ate a sandwich more than one hundred miles from home, sat in the warm, brightly lit hall listening to lawyers, then rode home again, Peter remained in one place: the third floor of a nursing hospital where he'd spent the last few months. He moved between his bed and a wheelchair, but never separated from the tubes and machines that allowed him to breathe. Peter could communicate through retinal eye technology, assuming that the computer wasn't crashing again and that there were folks within earshot who were willing to wait for its slow, robotic enunciation of Peter's words. Except for his eyebrows and some limited sideways movements of his left hand, Peter's body had been immobilized.

As I moved and breathed in the world, especially on this day, I thought of him.

It was raining in Albany and lawyers came barreling through the Court's doors with splattered suits. I watched young men and women following their senior colleagues into the building and remembered the years of behind-the-scenes, after-hours toiling at the firm. What were the other cases being argued? Who were these attorneys' clients? What was at stake in their cases?

I texted Peter and Joe Hall before turning off my phone, then greeted the appellate attorney, ADA Vincent Rivellese, who'd be arguing on behalf of the District Attorney's Office. He was experienced, composed, and ready. We spoke briefly, then I left him to his preparations and waited for the doors to open. I caught sight of Mr. Belair at the end of another anteroom, riffling through papers. When we lined up to enter, I turned to greet him. "Oh, hello," he said with warmth, extending his hand to shake mine before taking his seat at one of the counsel tables.

I took a seat behind the carved rail. There were two loud knocks and the door behind the judge's dais opened. Everyone stood as the judges entered. "Hear ye, hear ye, hear ye," the bailiff began in a loud, deep voice, calling the Court to order. A church bell tolled twelve times, marking high noon, as the black-robed judges, attorneys, and audience members took their seats.

There were two cases scheduled before ours: a dispute about mortgage-backed securities, whose value had plummeted after the 2008 crash; and another about a real estate developer's attempts to wield bankruptcy laws against his creditors on an unpaid loan. It was

America's previous decade, in a microcosm. The judges grappled with contractual details, statutes of limitation, big banks represented by big firms, the elusive location and nature of the real economic losses, and the even more elusive goal of justice. They formed a "hot bench," peppering the attorneys with questions.

After an hour, I wrapped my clammy hands in my cardigan, looking around to see whether I was sitting near an air vent. I wasn't. My chest felt tight. So much for my initial relief at not being on the spot and on duty: I was nonetheless nervous. What questions were the judges reserving for our case?

The chief judge, Janet DiFiore, thanked the attorneys on the second case and prepared for the next and last: "Appeal Number 86, the People of the State of New York versus Stan Li."

Belair arranged his papers on the lectern and hurtled into his argument: the medications prescribed were within regular therapeutic ranges and presented no risk if taken as prescribed. That's as far as he got before one of the judges interrupted: "Wasn't there some expert testimony that contradicts that position?" Belair disagreed, claiming that Dr. Gharibo had applied a "malpractice" standard and had been forced to concede that Dr. Li's prescriptions and dosages were in accordance with FDA guidelines. As Belair attempted to discredit Dr. Gharibo's testimony and offer evidence drawn from Dr. Li's own files, the judges challenged him: Weren't some of the records manufactured? Didn't Dr. Gharibo list a number of factors that raise significant concerns, such as the lack of medical justification for prescription, the combination of oxycodone with Xanax, the increases in Nicholas Rappold's dosages, the early visits? Wasn't there also statistical evidence about the large proportion of oxycodone prescriptions as compared to other controlled substances? Hadn't the People also proved that the doctor only accepted cash and imposed additional fees depending on the patient's lack of compliance?

As they rattled through these lists of factors, I remembered the slog to uncover evidence of each one, to gather evidence for court, to present it in court. As I listened to Mr. Belair's energetic defense of Dr. Li's medical practice, I remembered the questions we'd raised at the beginning of the investigation about the validity of our prosecution, about whether we were best positioned to right this particular wrong.

"Are you arguing," a judge interrupted Belair, "that a physician can never be found guilty of reckless manslaughter unless they administer the drugs themselves or are you saying that the elements of the crime were not established in this case?"

"Both," answered Mr. Belair.

ADA Rivellese took his turn at the lectern, emphasizing the volume of evidence we'd placed before the jury and the inevitable conclusion: "It was all about the money." He acknowledged the challenges of the Rappold case—only the Xanax prescribed by Dr. Li had been recovered from Rappold's car, not the oxycodone—but explained the synergistic effect of Xanax and oxycodone.

"How far back would you go?" one judge asked Rivellese during an exchange about the charge of reckless manslaughter and the links in the chain of causation. Would prosecutors now rely on this case to track deaths back to local pharmacists who might have an inkling of a customer's addiction, or even pharmaceutical companies? Rivellese gave the only sound legal answer: prosecutors still would need to be able to prove each element of the crime beyond a reasonable doubt, with or without this precedent.

On rebuttal, Belair faced an even hotter bench. As he insisted that none of Dr. Li's patients had come into the office in a state of overdose, looking sweaty or disheveled, one of the judges jumped in. "You identified the things that a criminal actor would deny that they observed," she said. When Belair hesitated, she continued: "He's the only one in the room."

I thought about the beautiful upstate New York counties spanning out around Albany, which had been devastated by the epidemics of misleading marketing, overprescription, heroin, addiction, overdose, and greed. I thought about the small towns like Hobart, New York, where opioid painkiller factories provided crucial employment opportunities while contributing to the state's greatest scourge. I thought about all the families who remained without answers about their children's overdoses or deaths, who just had to live with the pain.

I thought about Joe Hall and his team, who'd logged countless miles and hours painstakingly gathering evidence to obtain justice in just this one case—and all the others who might be out there doing the same on other cases—and all the cases that weren't being investigated for lack of resources or starting points—and all the families who might still suffer and lose loved ones before we could get a handle on our national addiction to profit. There were no official opioid overdose death statistics available yet for 2018, but even if the numbers decreased slightly, as it was hoped they would, each incremental loss was still catastrophic.

Leaving the warm, red-carpeted, beautiful chamber, I braced for another few weeks of uncertainty on the case. The judges wouldn't issue their decision for at least another month. What would they say? What would it mean, for this case and others like it, or bigger cases, against different criminal actors?

Dr. Li may have been the only doctor in the room in his basement clinic in Flushing, but he wasn't the only one in this epidemic of opioid overprescription, addiction, and overdose who witnessed the suffering but didn't care, and who filled his pockets with money as other people died. How far back will *we* go? Are we even able to comprehend and feel the tremendous loss of so many precious lives? It's an open question for all of us. We may be near the end of the Li case, but we're just getting started with a larger accounting in this country—and the epidemic may be about to take on global proportions.

• • •

On November 26, 2019, the New York State Court of Appeals upheld Dr. Li's manslaughter conviction in a 6–1 decision.

Author's Note

When Dr. Li sold prescriptions for oxycodone and Xanax out of his weekend basement clinic in Flushing, Queens, he risked the lives of his patients. This story of recklessness, indifference, tragedy, and greed is so cruel as to be nearly unbelievable. It is the opioid epidemic in a microcosm.

It is also a story, however, about the unlikely team of civilians and professionals who responded to this public health emergency.

In writing this book, I relied on my own memories of our four-year investigation and eighteen-week trial, more than seven thousand pages of trial transcript, conversations with teammates who have since left public service, press reports about the case, and the Centers for Disease Control's data about the opioid epidemic.

This book does not purport to be a journalistic overview of the opioid epidemic; it is a memoir from the trenches. It is a look back at a time when we hoped to be seeing the worst of it—before it got even worse. It is an expression of gratitude for the team, the work, and the resources that so many people devoted to stopping this killer in a white coat. It is a prayer for greater awareness and greater resources, so that we may interrupt the stream of tragedies.

I have tried to be transparent about the criminal justice system, the procedural aspects of an investigation and trial, as well as my own challenges as a prosecutor, woman, and mother working through divorce and depression. I can only tell my side of the story. There are different perspectives. Without doubt, any and all errors are entirely my own. At the time of this writing, the Li case was still pending appeal, so the Office of the Special Narcotics Prosecutor and the Manhattan District Attorney's Office could not, and did not, participate in this account.

During one of the first days of our long trial, a juror stood up at the close of the day's proceedings. Judge Michael Sonberg urged her to sit down. "You don't have to stand up," he said. "We stand up in honor of the jury; jurors don't have to stand up."

The trial jury deserves thanks and respect—but they are not the only ones.

Eddie Valora, our unlikely tipster, sounded the first alarm about Dr. Li. Valora saw a public health risk and decided to do something about it. He never could have guessed that, from his tip, a mammoth case and team would emerge to pursue justice for twenty different victims on behalf of the People of the State of New York. Trial witnesses are not allowed to hear each other testify, so he never had the satisfaction of hearing law enforcement and fraud detection professionals confirm what he had suspected. Nobody needs to be perfect or all-knowing to do good for others. I stand up in his honor.

Dr. Li's surviving patients, albeit sometimes reluctantly and always painfully, also performed a civic duty. They showed up, told the truth, and stood firm even though much of what they admitted did not reflect easily upon themselves. I have changed the names of certain witnesses featured in this book to protect whatever precious privacy they have regained since the trial. I stand up in honor of all the witnesses.

Andrea Howard, Kristin Delumen, Anne Kingsley, Erin Kingsley Markevitch, Margaret Rappold, Kathleen Haeg, Sybil Stearns, Armen Tamasi: they were caretakers, advocates, fighters, and helpless bystanders. They were fighting against broad, unseen, overwhelming forces: pharmaceutical companies, biased medical training, and greed. Each of them felt like they had not done enough, needed to do more, could have, should have . . . They felt alone. They are not alone. They are not at fault. I stand up in their honor.

The New York City doctors who individually treated Dr. Li's patients—bringing them out of respiratory depression or benzodiazepine withdrawal, pulling them back from suicidal ideation, responding to repeated demands for painkillers with perception and compassion—made a tremendous difference both in the moment of medical intervention and collectively at trial.

Dr. Christopher Gharibo, our medical expert, showed his passion for medicine and integrity during his many days of grueling preparation and testimony.

Dr. Andrew Kolodny answered my questions with patience and precision, both during the investigation and as I began writing this book. I stand up in honor of all these physicians and their colleagues as they continue their work on the front lines of a continuing public health disaster.

Kris Hamman, Director of the Prosecutors' Center for Excellence, and one of my workplace mentors, took the time to read and comment on the manuscript. Her husband, Alan Friedberg, aka Fry, our secret weapon from the world of medical malpractice law, devoted hours of his time to helping us understand and prepare for the medical testimony. He provided the best brand of feedback: direct, unvarnished, productive, peppered with humor, and delivered at twice the speed of regular humans. I thank them both, with profound respect.

My partners, Joe Hall and Peter Kougasian, are still my heroes. Joe Hall is still working around the clock to fight off lethal dealers and doctors. Peter is fighting for his life. I hold them in my heart and stand for them and their families.

Nancy Ryan played a crucial role in the case and in my life during these years of investigation and trial. She coached me with intelligence, patience, and humor, helping me to become a better attorney and team player. The first days that we spent talking about the case—hours upon hours of factual analysis and legal discussions—were some of the most educational and valuable days of my life. Her hard work, integrity, attention to detail, and thoughtfulness continue to set the bar for everything I do.

Bridget Brennan, Joe Tesoriero, Steve Goldstein: Thank you for your trust and for all the resources that you devoted to this case and the Prescription Drug Investigation Unit. I wish you all had been wrong when you warned of an imminent crisis. To all the wonderful people at the Office of the Special Narcotics Prosecutor for the City of New York and the New York County District Attorney's Office, too many to name but all unforgettable to me, who work long hours with limited resources to protect the public: thank you. Your friendship and support made it all possible and bearable.

Cynthia, Diana, Donna, Dawn, Denise, Lisa, Evelyn, Kristine, Jodi, Nancy, and all the stenographers who sat and transcribed testimony for hours upon hours: we saw and appreciated your hard work. You keep a crucial record of pain, truth, and conflict. Thank you.

Our grand jury of anonymous New Yorkers must rank among the most dedicated, effective, and worthy of thanks. They persisted despite medical conditions, caregiving responsibilities, and employment challenges; they sifted through masses of evidence and testimony, asked challenging questions, and came back as soon as the floodwaters of Hurricane Sandy retreated. I never knew their names, and everything they did and heard is a secret, but I would recognize their faces anywhere, and I am still thankful for their work.

Belair occasionally referred to me and Peter as his "brother and sister before the bar." It was sweet, though perhaps slightly sarcastic as well. We were supposed to be on the same team: adversarial but not adversaries. That worked a bit better between him and Peter than it did with me, but I respected his work: he defended his client with intelligence and zeal. I stand up for him and for the mission of criminal defense.

Judge Sonberg and his staff accomplished the impossible: They kept this complex case on track, maintaining a balance between the law, the logistics, the schedules, the attorneys, and the jurors. Meanwhile, they also had other cases on their dockets, and lives outside the courtroom. I stand up for them.

When you are a prosecutor, you receive an undue number of requests for tips on how to avoid jury service. There are people who show up and make it work, regardless of their employment status or salary levels, and it's a requirement for a reason: if people don't show up, the system can't be fair. Bricklayers don't call for public participation. Dentists don't make civilians observe operations. The banking industry does not invite public review of daily transactions. The criminal justice system, however, cannot function, let alone be just, without the participation of citizens.

Our trial jurors, those mysterious overlords of our fates who pledged to reach for impartiality and dutifully completed questionnaires, voir dire, and eighteen weeks of service, then reviewed the pieces of evidence one by one during deliberations to reach a discerning and nuanced verdict, deserve sincere admiration and thanks.

One baby arrived during our trial: a brown-haired doll, the daughter of our analyst and paralegal Jon Courtney. We waited anxiously for word of her birth. We cooed over her photos during the breaks. We flailed around without Jon during his paternity leave, relying on the help of the investigators to steer our heavy evidence cart up the steep hill from the back entrance of our building in the morning and back down in the evening and realizing, with respect to all his intellectual and labor-intensive contributions to the case, that he carried the load of many. Jon, his family, and his little girl have shown tremendous courage and heart in the face of adversity: I stand in their honor.

"Due to the complex and time-consuming nature of these cases, and skyrocketing numbers of referrals," Bridget wrote to the City Council in 2013, the year before the trial, "we are devoting more and more resources to these cases on a daily basis. As we persevere in our efforts to confront the prescription drug epidemic, the costs keep climbing. These prosecutions require experienced prosecutors and dedicated, trained investigators. The Assistant District Attorneys, investigators, and analysts who handle these cases for my office are increasingly spread thin."

Our team of investigators exemplified this trend. There were health scares, there were all the complications of lives and families, there were cases coming in so fast the Office could barely keep up, there were witnesses to be interviewed all over the city and the tristate area, and the team just kept showing up, knocking out task after task after task. Teamwork and public service drove their every move. They're still out there. They still need support.

This book would not exist without my agent, champion, defender, voice of reason, and steadfast truth-teller, Joy Tutela. She was the first to believe in the project and shepherded me through the proposal, drafting, and editing phases with humor, precision, and patience. The intuitive Jessica DuLong, a brilliant author, editor, doula, and marine engineer, swooped in for a few crucial weeks to help me restructure the first draft and then, with just a few days to spare, to polish the manuscript. Julia Cheiffetz, my valiant editor at Simon & Schuster, fought through busy times launching an important imprint to offer her penetrating comments and encouragement. Nicholas Ciani and the team of editorial assistants, copy editors, designers, attorneys, and production editors at Simon & Schuster performed meticulous and precious work on the book. My friends Katherine, Suzanne, Vistie, Mindi, Allison, Philip, Sally, and Jen provided invaluable support and guidance. Emilio Leanza, fact-checker extraordinaire, worked with tenacity and remarkable precision.

Peter Kougasian listened to the entire manuscript from the confines of his hospital bed as I read it aloud. He offered feedback using retinal technology, typing out his comments with his eyes, letter by letter; he squiggled his eyebrows; he shook his head slightly from side to side in reminiscence or agreement; or sometimes I looked up to see a single tear flowing down his sunken cheek. "I give you my permission," he once typed out, "to discuss your frustrations about my assignment to the case." We laughed and cried and critiqued our way through many pages and hours this way.

To this attentive and resolute team, I offer my sincere gratitude and admiration.

If I was able to do my job and then write this book, it was because my home team stood up for me, helped me, pushed me, and supported me through it all: Nina, Charlie, Lucie, and even little Althea; my beloved John; our parents; my brother; our extraordinarily kind, dependable, and professional childcare provider, Ms. Mohamed, who raised Charlie and Nina, then came back for another round; my friends; my therapists; our babysitters; and, of course, my fellow "soccer parents," who gave me pep talks on the sidelines of our children's games. Our dear friend and talented Clue detective Mike Steib deserves particular thanks and recognition for introducing me to Joy Tutela.

Among our team, our witnesses, our law enforcement partners, and our jurors, all the people joined together in the courtroom to keep the wheels of justice grinding along, there may have been differences in political beliefs and world views. At the time, we were all focused on discovering facts and we all knew the difference between true facts and not-true facts: we never disagreed with solid proof, or with one another, when there was solid proof. We followed the facts and we believed in accountability, on a personal level, as a team, and for society. We were all united behind two goals: seeking justice for those who died and preventing more deaths. I cherish the memory of that teamwork.

The hardest part of writing this book was reaching out to the families of victims and learning of more children lost to overdoses. It gives rise to helplessness and anger, because there are others who concealed facts and avoided accountability, all for the sake of money. I have to remind myself that there are other teams hard at work right now trying to uncover the extent of those crimes and those responsible for them; there are teams at work right now to save more lives. I stand up for them and invite you to stand with me.

Notes

CHAPTER 1: THE ONE TO START WITH

1. Harmon, Katherine. "Prescription Drug Deaths Increase Dramatically," *Scientific American*. Springer Nature America, Inc., April 6, 2010. https://www.scientificamerican.com/article/prescription-drug-deaths/.
2. Hedegaard, Holly, Margaret Warner, and Arialdi M. Miniño. "Drug Overdose Deaths in the United States, 1999–2016 §." CDC National Health Statistics report. Accessed October 10, 2019. https://www.cdc.gov/nchs/products/databriefs/db294.htm.
3. "Public Hearing 08-31-11 NYS Roundtable." New York State Senate, March 8, 2016. https://www.nysenate.gov/transcripts/public-hearing-08-31-11-nys-roundtable-hannon-klein-marcellino-scoped-finaltxt.

CHAPTER 4: THREE YEARS, EIGHT MONTHS, TWO DAYS

1. "Sales Careers at Purdue." Sales and Marketing Goals and Vision. Accessed October 7, 2019. https://web.archive.org/web/20101127204043/http://pharma.com/html/SalesCareers/salesmarketing.htm.

CHAPTER 5: WHO'S WITH ME?

1. Epi Data Brief: Opioid Analgesics in New York City: Prescriber Practices § (2012). https://www1.nyc.gov/assets/doh/downloads/pdf/epi/databrief15.pdf.
2. Ibid.
3. Ibid.
4. Drug Abuse Warning Network, *2010: National Estimates of Drug-Related Emergency Department Visits.* 2010: National Estimates of Drug-Related Emergency Department Visits, SMA Drug Abuse Warning Network,

2010: National Estimates of Drug-Related Emergency Department Visits § (2012). https://www.samhsa.gov/data/sites/default/files/DAWN2k10ED DAWN2k10ED/DAWN2k10ED.htm.

5. Ibid.

6. *2018 National Drug Threat Assessment.* 2018 National Drug Threat Assessment §. Accessed October 10, 2019. https://www.dea.gov/sites/default /files/2018-11/DIR-032-18 2018 NDTA final low-resolution.pdf.

7. Treatment episode data set (TEDS) 1999–2009: State admissions to substance abuse treatment services § (2011). https://wwwdasis.samhsa.gov /dasis2/teds_pubs/2009_teds_rpt_natl.pdf.

8. Ibid, p. 2.

9. "Prescription Painkiller Overdoses in the US Infographic | VitalSigns | CDC." Centers for Disease Control and Prevention. Accessed October 10, 2019. https://www.cdc.gov/vitalsigns/painkilleroverdoses/infographic .html.

10. "80.62 Use of Controlled Substances in Treatment." *New York Codes, Rules and Regulations.* Westlaw. Accessed October 10, 2019. https:// govt.westlaw.com/nycrr/Document/I4fcd2827cd1711dda432a117e6e0f345 ?viewType=FullText&originationContext=documenttoc&transitionType =CategoryPageItem&contextData=(sc.Default)&bhcp=1.

11. "80.65 Purpose of Issue." *New York Codes, Rules and Regulations.* Westlaw. Accessed October 10, 2019. https://govt.westlaw.com/nycrr/Document/I4fcd 4f22cd1711dda432a117e6e0f345?viewType=FullText&originationContext =documenttoc&transitionType=CategoryPageItem&contextData=(sc .Default).

12. "The Laws of New York Consolidated Laws Public Health Article 33: Controlled Substances, Title 5: Dispensing to Addicts and Habitual Users." New York State Senate, October 5, 2019. https://www.nysenate.gov/legisla tion/laws/PBH/3351.

13. "Official Compilation of Codes, Rules and Regulations of the State of New York." *New York Codes, Rules and Regulations.* Westlaw. Accessed October 10, 2019. https://govt.westlaw.com/nycrr/Document/I4fcdeb68 cd1711dda432a117e6e0f345?viewType=FullText&originationContext =documenttoc&transitionType=CategoryPageItem&contextData= (sc.Default).

14. "21 U.S. Code § 841—Prohibited Acts A." Legal Information Institute. Accessed October 10, 2019. https://www.law.cornell.edu/uscode/text/21 /841.

15. *Burrage v. United States*, 12-7515 (Supreme Court of the United States 2014).

CHAPTER 6: THE FRUITS OF OUR LABOR

1. GAO, U.S. Government Accountability Office. "Prescription Opioids: Medicare Needs to Expand Oversight Efforts to Reduce the Risk of Harm." November 6, 2017. https://www.gao.gov/products/GAO-18-15.

CHAPTER 7: SOFT TARGETS

1. "Training Materials." RxPATROL® Rx Pattern Analysis Tracking Robberies and Other Losses. Accessed October 10, 2019. http://www..com /TrainingVideos/.
2. "New York Consolidated Laws, Penal Law—PEN § 190.65." Findlaw. Accessed October 10, 2019. https://codes.findlaw.com/ny/penal-law/pen -sect-190-65.html.
3. "Opioid Overdose," Centers for Disease Control and Prevention. https:// www.cdc.gov/drugoverdose/epidemic/index.html.

CHAPTER 8: MODERN MEDICINE

1. *"Bayer Pharmaceutical Products and Technical Preparations."* The College of Physicians of Philadelphia Digital Library. Accessed October 10, 2019. https://www.cppdigitallibrary.org/exhibits/show/bad-medicine /item/6759.
2. "Title 21 United States Code (USC) Controlled Substances Act." Section 812. Accessed October 10, 2019. https://www.deadiversion.usdoj.gov /21cfr/21usc/812.htm.
3. "Synthetic Opioid Overdose Data | Drug Overdose | CDC Injury Center." Centers for Disease Control and Prevention. Accessed October 10, 2019. https://www.cdc.gov/drugoverdose/data/fentanyl.html.
4. Kornick, Craig A., Juan Santiago-Palma, Natalia Moryl, Richard Payne, and Eugenie A. M. T. Obbens. "Benefit-Risk Assessment of Transdermal Fentanyl for the Treatment of Chronic Pain." *Drug Safety* 26, no. 13 (2003): 951–73. https://doi.org/10.2165/00002018-200326130-00004.
5. Ibid.
6. Scholl, L., Seth Puja, M. Kariisa, N. Wilson, and G. Baldwin. "Drug and Opioid-Involved Overdose Deaths—United States, 2013–2017." *Morbidity and Mortality Weekly Report* 67 (5152) January 24, 2019; 67:1419–1427. doi: http://dx.doi.org/10.15585/mmwr.mm675152e1.

7. Office of the Special Narcotics Prosecutor for the City of New York. *2015 Annual Report*. New York, NY: Office of the Special Narcotics Prosecutor, 2016.

8. Prekupec, Matthew P., Peter A. Mansky, and Michael H. Baumann. "Misuse of Novel Synthetic Opioids." *Journal of Addiction Medicine* 11, no. 4 (2017): 256–65. doi:10.1097/adm.0000000000000324.

9. *2018 National Drug Threat Assessment* §. Accessed October 10, 2019. https://www.dea.gov/sites/default/files/2018-11/DIR-032-18 2018 NDTA final low-resolution.pdf.

10. Ibid.

11. Ibid, p. 27.

12. Department of Health. *Data Brief 104*. New York, NY: New York City Department of Health, 2018.

13. New York City Department of Health, *Epi Data Brief No. 116*, August 2019. https://www1.nyc.gov/assets/doh/downloads/pdf/epi/databrief116.pdf.

CHAPTER 9: HOPE IN A BOTTLE

1. *Commonwealth of Massachusetts v. Purdue Pharma L.P., et al.*, C.A. No. 1884-cv-018082 (BLS2) (Suffolk County Superior Court 2019).

2. *State of Tennessee v. Purdue Pharma, L.P.*, 1-173-18 (Knox County Circuit Court, Sixth Judicial District 2019).

CHAPTER 11: THE GATEKEEPERS

1. *Fueling an Epidemic*. U.S. Senate Homeland Security & Governmental Affairs Committee, Minority Staff Report, February 2018. https://www.hsgac.senate.gov/imo/media/doc/REPORT-Fueling an Epidemic-Exposing the Financial Ties Between Opioid Manufacturers and Third Party Advocacy Groups.pdf.

2. Meier, Barry. "In Guilty Plea, OxyContin Maker to Pay $600 Million." *The New York Times*, May 7, 2007.

3. Armstrong, David. "Purdue 2007 Agreed Statement of Facts." DocumentCloud. Accessed October 8, 2019. https://www.documentcloud.org/documents/5744917-Purdue-2007-Agreed-Statement-of-Facts.html.

4. Kolodny, Andrew, David T. Courtwright, Catherine S. Hwang, Peter Kreiner, John L. Eadie, Thomas W. Clark, and G. Caleb Alexander. "The Prescription Opioid and Heroin Crisis: A Public Health Approach to an Epidemic of Addiction." *Annual Review of Public Health* 36, no. 1 (2015): 559–74. https://doi.org/10.1146/annurev-publhealth-031914-122957.

5. National Center for Health Statistics data brief: Drug Overdose Deaths in the United States, 1999–2016, 294, 1999–2016 § (2017).

6. *New York v. Purdue Pharma L.P. et al.*, New York State Supreme Court, Suffolk County, No. 400016/2018.

7. Ibid.

8. Ibid.

9. Tigas, Mike, Ryann Grochowski Jones, Charles Ornstein, and Lena Groeger. "Dollars for Docs." ProPublica, June 28, 2016. https://projects .propublica.org/docdollars/doctors/pid/24637.

10. Raymond, Nate. "U.S. to Narrow Opioid Bribe Case Against Insys Founder, Others." Reuters. Thomson Reuters, July 24, 2018. https://www.reuters.com /article/us-insys-opioids/u-s-to-narrow-opioid-bribe-case-against-insys -founder-others-idUSKBN1KE2GD.

11. Tigas, Mike, Ryann Grochowski Jones, Charles Ornstein, and Lena Groeger. "Dollars for Docs." ProPublica, October 17, 2019. https://proj ects.propublica.org/docdollars/doctors/pid/320370/year/2014.

CHAPTER 13: THE KOUGASIAN RULE

1. *Commonwealth of Massachusetts v. Purdue Pharma L.P., et al.*, C.A. No. 1884-cv-018082 (BLS2) (Suffolk County Superior Court 2019).

CHAPTER 14: ANGEL

1. Stekel, Wilhelm. *The Beloved Ego Foundations of the New Study of the Psyche.* London: K. Paul, Trench, Trubner. 1921.

CHAPTER 16: SORRY FOR THE LOSS

1. "Governor Cuomo Signs Legislation to Combat Heroin, Opioid and Prescription Drug Abuse Epidemic." New York State official website, June 23, 2014. https://www.governor.ny.gov/news/governor-cuomo-signs-leg islation-combat-heroin-opioid-and-prescription-drug-abuse-epidemic-0.

Index